INFORMATION HISTORY IN THE MODERN WORLD

HISTORIES OF THE INFORMATION AGE

Edited by

Toni Weller

D1528145

palgrave
macmillan

First published 2011 by
PALGRAVE MACMILLAN

Palgrave Macmillan in the UK is an imprint of Macmillan Publishers Limited, registered in England, company number 785998, of Houndmills, Basingstoke, Hampshire RG21 6XS.

Palgrave Macmillan in the US is a division of St Martin's Press LLC, 175 Fifth Avenue, New York, NY 10010.

Palgrave Macmillan is the global academic imprint of the above companies and has companies and representatives throughout the world.

Palgrave® and Macmillan® are registered trademarks in the United States, the United Kingdom, Europe and other countries.

ISBN 978–0–230–23736–0 hardback
ISBN 978–0–230–23737–7 paperback

This book is printed on paper suitable for recycling and made from fully managed and sustained forest sources. Logging, pulping and manufacturing processes are expected to conform to the environmental regulations of the country of origin.

A catalogue record for this book is available from the British Library.

A catalog record for this book is available from the Library of Congress.

10   9   8   7   6   5   4   3   2   1
20 19 18 17 16 15 14 13 12 11

Printed in China

For Eileen and Ted Poulter.

*For Kimberley Lloyd and Laura Jones. Thank you both so much for
your enthusiasm, support and loyalty.*

And also for my wonderful husband, Ed. Thank you for everything.

CONTENTS

LIST OF FIGURES

ix

LIST OF ABBREVIATIONS

Abbreviations used in Chapter 7, 'A Valuable Handbook of Information':
The Staff Magazine in the First Half of the Twentieth Century as a Means of
Information Management.

Staff Magazines Researched and Cited

The name of each magazine is preceded by the abbreviations as it appears
in the notes. The companies that produced them and the field of business in
which the companies operated are given in brackets if the titles of the magazines are not self-explanatory in these regards.

APOC   *APOC Magazine* (Anglo-Persian Oil Company)
BPM   *BP Magazine* (British Petroleum)
CC   *Costing Comments* (Prudential Assurance Company)
CWM   *Cocoa Works Magazine* (Rowntree and Co., makers of cocoa and
        confectionery)
MA   *Marlbeck Annual* (Thomas Marshall [Marlbeck] Limited, garment
        manufacturer)
NI   *Naft-i-Iran* (Anglo-Persian Oil Company)
OM   *Our Magazine*: The Staff: The Staff Journal of the Motor Union
        Insurance Co., the United British Insurance Company and the
        Federated British Insurance Company
PR   *Progress* (Lever Brothers, soap manufacturer)
PSN   *Port Sunlight News* (Lever Brothers, soap manufacturer)
PSMJ   *Port Sunlight Monthly Journal* (Lever Brothers, soap manufacturer)
RG   *Ravensbourne Gazette*: Magazine of Cook, Son and Co. (Wholesale
        importers of clothes and furnishings)
SMBMC   *Staff Magazine of Brown, Muff and Co.*, Bradford (department store)
TA   *The Aquarius*: Magazine of the [London] Metropolitan Water
        Board Staff Association
TB   *The Beam*: Staff Magazine of Brown, Muff and Co., Bradford
        (department store)
TBD   *The Black Diamond*: For Circulation Among the Staff of William
        Cory & Son, Ltd., and Associated Companies (Coal shippers)

TBMB   *The Brown Muff Bulletin* (Brown, Muff and Co., department store)
TCTA   *The Call to Arms* (Lever Brothers, soap manufacturer)
TCWM   *The Carrow Works Magazine* (Colman's, makers of mustard and other condiments)
THCSM   *The Home and Colonial Stores Magazine*: A Link Between the Staffs of the Home and Colonial Stores Ltd. and its associate companies
TP   *The Pheasant*: Works Journal of Jurgens Limited (makers of margarine)
TPB   *The Prudential Bulletin* (Prudential Assurance Company)
TPL   *The Pipe Line* (Shell Oil)
TTM   *The Tanzaro Magazine*: Staff Magazine of Jewsbury and Brown Ltd. of Manchester, London and Liverpool (makers of non-alcoholic wines, juices and cordials)
TTR   *The Thalos Review*: The Official Organ of the London and Thames Oil Wharves and London Oil Storage Company Limited
WN   *Wates News* (Wates Limited, construction)
WHN   *Wates House News* (Wates Limited, construction)

ACKNOWLEDGEMENTS

The editor and publishers wish to thank the following for permission to use the specified material:

Figures 4.2–4.3 in Chapter 4, reproduced with kind permission of the Rickards Collection, Centre for Ephemera Studies, University of Reading.

Figures 4.4–4.7 in Chapter 4, reproduced with kind permission of the Diocese of London and the Guildhall Library, City of London.

Figures 4.8–4.15 in Chapter 4, reproduced with kind permission of the National Archives, London.

Figure 7.1 in Chapter 7, reproduced with the kind permission of Shell International.

Every effort has been made to trace the copyright holders but if any have been inadvertently overlooked the publishers will be pleased to make the necessary arrangement at the first opportunity.

NOTES ON CONTRIBUTORS

Alistair Black is Professor at the Graduate School of Library and Information Science, University of Illinois, USA. He is author of *A New History of the English Public Library* (Leicester University Press 1996), *The Public Library in Britain 1914–2000* (British Library 2000) and co-author of *The Early Information Society in Britain, 1900–1960* (Ashgate 2007) and, on the history of public library design, *Books, Buildings and Social Engineering* (Ashgate 2009).

Paul Dobraszczyk is a research fellow in the Department of Typography & Graphic Communication, University of Reading, UK, for the AHRC-funded project 'Designing information for everyday life, 1815–1914'. He is the author of *Into the Belly of the Beast: Exploring London's Victorian sewers* (Spire Books 2009) and has published many articles on Victorian visual culture.

Mike Esbester is a research fellow in the Department of Typography & Graphic Communication at the University of Reading, UK, working on the AHRC-funded project 'Designing information for everyday life, 1815–1914'. He has published articles from the project in *Book History* and the *Journal of Design History* and also articles based on his doctoral research on the history of safety education and railway safety.

Edward Higgs is Professor in the Department of History at the University of Essex, UK. He has published widely on the history of censuses and surveys, civil registration, women's work, the impact of the digital revolution on archives and the history of identification. He is the author of *The Information State in England* (Palgrave 2004).

Dave Muddiman was, until 2008, Principal Lecturer in the School of Information Management, Leeds Metropolitan University, UK. In his early academic career his research and publications focused on the sociology and recent history of the public library service, but in the late 1990s, he became fascinated by the history of the rise of information, in particular during 1870–1945. Since then he has authored a number of papers – on H. G. Wells, J. D. Bernal and the early history of ASLIB – and in 2007, with Alistair Black and

Helen Plant, he published *The Early Information Society: Information Management in Britain before the Computer* (Ashgate 2007). Dave's own information career continues on an ad hoc basis: in addition to part-time teaching and research he is currently Reviews Editor of *Journal of Librarianship and Information Science* and a contributor to the latest edition of the *Encyclopaedia of Library and Information Sciences* (Taylor and Francis).

W. Boyd Rayward is Professor Emeritus in the Graduate School of Library and Information Science at the University of Illinois and in the School of Information Systems, Technology and Management at the University of New South Wales. He was editor of *the Library Quarterly* from 1975 to 1980. He is co-editor with Alistair Black of *Library Trends*. Among his publications are a study of the life and work of Paul Otlet (1975) (translated into Russian and Spanish), a book of translations into English of a selection of Otlet's papers (Elsevier 1990) and most recently the edited book *European Modernism and the Information Society* (Ashgate 2008). He has edited and contributed to special issues on aspects of library and information history of the journals, *IEEE Annals of the History of Computing, Information Processing and Management* and *Library Trends*.

Laura Skouvig is Associate Professor at the Royal School of Library and Information Science in Copenhagen. Besides research on Danish library history, she has focused on the theories of Michel Foucault and their relevance for library and information science. She is board member of the Danish Library History Association, co-editor of the journal *Danish Library Research* and a member of the editorial board of *Library and Information History*.

Paul Stiff, who worked in book publishing before turning to academic life, is a professor in the Department of Typography & Graphic Communication at the University of Reading and principal investigator for the project 'Designing information for everyday life, 1815–1914', funded by the Arts and Humanities Research Council. From 1985 to 2000 he edited *Information Design Journal*; in 1996 he founded, and edits, the *Typography Papers* book series.

Paul Sturges, OBE, is a Professor Emeritus at Loughborough University, UK and a Professor Extraordinary, University of Pretoria, South Africa. His more than 150 articles, reports and books in information science include several on aspects of information history, and on the information environment of the developing world. Recently he has researched, written and lectured throughout the world on aspects of the ethics of information, including comedy as freedom of expression.

Luke Tredinnick is Senior Lecturer in Information Management at London Metropolitan University, UK. He specializes in digital culture, theories of the information age and new media practices. He is author of *Why Intranets Fail (And How to Fix Them)* (Chandos 2004), *Digital Information Contexts: Theoretical Approaches to Understanding Digital Information* (Chandos 2006) and *Digital Information Culture: The Individual and Society in the Digital Age* (Chandos 2008). He has also written various papers on post-structuralism, complexity theory and the World Wide Web.

Toni Weller is Senior Lecturer in History at De Montfort University, Leicester, UK and an Honorary Fellow of the Department of Information Science, City University, London, UK. She is author of *Information History: An Introduction – Exploring an Emergent Field* (Chandos 2008) and *The Victorians and Information: A Social and Cultural History* (VDM Verlag 2009). She is also editor of the international journal, *Library & Information History*. Her research focuses on social and cultural information history in nineteenth-century England and upon the origins of the information age. She is currently researching a new project on women as information objects in Britain, 1870–1920.

1
INTRODUCTION

Toni Weller

INFORMATION HISTORY

Since the last decades of the twentieth century, information has become increasingly commonplace: an everyday commercial and cultural commodity, ubiquitous in our daily lives. The *idea* of information has taken on a new importance and value. Theorists such as Frank Webster, Manuel Castells, Anthony Giddens and Jürgen Habermas have discussed the notion of our contemporary world as an 'information society', as information has become recognized 'as a distinguishing feature of the modern world'.[1] The issues of the information age surround us in public debate, in political discourse and in cultural considerations: the 'surveillance state', personal privacy, information design, the collection of information, information access and information dissemination, amongst many other issues.

From the late 1990s there has emerged a train of historical thought which questions the origins of these themes; asking to what extent they are a product of this new information age, and to what extent they are age-old debates brought into popular focus by the new emphasis on all things 'information'.[2] Such a line of thinking also has also begun to challenge the way we think of information historically. Hobart and Schiffman suggested in 2000 that to a society immersed in information, 'the claim that information once did not exist, that it has a history, sounds absurd'.[3] However, until the late 1990s and early 2000s, scholars had not explored the idea of information historically at all. The old adage that the present affects the way we study the past, or, more to the point, that present issues can influence what we deem important to study about the past, has proved itself to be as true as ever. In previous generations, the 1960s witnessed a new historiography of crime following social challenges to the establishment after the Second World War.[4] The 1970s saw an interest in

1

women in history when the dominant issue of the day was feminism.[5] Likewise, the late 1990s and 2000s have seen a new exploration of the multifarious roles, uses and meanings of information in past societies, emerging from our contemporary fascination with information debates and concerns. As Peter Burke has argued, 'we should not be too quick to assume that our age is the first to take these questions [of information] seriously'.[6] This 'information turn' in scholarly thinking forms the basis of this collection of essays.

The book attempts to draw some of this work together; to explore information in the context of the history of the modern world; and to suggest some alternate histories of the contemporary information age. The contributors to this book do not suggest any kind of inevitable Whiggish progression towards 'the information age'; rather, they explore the concept of information in a variety of historical contexts. The chapters in this volume are discrete histories in their own right, but they are drawn together by a common historiography of information. A recent review of the literature of information history over the past decade suggested that such scholarship has two key features in common:

> The first is an overt and explicit recognition that the historical study of information adds a new perspective to more traditional histories, that they complement each other, but that the information discourse is something new. This is definitely a phenomenon of the last ten to fifteen years... The second is a sense, from the authors, that they are in some way contributing to a bigger picture, building up a new chronology and historiography of information, that the whole is greater than the sum of its parts.[7]

These commonalities can be applied to each of the chapters of this book. As individual studies they are fascinating; as a whole they offer a bigger picture of how the history of information can challenge our understandings of the modern information age, and add other perspectives to more established historical discourses.

Consequently, these chapters do not define or differentiate between information, knowledge, facts, wisdom or any other variants on the theme. There has been a great deal of literature on how these ideas should be defined, particularly within the library and information-science community,[8] but such definitions can be counterproductive in historical studies. In fact, the need to define information *explicitly* in this way is a recent development of the information age. As research into nineteenth-century Britain has shown, past societies did not feel the need to differentiate between such concepts, and we should not impose definitions upon the past.[9] Information is heterogeneous. It 'is multifaceted, so... multiple definitions apply concurrently'.[10] The multiple definitions that information has been afforded in recent decades are a good example of the 'language game' of Ludwig Wittgenstein, in which the meaning of a word should be identified by the way in which it is used, rather than by any single definition.[11] In this book therefore, the concept of information is defined and explored in relation to the specific historical context of each chapter, which changes according to focus and historical interpretation.[12] This is not so much a grand narrative; it is a grand perspective.

THE MODERN WORLD

The chronology of information history in the modern world does require some definition, however. The idea of modernity is complex, usually associated with the rise of nationalism and empire, capitalism, secularization and the growth of the state.[13] Such associations mean that the concept of the 'modern' world tends to be dated from the middle of the eighteenth century onwards, although others have posited its origins much earlier or much later.[14] Whilst there is no chronological restriction on the historical study of information – recent studies have explored information in the Roman Empire and in early modern Japan and Europe, for example[15] – this volume focuses on the era of the post-Enlightenment and post-industrial world from 1750 onwards. This era witnessed critical changes in scientific and cultural thinking and experience which had profound consequences for the way in which information was perceived and used within society.

Politically, the second half of the eighteenth century and the first decades of the nineteenth saw huge changes to the established order. In America, the War of Independence in the late 1770s and the Civil War almost a century later helped to establish the United States as a new political player. The revolution of 1789 in France and the subsequent revolutionary wars sent tremors throughout Europe which were still being felt in the revolutions of 1848. Both American and French conflicts emphasized the idea of liberties, civil rights and freedom of expression. Access and dissemination of information took on greater significance. Whilst largely stifled in the immediate aftermath by the reactionary conservative governments of Europe, more liberal ideals associated with Enlightenment traditions began to emerge in the salons and coffee houses of the West as well as through informal information exchanges. Publications such as *Tatler* put down coffee houses as their editorial addresses, and different locations specialized in different types of information: political, shipping, society or economic.[16]

It was not just coffee houses that utilized the liberal ideas of expression. The late eighteenth and nineteenth centuries saw a tremendous growth in print culture throughout the world. This was the era of the periodical and the newspaper, aided by the application of steam technology to printing and the abolition of taxes on paper.[17] Most cities in Europe had their own publications. Cheap 'penny magazines', based on the original *Penny Magazine* in England, were aimed at the new working classes, and had wide distribution in both Europe and America. The movements for education and political reform questioned to what extent the masses should have access to 'useful' information, pointing to the dangers of an informed radical mass.[18] The revolutionary decades of 1780 to 1820 saw much state censorship of the radical press throughout Europe, but this did not prevent the growth of cheap publications which drew attention to the political and social issues of the day.[19] Books were published on topics of all kinds, from science and geography to music, history and art. Education became a popular subject for books, following John Locke's influential essay of 1693, *Some Thought Concerning Education*, reprinted in numerous editions throughout the nineteenth century.[20] By the early twentieth century state-provided formal education had became the norm, and literacy rates rose accordingly.

Not only were more books, periodicals and newspapers being published than ever before, but the communications revolution meant that information could be shared much more quickly and effectively. Throughout Europe and North America the number of railway lines soared during the mid-nineteenth century, carrying passengers, publications – and ideas – with them. The telegraph, telephone and postal systems helped to communicate and disseminate information, with the technological developments of the latter twentieth century allowing unprecedented democratization and access to information via digital technologies and the internet.[21] Such openness and dissemination brought their own problems, and issues of theft, censorship and transgression arose. Criminals utilized new communication and information technologies just as much as they had done with earlier technologies and tools.[22] Dissent could be communicated just as easily as acquiescence.

By the late nineteenth century the growth of imperialism and colonial conflict was creating new tensions and uncertainties on a global scale, which escalated through the two world wars of the twentieth century. Political tensions reached their peak in the Cold War between the capitalist West and the communist East from the 1950s, only to be succeeded by new forms of terrorism through the 1980s and on into the twenty-first century.[23] This post- 9/11 environment has given rise to an ongoing 'information war' about who controls opinion and propaganda most effectively.[24] Habermas' informed public sphere of the nineteenth century has arguably become a global arena for control of information. Information then, in all its variety of manifestations, has played an important role in the modern world.

The word 'information' was not new to the late eighteenth century. Its etymological origin stemmed from the Middle Ages, where it was derived from the medieval Latin *informationem* and old French *enformacion*, meaning 'formation of the mind, or teaching'.[25] However, although the word had been in use for several centuries, the 1800s witnessed a shift in the way people, in the West at least, understood, conceptualized and used information.[26] For Neil Postman, 'the eighteenth century generated a tumult of new information; along with new media through which information [was] communicated'.[27]

More specifically, it was not just that new information was available but, more significantly, that for the first time people began to view information as a category in its own right. There was a profound shift in conceptual understanding during the nineteenth century. Information was no longer a 'rhetorical instrument' used to convince, persuade or inform, but instead became divorced from content and specific purpose.[28] For Postman, this was intrinsically linked to the new technologies of industrialization: the telegraph, telephone and photograph each allowed the isolation of information, and its separation from the earlier traditions of information content, persuasion and rhetoric. However, such a conceptual shift should not be located entirely within changes in technology. Ronald Day has argued that language and political agency have also influenced such changing perceptions, and that the growth of bureaucracy and documentation in the late nineteenth century introduced a modern culture of information.[29] I have argued elsewhere that the technological processes and tools of the post-1750 period were only part of the story, and that the social and cultural acceptance of information raised nascent questions of personal and public information personas; of visual information; and of the collection and display of information artefacts.[30] During the nineteenth century then, there was a shift from pre-modern to modern understandings of information.[31] Information was discussed explicitly as an idea, as a concept, rather than forming a more implicit part of education or polemic. There was not just a move towards the modern world from 1750 in terms of bureaucracy, nationalism, politics and so forth; there was also a move towards a more recognizably modern way of conceptualizing information. The chapters of this book focus on the period during this shift. The modern world, so far as this volume is concerned, is not just linked to the traditional discourses of the Enlightenment and industrialization. It argues that alongside this broader historical context from 1750, we can also see early traces of the modern conceptual values and the ubiquitous nature of information that have now become so evident in our own contemporary society.

Following on from this argument, there are two exceptions to the general post-1750 emphasis of the book. In Chapter 2 Edward Higgs explores personal identification in England in the five centuries since 1500, but he argues that there were very modern concerns with identity and trust which necessitated 'the development of forms of personal identification based on the storage and retrieval of information'.[32] The majority of the chapter deals with the post-industrial period from 1750 onwards, but in this context modern concerns over personal privacy can be identified much earlier than the industrial revolution.

The second exception to the general post-1750 emphasis is Chapter 3, in which W. Boyd Rayward discusses the lives of four men in mid-seventeenth-century France and England. He argues that the protagonists 'were actively participating in a pre-modern information society that was on the cusp of the enormous changes that were to usher in our modern world and create the information infrastructures that support it'.[33] His chapter offers a glimpse of what was happening on the very edge of the nascent modern information world.

CONTRIBUTING CHAPTERS

The chapters follow a roughly chronological order, although there is a degree of temporal overlap between them. This introductory chapter offers some background to the field of information history and attempts to set the contextual scene for the chapters that follow. In Chapter 2, 'Personal Identification as Information Flows in England, 1500–2000', Edward Higgs examines the ways in which identification and the body are turned into information in database systems and communicated around the world. He provides a grand narrative of identity and personal information flows since 1500, challenging the accepted notion that the pre-industrialized world was based on trust and recognition. He argues that the nineteenth-century development of credit rating agencies, and anthropometric and fingerprinting systems of identification which were intended to be communicated down telegraph lines, developed themes and concerns which were already long-established, and that the role of warfare and welfare during the twentieth century continued this tradition. Although the focus of the chapter is on England, there are arguably parallels to be made with continental Europe and North America.

Boyd Rayward continues the theme of information flows and networks in Chapter 3, 'Information for the Public: Information Infrastructure in the Republic of Letters'. He discusses the interlinking case studies of four men involved in the intellectual development of Europe during the seventeenth century through the Republic of Letters – Théophraste Renaudot, Gabriel Naudé, Samuel Hartlib and John Dury. He argues that the history of how societies, in times of violent and far-reaching social and political change, such as the period covered by this chapter, struggle to manage the information on which their security and identity to a large extent depend, is critical to our understanding of our own information age. During a period of profound political and social disturbances in the mid-seventeenth century new social and institutional practices of managing information became central to the way information was communicated. The information impact of war, instability and threat discussed here in relation to mid-seventeenth-century France and England are also evident in other chapters discussing Britain between the sixteenth and twentieth centuries, and in twentieth-century Africa (see Chapters 2, 4, 6 and 8).

In Chapter 4, 'Designing and Gathering Information: Perspectives on Nineteenth-Century Forms', Paul Stiff, Paul Dobraszczyk and Mike Esbester explore the notions of information design during the nineteenth century, using the ephemera of material printed forms to show the impact on state interaction and contemporary discourses of information- gathering. They discuss the importance of historical information design, using examples of the administrative tax and census form to conclude that there was a conceptual shift in the way citizens read and wrote information through official state documents. They argue that while the state demanded compliance in the completion of such forms, citizens often either refused, or were unable to comply with, such conformity. Building on the ideas expressed by Edward Higgs in Chapter 2, Stiff et al. offer a more subtle interpretation of the collection of information on individuals, and its socio-cultural impact.

Laura Skouvig takes a look at the impact of nineteenth- and early twentieth-century industrialization in Denmark in Chapter 5, 'Broadside Ballads, Almanacs and the *Illustrated News*: Genres and Rhetoric in the Communication of Information in Denmark 1800–1925'. She offers a view from the peasant classes, and describes the ways in which they used and disseminated information. More specifically, she asks what the media landscape looked like and how it worked as the channel for dispersing information during the long nineteenth century in Denmark. She explores how the need for information was defined and how information was dispersed through the medium of the broadside ballad. This offers an interesting comparison with other chapters which focus on Britain during this period, particularly with those by Paul Stiff et al. and Alistair Black (Chapters 4 and 7) which engage with cultural information and information design.

Moving more fully into the twentieth century, Dave Muddiman offers a case history of the Imperial Institute in London in Chapter 6, 'Information and Empire: The Information and Intelligence Bureaux of the Imperial Institute, London, 1887–1949'. He argues that information played a key role in nationalism and imperialism, from the late nineteenth into the twentieth century, in the development of the information-intensive societies we recognize today. As demonstrated by the chapters of Edward Higgs, Boyd Rayward, Paul Stiff et al. and Paul Sturges (Chapters 2, 3, 4, and 8), the rhetoric of the information state seems to become more powerful in periods of conflict or threat, when it is intrinsically linked to information culture and discourse.

Alistair Black looks at the development of information management during the first half of the twentieth century in Chapter 7. In 'A Valuable Handbook of Information: The Staff Magazine in the First Half of the Twentieth Century as a Means of Information Management', he argues that the origins of managing information can be found in the early company magazine rather than in the advent of the microprocessor and the internet. Complementing the chapters by Laura Skouvig and Paul Stiff et al. (Chapters 4 and 5), Black's account shows the significance of the way information is presented and managed visually through cultural mediums.

In Chapter 8, 'Modelling Recent Information History: The "Banditry" of the Lord's Resistance Army in Uganda', Paul Sturges uses information history as a tool to re-examine military conflicts, focusing on Ugandan liberation struggles dating from the 1980s as information wars. Contrary to views which present such tensions as battles over political or economic power, Sturges argues that it is information which is the dominant currency. He concludes that his graphical model of an information conflict could be usefully applied to contexts much broader than political liberation struggles; anywhere in fact where there is competition and discord between factions. Although the majority of information history research is currently dominated by Western scholars or subjects (mostly due to the relative youth of the field), there is no reason why it should remain so as the field expands. Indeed, modernity is not synonymous with Westernization, and its key processes and dynamics can be found in all societies.[34] This chapter provides an interesting contrast to the information histories of the Western world.

In the penultimate chapter, 'Rewriting History: The Information Age and the Knowable Past', Luke Tredinnick brings us right up to the contemporary present, exploring how the mutability of digital records and the participatory nature of digital discourse are changing the relationship between the recorded past and lived present, drawing on postmodern historiography around the nature of writing and text. Tredinnick argues that information history offers a way of rethinking both the nature of history and our relationship with the past, in an era which is more ephemeral and ontologically unstable than ever before. In Chapter 9 we witness a full circle from the conceptual shifts towards information during the nineteenth century discussed above, from pre-modern to modern, to perhaps a more subtle postmodern view of information discourse in the twenty-first century.

In the concluding chapter, 'Information History in the Modern World', I attempt to bring together some of the broader themes emerging from the rest of the book. This chapter explores the ideas of identity, the management and control of information, surveillance, conflict, the information state, information design and challenges to the way we view the information age more holistically, drawing on the previous chapters for examples. I argue that despite differences in temporal and geographical emphasis, there is a great deal of consistency in the arguments presented on the historical study of information in the modern world. By presenting this collection of essays together in one volume, a new collective picture of information history emerges.

A FINAL THOUGHT

The subtitle of this book is *Histories of the Information Age*. The plural is significant. There is no single history of information; as with any historical subject, it is open to a range of definitions and contextual interpretation. The information turn which emerged at the end of the 1990s, and has continued to gain momentum, suggests a richness of unexplored avenues. As contemporary concerns and debates about information continue to flux, information history offers a way of exploring and reflecting our own shifting attitudes to information and the information society. I argued in a recent article on the changing historiography of information between 2000 and 2009 that we can trace 'a shift in how historical understandings of information have changed; from technological to political to a cultural emphasis'[35] as the decade has progressed, but which have all retained a commonality of purpose and overview. The chapters in this volume, while eclectic in their subject matter, also share a consistent intent and justification: to contribute to a bigger information discourse.

It is hoped that this collection of essays will act as an introduction to these bigger themes and historiographical developments. Information history has many facets, and the chapters here showcase just some of them: the information state, information collection, identification, personal privacy, information design, public and private information, and information culture. Each chapter has comprehensive bibliographical notes which suggest further readings in these areas and others. By all means read the chapters as individual articles, but also read them as part of a larger and more subtle discourse of information history.

NOTES

1. F. Webster (2002), *Theories of the Information Society* (London: Routledge), p. 1. See also J. Habermas (1962), *The Structural Transformation of the Public Sphere* (Cambridge: Polity); A. Giddens (1990), *The Consequences of Modernity* (Cambridge: Polity); M. Castells (1996–98), *The Information Age* (Oxford: Blackwell).
2. Good coverage of the literature prior to 2000 can be found in A. Black (1995), 'New Methodologies in Library History: A Manifesto for the "New" Library History', *Library History*, 1, pp. 76–85; A. Black (1997), 'Lost Worlds of Culture: Victorian Libraries, Library History and Prospects for a History of Information', *Journal of Victorian Culture*, 2 (1), pp. 124–41; A. Black (1998), 'Information and Modernity: The History of Information and the Eclipse of Library History', *Library History*, 14 (1), pp. 39–45; A. Black (2006), 'Information History', in B. Cronin (ed.), *Annual Review of Information Science and Technology Volume 40* (New Jersey: Information Today Inc), pp. 441–74; T. Weller (2007), 'Information History: Its Importance, Relevance, and Future', *Aslib Proceedings*, 59 (4/5), pp. 437–48; T. Weller (2008), *Information History – An Introduction: Exploring an Emergent Field* (Oxford: Chandos).
3. M. Hobart and Z. Schiffman (2000), *Information Ages: Literacy, Numeracy and the Computer Revolution* (Maryland: Johns Hopkins University Press), p. 2.
4. For discussion of this see, for example, C. Emsley and L. Knafla (eds) (1996), *Crime History and Histories of Crime: Studies in the Historiography of Crime and Criminal Justice in Modern History* (Santa Barbara: Greenwood Press); M. Arnot and C. Usborne (eds) (1999), *Gender and Crime in Modern Europe* (London: UCL Press).
5. For example, see N. Cott (1977), *The Bonds of Womanhood* (New Haven: Yale University Press); N. Cott and E. Pleck (eds) (1979), *A Heritage of Her Own: Toward a New Social History of American Women* (New York: Simon and Schuster); K. Offen (1998), 'Defining Feminism: A Comparative Historical Approach', *Signs*, 14 (1), pp. 119–57.
6. P. Burke (2000), *A Social History of Knowledge: From Gutenburg to Diderot* (Cambridge: Polity Press).
7. T. Weller (2010a), 'An Information History Decade: A Review of the Literature and Concepts, 2000–2009', *Library & Information History*, 26 (1), pp. 83–97.
8. See, for example, C. Shannon and W. Weaver (1949), *The Mathematical Theory of Communication* (Urbana: University of Illinois Press); G. Stigler (1961), 'The Economics of Information', *Journal of Political Economy*, 69 (3), pp. 213–25; N. Belkin (1990), 'The Cognitive Viewpoint in Information Science', *Journal of Information Science*, 6 (91), pp. 11–15; M. Buckland (1991), 'Information as a Thing', *Journal for the American Society for Information Science*, 42 (5), pp. 351–60; J. Eaton and D. Bawden (1991), 'What Kind of Resource is Information?',

International Journal of Information Management, 1 (2), pp. 156–65; T. Haywood and J. Broady (1994), 'Macroeconomic Change: Information and Knowledge', *Journal of Information Science*, 20 (6), pp. 377–88; D. Kaye (1995), 'The Nature of Information', *Library Review*, 44 (8), pp. 37–48; C. Meadow and W. Yuan (1997), 'Measuring the Impact of Information: Defining the Concepts', *Information Processing and Management*, 33 (6), pp. 697–715; J. Rowley (1998), 'What is Information?', *Information Services and Use*, 18 (4), pp. 243–54; C. Oppenheim, J. Stenson and R. Wilson (2003), 'Studies on Information as an Asset III: Views of Information Professionals', *Journal of Information Science*, 30 (2), pp. 181–90; C. Zins (2006), 'Redefining Information Science: From "Information Science" to "Knowledge Science"', *Journal of Documentation*, 62 (4), pp. 447–61.

9. See T. Weller and D. Bawden (2006), 'Individual Perceptions: A New Chapter on Victorian Information History', *Library History*, 22 (2), pp. 137–56; Weller, *Information History*; Weller (2009), *The Victorians and Information: A Social and Cultural History* (Saarbrücken: VDM Verlag); Weller (2010a), *An Information History Decade*.

10. S. Braman (1989), 'Defining Information: An Approach for Policymakers', *Telecommunications Policy*, 13 (3), pp. 234–5.

11. L. Wittgenstein (1985), *Philosophical Investigations* (Oxford: Blackwell).

12. For more discussion on defining information in relation to historical context see Black, 'Information and Modernity, pp. 39–45; Weller, *Information History*; Weller, *Information History: An Introduction*; Weller, *The Victorians and Information*.

13. See, for example, A. Giddens (1998), *Conversations with Anthony Giddens: Making Sense of Modernity* (Stanford: Stanford University Press); and C. Barker (2005), *Cultural Studies: Theory and Practice* (London: Sage).

14. S. Toulmin (1990), *Cosmopolis: The Hidden Agenda of Modernity* (New York: Free Press) offers the argument that modernity could begin as early as the fifteenth century, or as late as the second half of the twentieth century.

15. See, for example, A. Lee (2006), *Information and Frontiers: Roman Foreign Relations in Late Antiquity* (Cambridge: Cambridge University Press); J. König and T. Whitmarsh (eds) (2007), *Ordering Knowledge in the Roman Empire* (Cambridge: Cambridge University Press); M. Berry (2007), *Japan in Print: Information and Nation in the Early Modern Period* (California: University of California Press); and F. de Vivo (2007), *Information and Communication in Venice: Rethinking Early Modern Politics* (Oxford: Oxford University Press).

16. M. Ellis (2004), *The Coffee House: A Cultural History* (London: Weidenfield & Nicolson) has a good discussion of this phenomenon.

17. E. Eisenstein (1979), *The Printing Press as an Agent of Change: Communication and Culture in Early Modern Europe* (Cambridge: Cambridge University Press); R. Altick (1998), *The English Common Reader: A Social History of the Mass Reading Public, 1800–1900* (Ohio: Ohio State University Press).

18. Weller, *The Victorians and Information*, pp. 25–56, 87–120.

19. See, for example, R. Goldstein (2000), *The War for the Public Mind: Political Censorship in Nineteenth Century Europe* (Westport: Praeger Publishing).

20. J. Locke (1693), *Some Thoughts Concerning Education* (London). See G. Boyce, J. Curran and P. Wingate (eds) (1978), *Newspaper History from the Seventeenth Century to the Present Day* (London: Constable); Burke, *A Social History of Knowledge*; A. Raunch (2001) *Useful Knowledge: The Victorians, Morality and the March of Intellect* (London: Duke University Press).

21. See, for example, M. Daunton (1985), *Royal Mail: The Post Office Since 1840* (London: Athlone); J. Beniger (1986), *The Control Revolution: Technological and Economic Origins of the Information Society* (Boston: Harvard University Press); T. Haywood (1995), *Info-Rich, Info-Poor: Access and Exchange in the Global Information Society* (London: Bowker-Saur); P. Hall and P. Preston (1988), *The Carrier Wave: New Information Technologies and the Geography of Innovation, 1846–2003* (London: Unwin Hyman); T. Weller and D. Bawden (2005), 'The Social and Technological Origins of the Information Society, 1830–1900,' *Journal of Documentation*, 61 (6), pp. 777–802.
22. D. Phillips (1993), 'Crime, Law and Punishment in the Industrial Revolution', in P. O'Brien and R. Quinault (eds), *The Industrial Revolution and British Society* (Glasgow: Bell & Bain Ltd), pp. 156–82.
23. See, for example, C. Bartlett (1984), *The Global Conflict: The International Rivalry of the Great Powers 1880–1990* (Harlow: Longman); E. Hobsbawm (1995), *Age of Extremes: The Short Twentieth Century 1914–1991* (London: Abacus); B. Bond (1998), *War and Society in Europe, 1870–1970* (Montreal: McGill-Queen's University Press); and, G. Wawro (1999), *Warfare and Society in Europe, 1792–1914* (London: Routledge).
24. N. Snow (2003), *Information War: American Propaganda, Free Speech and Opinion Control Since 9/11* (New York: Seven Stories Press); H. Tumber and F. Webster (2006), *Journalists under Fire: Information War and Journalistic Practices* (London: Sage).
25. *Chambers Dictionary of Etymology* (1998) (Chambers), p. 527; *The Oxford Dictionary of Word Histories* (2002) (Oxford: Oxford University Press), p. 272; *The Oxford English Dictionary* (Oxford: Oxford University Press).
26. For more on this see N. Postman (1999), 'Information', in *Building a Bridge to the Eighteenth Century* (New York: Vintage), pp. 82–98; R. Day (2001), *The Modern Invention of Information* (Edwardsville: The Southern Illinois Press); Weller and Bawden, *Individual Perceptions;* Weller, *The Victorians and Information*; Weller (2010b), 'The Victorian Information Age: Nineteenth Century Answers to Today's Information Policy Questions?', *History & Policy*, (June) available at http://www.historyandpolicy.org/papers/policy-paper-104.html.
27. Postman, *Information*, p. 82.
28. Postman, *Information*, pp. 87–8.
29. Day, *The Modern Invention*, pp. 1–37.
30. Weller, *The Victorians and Information*.
31. For more on the shift from pre-modern to modern conceptualizations of information see Weller, *The Victorians and Information*.
32. Chapter 2, this volume.
33. Chapter 3, this volume.
34. S. Eisenstadt (2003), *Comparative Civilizations and Multiple Modernities* (Leiden and Boston: Brill); G. Delanty (2007), 'Modernity', in G. Ritzer (ed.), *Blackwell Encyclopedia of Sociology* (Malden: Blackwell Publishing).
35. Weller, *An Information History Decade*, p. 95.

2

PERSONAL IDENTIFICATION AS INFORMATION FLOWS IN ENGLAND, 1500–2000

Edward Higgs

INTRODUCTION

The study of the social uses of information seems appropriate to the contemporary 'Information Age'. However, as the contributions to this book reveal, the historical study of information is also important in helping the present to understand its past. This is certainly the case with respect to the history of the techniques and technologies used to identify people as particular individuals from the early-modern period onwards. Seeing the history of identification in terms of information flows might seem, at first, a little perverse. After all, identifying someone is surely a grasping of their essential being, rather than the provision of information? The former may be true when identifying a friend in a public place, or a loved-one in a morgue, but it is more difficult to see this process in action when one has to identify a stranger. Here it is necessary to have some sign, token, or information, which can be used to verify that the person is who they say they are. This is especially true when individuals are identifying not their bodies, but personalities that are social conventions – their legal persona, or their citizenship. Thus, signatures do not identify bodies but juridical persons, and have the force of law long after the body has ceased to exist. As will be argued here, identification in this more extensive sense has always involved information flows. There are also cases where individuals do not want to be identified and take considerable pains to prevent this, as with criminals and impostors. Even here one cannot rely on the direct identification of witnesses, as numerous cases of mistaken identity have revealed.[1]

An attentive reader might grant the possibility of writing a history of identification as information flows, but might baulk at the idea of pushing this history back into the early-modern period, say before 1760. Before the industrial revolution, England was a land of small, immobile communities in which there were no strangers, and people lived a life of face-to-face interaction that engendered trust, or so the accepted idea goes. In such communities, we are told, there was little need of identification as a flow of information. This is certainly a popular understanding of 'Merry England', and even one found, in passing, in some histories of identification.[2] However, this notion of early-modern England as a country without strangers, and founded on trust, is almost completely fallacious. Recent historical research has shown that at least since the fourteenth century English men and women moved home over their lifetimes as frequently as we do today.[3] The fear of the wandering stranger, or poor vagrant, was so pervasive in the sixteenth and seventeenth centuries that it even spawned a vast draconian system of repression in the Vagrancy Laws.[4] Of course, people moved much less on a day-to-day basis, and worked and lived in the same locale, but there were still plenty of strangers who needed to be identified.

Similarly, people in the period often had to place their trust in strangers because so many purchases were on the basis of credit agreements made before witnesses, and this hardly led to the creation of a society based on trust. Thus, by the late sixteenth century the amount of civil litigation in England might have been as high as 1,102,367 cases per year, one suit for every household in the country. This can be compared to England and Wales in the mid- 1990s, where the rate of civil litigation was only a quarter of this figure.[5] The serious problems caused by forgery, and other forms of 'identity theft', explain why William Blackstone in his mid-eighteenth-century *Commentaries* declared that 'there is now hardly a case possible to be conceived wherein forgery, that tends to defraud, whether in the name of a real or fictitious person, is not made a capital crime'.[6] The pillory, fines and imprisonment were the penalties in those rare cases that were not subject to capital punishment.[7] There was thus ample scope for the development of forms of personal identification based on the storage and retrieval of information.

IDENTIFICATION IN EARLY MODERN ENGLAND

The story of Martin Guerre, the sixteenth-century French impostor who was the subject of a classic historical monograph by Natalie Zemon Davis, and a number of films, shows that much identification in the early-modern world did indeed depend upon personal information. Arnaud du Tihl was able to impersonate Guerre, who was away at the wars, because he was accepted as Guerre by the latter's wife and her family.[8] But there were still numerous ways in which identification might depend on information systems before the modern period.

This can be seen most clearly in the state welfare system instituted under the Tudor and Stuart Poor Laws. In essence, the Poor Law system laid down that the 'respectable, impotent poor', who could prove that they had a 'settlement', or 'belonged', in a parish, should be given relief paid out of a parish-based tax, the poor rate. People obtained a settlement in a parish via birth, marriage, the ownership or renting of property, paying parish rates, or residence or employment for a stipulated period. By the eighteenth century, parishes were able to send funds to other parishes to support 'their' parishioners who lived elsewhere.[9] The whole system was administered by the overseers of the poor, drawn from the wealthier inhabitants of the parish, and supervised by the gentry-magistrates, the justices of the peace.[10]

The workings of this system created vast flows of enquiries and answers between the hundreds of thousands of overseers who ran the Poor Law system until its demise in the early twentieth century. This functioned as a distributed information system, with officials drawing on information about would-be welfare claimants to identify if they had settlements, or were chargeable elsewhere. The dispersal of information in different parishes necessitated a constant exchange of correspondence. Documentation also helped to underpin parts of this elaborate welfare system. The parochial registers provided information about baptisms, marriages and burials, which could be used to solve all manner of practical disputes about who had a settlement in a parish.[11] These documents had been instituted in 1538 by Henry VIII's vicar-general, Thomas Cromwell, who saw them as a useful means 'for the avoiding of sundry strifes, processes and contentions rising from age, lineal descent, title of inheritance, legitimation of bastardy, and for knowledge whether any person is our subject or no'.[12]

Identification under the Poor Laws could also take the form of documents held by the poor themselves. Documentary forms of identification were made mobile in the late seventeenth and eighteenth centuries in the form of the settlement certificate. This was a paper, signed by the magistrates, which named a migrant and indicated that he or she had a poor law settlement in a particular parish. This guaranteed that the officers and ratepayers of the parish of settlement would relieve the pauper no matter where he or she actually lived, whether that was in the parish of settlement itself or, increasingly as the decades passed, in the parish where the pauper resided. A somewhat different form of documentation was the 'beggar's licence', authorizing a person to beg within a hundred parishes, an area called a hundred or wapentake. Such a document identified an individual as a pauper, with the geographical and moral context that gave that individuality meaning. The licence usually identified the pauper and his or her parish; it also provided a brief description of the reason for their poverty, and by implication the deservingness of their case.[13] Linked to such licences were certificates allowing the unemployed, those left destitute by fire, shipwrecked sailors or maimed soldiers, to travel in search of jobs, home ports or places of settlement.[14] As with all sorts of documentary evidence, these forms of identification were endlessly forged.[15]

In this period seals and signatures could identify the will of the juridical person on documents, but as the laws on forgery indicate, they were hardly foolproof methods of identification. The answer to this problem, if an expensive one, was to have one's documents given an official status through holding them in registries. On the Continent that was often done through the institution of the public, or private, notary, who wrote out documents, signed them himself, and then preserved them in his own records.[16] In England, however, this function was carried out by the courts of law such as Chancery.[17] As banks developed from the seventeenth century onwards, they dealt with the problem of forgery through the creation of registries of specimen signatures, a system that survived down into the twentieth century.

An alternative way of dealing with juridical identity was to incorporate it into a document that passed from hand to hand, the early-modern equivalent of packet-switching. This can be seen in the more formal credit instruments used by merchants for long-range transactions in the early-modern period – the bill obligatory, bill of debt, or bond. These were sealed documents which typically combined acknowledgements of debt with an undertaking to settle them, and contained the names of the parties, the amount of the debt and the date or dates for repayment. Such documents were often assigned to others by signed endorsements on the back, so that the assignee took the place of the assignor, and they became a means of circulating credit. Moreover, merchants often acknowledged debts with 'bills', 'bills of hand', or promissory notes, which were open documents and merely signed. Increasingly, however, the principal financial instrument used in inland banking was the inland bill of exchange – an unconditional order in writing, addressed by one person to another, signed by the person giving it, requiring the person to whom it was addressed to pay on demand, or at a fixed date, a certain sum of money to the bearer or to a specified person. This can still be seen in the wording on the front of modern British bank notes: 'I promise to pay the bearer on demand the sum of ...', with the signature of the chief cashier of the Bank of England.[18]

In the case of the criminal, the body itself became the site of information exchange, through being marked with signs of infamy. Branding and ear-boring, as a means of marking the deviant status of the criminal, had been statutory punishments in England from the late fourteenth century. A labour statute of 1361 declared that fugitives were to be branded on the forehead with 'F' for 'falsity'. The Vagabonds Act of 1547 ordered that vagrants should be branded with a 'V' on their breast.[19] Ear-boring was introduced in 1572, when a statute was passed requiring all vagabonds to be 'grievously whipped and burned through the gristle of the right ear with a hot iron'. By an Act of 1604, 'incorrigible rogues' were to be 'branded in the left shoulder with a hot burning iron of the breadth of an English shilling with a great Roman "R" upon the iron'.[20] Similarly, at the Old Bailey convicts who successfully pleaded benefit of clergy, and those found guilty of manslaughter instead of murder, were branded on the thumb (with a 'T' for theft, 'F' for felon, or 'M' for murder), so that they would be unable to receive this benefit more than once.[21]

Given that policing in the early-modern period was a widely distributed system, based on local parish constables and justices of the peace, it should come as no surprise that descriptions of criminals were widely circulated. By the early seventeenth century the physical pursuit of criminals across parish and county boundaries had often been replaced by the bureaucratic proce-dure of issuing written warrants of 'hue and cry' to be circulated amongst law enforcement officers. The written warrant, designed to be passed from hand to hand between officials, necessitated the introduction of a prose description of the wanted person. Constables' accounts for Manchester in the period 1612 to 1631 list on average 12 issues of such warrants per year.[22] In London at the same time, court books were full of descriptions of wanted criminals.[23]

In 1771 John Fielding, the blind London magistrate and brother of Henry Fielding, took the logical step of bringing the descriptions of wanted criminals found in the warrants of hue and cry together into a single publication. In that year he began publishing the *Quarterly Pursuit* and the *Weekly or Extraordinary Pursuit*, which later became the *Hue and Cry*. Fielding was in correspondence with magistrates all over London and the provinces, and asked them to send him details of criminals. He collated this information and sent the results to the magistrates on a weekly and quarterly basis, including 'an exact descrip-tion of their persons'. In the late eighteenth century, however, official systems for disseminating deviant identifications were increasingly overshadowed by the private use of newspapers, and other printed periodicals and handbills, for the same purpose. This reflected the rapid spread of printing in the provinces, as well as improvements in postal, coaching and carrying services, and in the road network itself. Associations for the prosecution of felons were set up, and subscribers could use these to place adverts and offer rewards.[24] In addition to newspaper advertisements, printed handbills provided a much deeper, and more clearly targeted, penetration of the potential audience at the local level, especially in rural areas where the circulation of newspapers was limited.[25] Such handbills could often provide more detail in descriptions, to aid identification.

Thus, forms of identification in the early-modern period were therefore heavily dependent on information systems within dispersed political and commercial systems.

IDENTIFICATION DURING THE INDUSTRIAL REVOLUTION

The period of the classic Industrial Revolution, from about 1760 to 1850, was a time of vast population movements, urbanization and increasing anonymization. However, perhaps surprisingly, it did not see much in the way of innovations in forms of identification. Indeed, some forms of identification, such as settlement certificates, declined in importance.[26] Similarly, the identification of aliens came and then went, with the registration systems of the French Revolution and Napoleonic period being dismantled by the 1836 Aliens Act.[27] The nineteenth century as a whole saw the relaxation of restrictions on international movement, at least in Europe, with the virtual abandonment of the use of passports.[28] However, the century did see the start of the creation of centralized databases in which identification depended on the storage and retrieval of information. These were a means of identification of the citizen, the consumer and the deviant.

In 1836 the system of parochial registration of baptisms, marriages and burials was replaced by a new centralized system for births, marriages and deaths. Vital events were to be registered locally, but copies of the certificates were to be sent to a new General Register Office (GRO) in London. The establishment of the GRO initially reflected a desire to improve the recording of lines of descent, and so underpin property rights. A centralized system meant that solicitors no longer needed to visit numerous dispersed parish registries to substantiate claims of lineal descent. In the *Twenty-second Annual Report of the Registrar General for 1859*, for example, the second Registrar General, George Graham, noted that in that year there were 4,110 successful searches in the registers at the GRO – 1,662 births, 1,866 deaths and 582 marriages. Of such searches leading to the issuing of certificates, the 'greater number ... are for legal purposes, and are applied for by solicitors'.[29] By 1866 the GRO was issuing just over 10,000 certificates a year, and this figure had doubled by 1875.[30] However, by 1877 Graham was noting that besides their use for pedigree purposes:

> A considerable number of applications for birth certificates are made by candidates for civil service clerkships, for boys about to be apprenticed, and for boys about to be employed as messengers, etc. for post office purposes.[31]

This reflected, no doubt, the restrictions placed on the employment of children under a certain age by the Factory and Education Acts. The development of such certificates as a general means of identification was already foreshadowed here, and came into its own in the more centralized welfare systems of the twentieth century. The GRO certainly experienced a rush of people during the First World War requiring such certificates to prove entitlement to war pensions, or eligibility for service in the military and in munitions works.[32]

The development of a mass commercial society also created a need to identify individuals as credit risks, which led to the storing and dissemination of information. As early as 1776, the London Guardians, or the 'Society for the Protection of Trade Against Swindlers and Sharpers', had been established in the metropolis to pool information about fraudsters.[33] Similar societies grew up in commercial and industrial centres in the provinces. By 1854 the Leicester Trade Protection Society had connections with affiliates and agents in 469 towns at home and abroad, and there was a National Association of Trade Protection Societies (NATPS) co-ordinating the work of provincial organizations from 1866 onwards.[34] By combining their own private records of recalcitrant debtors with published press reports of local bankruptcies, insolvencies and county-court litigation, guardian societies built up a wealth of information on consumers, which were made available to subscribers. A year after beginning to conduct business the NATPS claimed to have received 75,000 credit enquiries. The National Association developed a 'telegraphic code' to encourage the rapid exchange of information on debtors via the telegraph system, with keywords such as 'safe', 'good' and 'with care' defining levels of creditworthiness.[35]

The Victorian period also saw the identity of the criminal turned into centralized information systems. Identification of the deviant increasingly meant the generation, storage and retrieval of information about aspects of the criminal body. Both the Habitual Criminal Registry, and the later

Metropolitan Police Convict Supervision Office set up in 1880, maintained registers for criminal identification. These contained physical descriptions, records of 'distinguishing marks' and increasingly photographs.[36] However, despite the publication of alphabetical registers of habitual criminals giving names, 'distinctive marks' and descriptions, such means of identification were seldom used by the police. This was because the information they contained could not be easily retrieved, since it was necessary to have a name to use the registers properly, which somewhat negated their use as a means of identification.[37] In addition, the sepia photographs of the time could not easily be classified and indexed, especially by colour of eyes or hair, and the whole collection might have to be searched to find a particular individual. Criminals could look alike, disguise their appearance, 'mug' in front of the camera, or change as they grew older.[38]

The first attempt to create a criminal identification system that allowed systematic retrieval was anthropometrics. This was the method of identification through bodily measurement invented by Alphonse Bertillon in late-nineteenth-century France. The anthropometric technique involved elaborate measurements of parts of the body of a criminal. These were recorded on a card along with carefully controlled discursive descriptions of features and distinctive marks, and a photograph. The measurements were used to classify individuals and to allow for easy retrieval of information when they were re-measured at a later date, although it was the peculiar marks and the photographs that were then used for identification.[39] In addition, precise descriptions and standardized abbreviations formed the basis of Bertillon's 'portrait parlé', whereby a trained operator could transmit via the telegraph a usable physical description of a criminal to another operator entirely in words, numbers and coded abbreviations.[40] The identification of the deviant was thus reduced to standardized information which could be stored in an information system, retrieved at a later date and transmitted over a distance.

However, Bertillonage had serious drawbacks as a forensic technique in Britain. These included the requirement for costly instruments that required calibration; training for operatives on the decimal, rather than imperial, scale; the possibility of error in transcribing measurements; the time needed to take measurements (each taken three times); and the complicated procedure for searching through records.[41] On the recommendation of the 1900 Belper Committee on the Identification of Criminals, fingerprinting replaced anthropometrics as the principal means of criminal identification.[42] Although fingerprinting has a long history, the creation of a fully effective means of classifying fingerprints was the achievement of Sir Edward Henry when Inspector General of Police in Bengal in the 1890s, although he may merely have been taking credit for the work of his Indian subordinates. The title of his monograph describing the new system, published by the Indian authorities in 1896, 'Bengal Police: Instructions for Classifying and Deciphering Finger Impressions and for Describing them with Sufficient Exactness to Enable Comparison of the Description with the Original Impression to be Satisfactorily Made', reveals the centrality of information retrieval in his method.[43] Henry subsequently introduced the new system into the Metropolitan Police when he became Assistant Commissioner in charge of CID at Scotland Yard in 1901.[44] As with anthropometrics, criminal identification was reduced to information that could be stored, retrieved and subsequently transmitted by telegraph in coded form.[45]

IDENTIFICATION IN THE TWENTIETH CENTURY

The twentieth century saw an increasing generalization of identification through database systems as state and commercial organizations grew in scale and centralization. It was also a period in which total war created new, unprecedented forms of identification. Before the First World War it was not mandatory for those travelling abroad to apply for a passport. During the eighteenth and nineteenth centuries, possession of a passport was confined largely to merchants and diplomats, and the vast majority of those travelling overseas did so with no formal documentation.[46] England's *laissez-faire* policy on passports for its own citizens foundered during the global conflict of the First World War, when all foreigners, and some British subjects, came to be seen as potential enemies or fifth-columnists. In November 1915 an Order in Council was issued to amend the Defence of the Realm (Consolidation) Regulations of 1914. Among the amendments made was the addition of a requirement that

A person coming from or intending to proceed to any place out of the United Kingdom as a passenger shall not, without the special permission of a Secretary of State, land or embark at any port in the United Kingdom unless he has in his possession a valid passport issued to him not more than two years previously, by or on behalf of the Government of the country of which he is a subject or a citizen[47]

In 1915 a one-page British passport, folding into eight with a cardboard cover, came into use. In addition to the photograph and signature, it contained a description of the holder and was valid for two years. In the aftermath of the War the 1914 regulation remained in force, as all Western countries erected passport systems to control their boundaries.[48] Identification as one crossed borders came to depend upon the production of an authorized document, which could be referred back to a registry of information supplied when the passport was applied for.

Similarly, both world wars led to the creation of identification systems based on national registries, and in the case of the Second World War, to the issue of ID cards. Both systems were used for conscription and rationing, and depended upon the storage and accessing of information. During the First World War a census of the country was carried out. On the basis of this citizens were given certificates containing their address, to show that they had been registered, and had to inform the authorities if they moved house, at which time they were issued with a new certificate. These certificates contained no form of individual identification, and the whole system was kept up to date through the imposition of fines for non-registration, and through the activities of 'revisers', who visited houses checking on their occupants.[49] When a new National Registration system was planned in the late 1930s, as another war loomed, it was decided to tie the system more closely in with rationing. Although the original identification of citizens for registration, and the issuing of identity cards, was again based on a census, the rationing system helped to maintain it. To get a ration book it was necessary to show an ID card, and the former would be sent to the address on the latter. There was thus a means of checking on changes of address, and picking up people who had not been caught by the census.[50] The thoroughness and universality of the resulting identification system far exceeded that created in the totalitarian regime of Nazi Germany.[51] However, there were limits to how far the British state would push such forms of total identification. Thus, both systems of national registration did not survive for very long under peace-time conditions,[52] and the forms of identification on ID cards were minimal. The general blue card issued to the bulk of the population in the Second World War did not even carry a photograph.[53]

Nor were biometric systems applied to ordinary citizens. Proposals just after the First World War to fingerprint everyone receiving pensions and benefits foundered because officials thought that the general public would not accept means of identification associated with criminals being applied to the 'respectable'.[54] Instead the central state fell back on the traditional sources of identification for welfare claimants and citizens, the community and documentation. However, these means of identification were given a new, bureaucratic form, indeed they came to be embedded physically in forms that mediated the flow of information between the state and the public. Communal means of identification were carried over into the 'recommender system'. This involved some person with semi-official status in the local community countersigning the application forms of claimants, to vouch for their identity and the information they supplied. By the 1930s those claiming pensions from the Ministry of Pensions had to obtain a 'life certificate' proving their identity, which was attested by officials or professionals – a minister of religion, a magistrate, a physician or surgeon, an officer of HM forces, a secretary of a friendly society, a postmaster or mistress, a police officer, a civil servant earning more than £200 a year, a solicitor, a bank manager, an accountant, a head teacher, or a chief area officer of the Ministry of Pensions.[55]

Today the documentary technique of identification has generally superseded the recommender system, with modern benefit offices requiring a mosaic of documents for checking and cross-referencing, including:

- Valid passport/ID card
- Two or more passports if of dual/multinationality
- Home Office documents
- Work permit
- Letter from employer/contract of employment
- Evidence of actively seeking work
- Payslips
- Mortgage/rental agreement confirming where residing
- Marriage/birth certificate/deed poll
- Student loan documentation
- Certificate of incorporation
- Memorandum of association
- Articles of association
- Stock transfer form
- Schedule D taxation form
- Services contract
- Invoices
- Letter from accountant
- Letter from client
- Letter from college, including details of type and length of course and weekly hours
- Student ID card
- Full driving licence.[56]

Many of these documents can, of course, be cross-referenced with each other, and with the electoral register, that great fall-back for all official forms of identification. Individual identification no longer depends on the personal knowledge of members of the community but upon the possession of documentation that can be linked with official or commercial information systems.

This process has been facilitated by the development of integrated IT systems within government that allow data-sharing and data profiling.[57] Rather than creating a single identification system, the state has fallen back on the dispersed information systems familiar in earlier periods.

THE 2006 IDENTIFICATION CARD ACT

However, the proposed national registration system to be established under the 2006 Identity Cards Act, if ever established, will cut across many of the traditional features of identification in Britain. This will involve the creation of a central national register, and the issuing of ID cards containing digitized biometrics. The identity card is intended as a means of fighting crime and terrorism, preventing identity theft, enabling e-government, and as a general all-purpose method of identification.[58] The creation of a centralized information system to store identification data is a departure from the usual decentralized systems of identification. Similarly, the use of biometrics to identify citizens collapses the distinctions between citizens, juridical persons and criminals that have existed for centuries. So how did this shift come about?

At one level one might explain this in terms of the statism inherent in Labour Party thinking over a long period. Fabian socialists supported the extension of the First World War registration system; the Attlee government maintained the Second World War registration system till its electoral defeat in 1951; and New Labour has sought to establish a new national registration system.[59] On this reading, the drive to introduce ID cards will disappear if Labour loses power and is replaced by a Conservative administration. However, this explanation is perhaps too glib. After all, the Conservative administration of the 1990s had attempted to introduce a voluntary identity card scheme, in the face of Labour Party opposition.[60] Similarly, the Conservative Party supported, in principle, an ID Card Bill introduced in Parliament in 2004, so their opposition to the 2006 Act may be more tactical than principled. In addition, the drive to introduce biometric ID cards is something that can be found in many countries throughout the contemporary world.[61]

Part of the reason for this shift may be the perceived success of modern biometric databases. This can be seen in the development of the use of DNA profiling in police work. Consequent upon the development of DNA sequencing for identification purposes by Sir Alec Jeffreys in the 1980s,[62] the United Kingdom has developed a database of genetic information for forensic identification. The United Kingdom's National DNA Database is the largest in the world, containing 5.2 per cent of the UK population compared with 0.5 per cent in the United States of America, and by the end of 2005 it held over 3.4

million DNA profiles.[63] Plainly, there are issues about the probabilistic nature of DNA identification, and the use that is made of the technique in court,[64] but it has now established itself in the official and popular mind as a key resource. Other forms of biometric databases are also being developed internationally for the identification of those crossing borders. The International Civil Aviation Organization, an agency of the United Nations, has a 'Machine Readable Travel Document' initiative, whilst the United Arab Emirates has already archived over 1 million iris scans of people for the purposes of border control.[65]

However, the existence of successful technologies does not mean that they will necessarily be used, and there are other factors at play here than technological determinism. National registration and identification systems in Britain have always been associated with times of danger and risk, especially during wartime, and there is a sense in which the contemporary British state and society also feel themselves at war, whether with 'terror', crime, or 'anti-social behaviour'.[66] The difference from the two world wars is, perhaps, that the enemy is seen not just as an external threat but as, potentially, any member of society. This is part of a general decline of trust in interpersonal relationships.[67] In this climate of fear, databases no longer use information to identify individuals as citizen, or even as criminals, but as risks. Information is gathered to sort people into risk categories for the purposes of surveillance, control and intervention.[68]

In this the British state is perhaps aping the use made of information systems by commercial organizations for identifying customers. Since the late 1960s businesses have been collecting information on their customers as part of their ongoing operations. In 1965 IBM developed a magnetic strip on which data could be stored in binary form, to be used with plastic cards for electronic reading. In 1967 Barclays Bank installed the first cashpoint in London using tokens, which soon led to the modern automated teller machine (ATM). In 1974 there were 14,908 branches of banks in Britain and no ATMs, whilst in 1999 there were 11,044 branches and 17,892 ATMs.[69] This led to the development of the use of passwords and personal identification numbers (PINs), through which customers supplied a common key that could be interpreted via computer databases. The subsequent use of such cards in electronic point of sale (EPOS) systems further extended the dependence of identification on information systems.[70] Identity ceased to reside in individuals and began to be located in computer databases, hence the capacity for it to be stolen. At the same time, the credit-rating agencies that grew out of mail-order businesses were developing database systems in order to establish the commercial risk presented by lending to named individuals.[71] In the 1990s supermarkets also began to collect vast amounts of information on shoppers via store loyalty cards, in order to profile them for targeted mailing and offers.[72] Information about individuals has become both a commodity and a unit of production, and is at the heart of business models.

The modern British state has been captured by commerce, both in terms of the number of state functions now outsourced to businesses, and the way in which the state now sees itself as running a business – 'UK PLC'. It should come as no surprise, therefore, that like any other commercial organization it sees the use of information on identity as a key to one of its key business processes, social control. The desire to change citizens into consumers who choose state services via e-government websites is part of this process.[73] To some extent the drive to create large database systems for identification purposes also represents the commercial interests of the large commercial vendors of such systems.[74] Since this neo-conservative agenda has been accepted throughout much of the world, the widespread interest in the use of national ID card systems becomes understandable.

CONCLUSION

Whatever the fate of the system laid out in the 2006 Identification Card Act, it is unlikely that the link between information and identification will be broken. Identification over distance and time has inevitably involved flows of information, and this has been the case since the early modern period. Today information may be more centralized and integrated, but this process has been driven by changes in the nature of modern states and commercial organizations, rather than by changes in the nature of human identity as such. However, the effect has been to de-centre identity, to place it outside the individual, and to decompose the latter into a bundle of risks, and genetic potentialities and lineages.

NOTES

1. Devlin Committee on Evidence of Identification in Criminal Cases 1975–76, *Report of the Devlin Committee on Evidence of Identification in Criminal Cases*. British Parliamentary Papers, XIX, pp. 9–66.
2. S. A. Cole (2001), *Suspect Identities: A History of Fingerprinting and Criminal Identification* (London: Harvard University Press), p. 15; C. Sengoopta (2003), *Imprint of the Raj: How Fingerprinting was Born in Colonial India* (London: Macmillan), p. 9.
3. See, for example, K. Wrightson (1982), *English Society 1580–1680* (London: Hutchinson), p. 42; D. Rollison (1999), 'Exploding England: The Dialectics of Mobility and Settlement in Early Modern England', *Social History*, 24, pp. 11–12;

C. Dyer (2007), 'Were Late Medieval English Villages "Self-Contained"', in C.Dyer (ed.) *The Self-Contained Village? The Social History of Rural Communities 1250–1900* (Hatfield: University of Hertfordshire Press), pp. 14–15.

4. A. L. Beier (1985), *Masterless Men: The Vagrancy Problem in England 1560–1640* (London: Methuen).

5. C. Muldrew (1998), *The Economy of Obligation: The Culture of Credit and Social Relations in Early Modern England* (London: Macmillan), p. 236.

6. Avalon Project at Yale Law School. *Blackstone's Commentaries on the Laws of England* [online]. Available at: http://www.yale.edu/lawweb/avalon/blackstone/bk4ch17. htm [Date accessed 18 September 2008].

7. K. M. Koppenhaver (2007), *Forensic Document Examination: Principles and Practice* (Totowa, NJ: Humana Press), p. 47.

8. N. Z. Davis (1983), *The Return of Martin Guerre* (London: Harvard University Press).

9. K. D. M. Snell (2006), *Parish and Belonging: Community, Identity and Welfare in England and Wales 1700–1950* (Cambridge: Cambridge University Press), pp. 85–6.

10. For a general introduction to the Poor Laws, see P. Slack (1990), *The English Poor Law, 1531–1782* (Basingstoke: Macmillan Education).

11. S. Szreter (2007), 'The Right of Registration: Development, Identity Registration, and Social Security – A Historical Perspective', *World Development*, 35, p. 76.

12. G. R. Elton (1972), *Policy and Police: The Enforcement of the Reformation in the Age of Thomas Cromwell* (Cambridge: Cambridge University Press), pp. 259–60.

13. S. Hindle (2006), 'Technologies of Identification under the Old Poor Law', *The Local Historian*, 36, pp. 222–4.

14. P. Slack (1988), *Poverty and Policy in Tudor and Stuart England* (London: Longman), p. 97.

15. Hindle, *Technologies of Identification*, p. 227; P. Griffiths (2008), *Lost Londons: Change, Crime and Control in the Capital City, 1550–1660* (Cambridge: Cambridge University Press), p. 121.

16. B. Fraenkel (1992), *La Signature: Genèse d'un Sign* (Paris: Gallimard), pp. 26–9, 92–6.

17. Public Record Office (1963), *Guide to the Contents of the Public Record Office*, Vol. I. Legal Records, etc. (London: HMSO), pp. 16–17.

18. E. Kerridge (1988), *Trade and Banking in Early-Modern England* (Manchester: Manchester University Press), pp. 39–42, 57.

19. 1 Edw. 6, c.3.

20. Beier, *Masterless Men*, pp. 159–60.

21. Proceedings of the Old Bailey, London [online]. Available at: http://www. oldbaileyonline.org/static/Punishment.jsp#branding [Date accessed 10 October 2008].

22. C. B. Herrup (1984), 'New Shoes and Mutton Pies: Investigative Responses to Theft in Seventeenth-Century Sussex', *The Historical Journal*, 27, p. 816.

23. Griffiths, *Lost Londons*, pp. 255–7.

24. J. Styles (1985), 'Print and Policing: Crime Advertising in Eighteenth-century England', in D. Hay and F. Snyder (eds) *Policing and Prosecution in Britain 1750–1850* (Oxford: Clarendon Press), pp. 55–63.

25. Griffiths, *Lost Londons*, p. 381.

26. K. D. M. Snell (1992), 'Settlement, Poor Law, and the Rural Historian: New Approaches and Opportunities', *Rural History*, 3 (2), p. 159.
27. 6 & 7 Will. 4, *c*.11
28. National Archives, London. Domestic Records Information 60: Passport Records, London [online]. Available at: http://www.nationalarchives.gov.uk/catalogue/RDleaflet.asp?sLeafletID=109&j=1. [Date accessed 30 June 2009].
29. General Register Office (1861), *Twenty-second Annual Report of the Registrar General (ARRG) for 1859* (London: HMSO), p. xlv.
30. General Register Office (1897), *Fifty-ninth ARRG for 1896* (London: HMSO), p. xxxvi.
31. General Register Office (1877), *Thirty-eighth ARRG for 1875* (London: HMSO), p. liii.
32. General Register Office (1916), *Seventy-seventh ARRG for 1914* (London: HMSO), p. viii; General Register Office (1918), *Seventy-ninth ARRG for 1916* (London: HMSO), lxxxvii.
33. M. Finn (2001), 'Scotch Drapers and the Politics of Modernity: Gender, Class and National Identity in Victorian Tally Trade', in M. Daunton and M. Hilton (eds), *The Politics of Consumption: Material Culture and Citizenship in Europe and America* (Oxford: Berg Publishing), p. 101.
34. M. Finn (2003), *The Character of Credit: Personal Debt in English Culture, 1740–1914* (Cambridge: Cambridge University Press), p. 291.
35. Finn, *Character of Credit*, pp. 291–301.
36. E. Higgs (2004), *The Information State in England: The Central Collection of Information on Citizens since 1500* (Basingstoke: Palgrave), pp. 95–7.
37. Committee on Identifying Habitual Criminals (1893–94), Report of a Committee Appointed by the Secretary of State to Inquire into the Best Means Available for Identifying Habitual Criminals, British Parliamentary Papers, LXXII, 215–16; National Archives, London, MEPO 6/90 Pt 2, Registry of Criminals, p. 8; National Archives, London, HO 144/184/A45507, Report on the Working of the Prevention of Crimes Acts by the Convict Supervision Office, p. 4.
38. National Archives, London, HO 45/9320/16629C, Prisons and Prisoners (4), Other: Prevention of Crimes Act, 1871, Regulations for Photographing Prisoners; Committee on Identifying Habitual Criminals 1893–94, pp. 12–19; National Archives, London, HO 144/530/A6508 (14); N. Davie (2005), *Tracing the Criminal: The Rise of Scientific Criminology in Britain 1860–1918* (Oxford: The Bardwell Press), p. 94.
39. Cole, *Suspect Identities*, p. 45.
40. A. Bertillon (1893), *Identification Anthropométrique: Instructions Signalétiques* (Melun: Imprimerie Administrative), pp. 137–44; Cole, *Suspect Identities*, pp. 47–8; P. Becker (2001), 'The Standardized Gaze: The Standardization of the Search Warrant in Nineteenth-century Germany', in J. Caplan and J. Torpey (eds) *Documenting Individual Identity: The Development of State Practice in the Modern World* (Oxford: Princeton University Press), pp. 139–63.
41. A. M. Joseph (2001), 'Anthropometry, the Police Expert, and the Deptford Murders: The Contested Introduction of Criminals in Late Victorian and Edwardian Britain', in J. Caplan and J. Torpey (eds), *Documenting Individual Identity*, 170–1; Cole, *Suspect Identities*, pp. 35–6.

42. Higgs, *The Information State*, p. 114.
43. E. R. Henry (1896), 'Bengal Police: Instructions for Classifying and Dechipering Finger Impressions and for Describing Them with Sufficient Exactness to Enable Comparison of the Description with the Original Impression to be Satisfactorily Made' (India).
44. Sengoopta, *Imprint of the Raj*, pp. 120–83.
45. Cole, *Suspect Identities*, pp. 25–8.
46. National Archives, London, Domestic Records Information, p. 60.
47. National Archives, London, Domestic Records Information, p. 60.
48. National Archives, London. History of Passports [online]. Available at: http://yourarchives.nationalarchives.gov.uk/index.php?title=History_of_Passports. [Date accessed: 30 June 2009].
49. R. Elliot (2006), 'An Early Experiment in National Identity Cards: The Battle over Registration in the First World War', *Twentieth-century British History*, 17 (2), pp. 145–76; National Archives, London (1915), RG 900/1, Specimen Documents National Registration Acts; National Archives, London (1915–18), RG28/13, Miscellaneous Memoranda and Instructions.
50. National Archives, London (1939–41), RG28/146, Ration Books and Identity Cards: Original Issue, 1939–41.
51. G. Aly and K. H. Roth (2004), *The Nazi Census: Identification and Control in the Third Reich* (Philadelphia: Temple University Press), 52–3, 119–20, 140–7.
52. Higgs, *The Information State*, 134–44.
53. S. Thompson (2008), 'Separating the Sheep from the Goats: The United Kingdom's National Registration Programme and Social Sorting in the Pre-electronic Era', in C. J. Bennet and D. Lyon (eds), *Playing the Identity Card: Surveillance, Security and Identification in Global Perspective* (London: Routledge), 150–4.
54. E. Higgs (2010), 'Fingerprints and Citizenship: The British State and the Identification of Pensioners in the Inter-war Period', *History Workshop Journal*, 69, pp. 52–67.
55. National Archives, London (1929–39), PIN 15/2594, Identification of Pensioners.
56. Social Security Office (2003), 'How to Prove Your Identity for Social Security' (Leeds: Social Security Office).
57. Higgs, *The Information State*, pp. 171–6.
58. D. Wills (2008), 'The United Kingdom Identity Card Scheme: Shifting Motivations, Static Technologies', in C. J. Bennett and D. Lyon (eds), *Playing the Identity Card*, pp. 173–6.
59. Higgs, *The Information State*, pp. 134–44.
60. Higgs, *The Information State*, pp. 184–5.
61. London School of Economics (2005), *The Identity Project: An Assessment of the UK Identity Cards Bill and its Implications* (London: London School of Economics), pp. 48–90; C. J. Bennett and D. Lyon (eds), *Playing the Identity Card*, passim.
62. P. Gill, A. Jeffreys and D. Werrett (1985), 'Forensic Application of DNA "Fingerprints"', in *Nature* (December), 577–9.
63. Home Office website, the National DNA Database [online], London. Available at: http://www.homeoffice.gov.uk/science-research/using-science/dna-database/. [Date accessed 15 July 2009].

64. M. Lynch, S. A. Cole and R. McNally (2008), *Truth Machine: The Contentious History of DNA Fingerprinting* (London: University of Chicago Press); R. Williams and P. Johnson (2008), *Genetic Policing: The Use of DNA in Criminal Proceedings* (Cullompton: Willan Publishing).

65. J. M. Stanton (2008), 'ICAO and Biometric RFID Passport: History and Analysis', in C. J. Bennett and D. Lyon (eds), *Playing the Identity Card*, pp. 253–67; Z. Karake-Shalhoub (2008), 'Population ID Card Systems in the Middle East', in C. J. Bennett and D. Lyon (eds), *Playing the Identity Card*, pp. 128–41.

66. F. Furedi (2002), *Culture of Fear: Risk-taking and the Morality of Low Expectation* (London: Continuum).

67. A. Offer (2006), *The Challenge of Affluence: Self-Control and Well-being in the United States and Britain since 1950* (Oxford: Oxford University Press), pp. 121–31.

68. D. Lyon (2003), 'Surveillance as Social Sorting: Computer Codes and Mobile Bodies', in D. Lyon (ed.), *Surveillance as Social Sorting: Privacy, Risk, and Digital Discrimination* (Abingdon: Routledge), pp. 13–30.

69. D. Consoli (2003), *The Evolution of Retail Banking Services in the United Kingdom: A Retrospective Analysis* (Manchester: Centre for Research on Innovation and Competition, University of Manchester), pp. 8–9.

70. E. Schoeters (1980), 'The "Dematerialisation" of Payment Systems', *The Banker*, 130 (March), pp. 101–5.

71. S. O'Connell (2009), *Credit and Community: Working-Class Debt in the UK Since 1880* (Oxford: Oxford University Press), pp. 114–15.

72. M. Evans (1999), 'Food Retailing Loyalty Schemes and the Orwellian Millenium', *British Food Journal*, 101 (2), pp. 132–47.

73. E. Vidler and J. Clarke (2005), 'Creating Citizen-Consumers: New Labour and the Remaking of Public Services', *Public Policy and Administration*, 20 (2), pp. 19–37.

74. K. Gates (2008), 'The United States Real ID Act and the Securitization of Identity', in C. J. Bennett and D. Lyon (eds), *Playing the Identity Card*, pp. 228–30.

3

INFORMATION FOR THE PUBLIC: INFORMATION INFRASTRUCTURE IN THE REPUBLIC OF LETTERS

W. Boyd Rayward

In this chapter I tell briefly the story of the overlapping lives of four men of the mid-seventeenth century: Théophraste Renaudot (1586–1653), Gabriel Naudé (1600–53), Samuel Hartlib (1600–62) and John Dury (1596–1680). Two were French and two English. Each of their lives has been touched on in the course of larger historical accounts related to social and religious history, the history of science and of scholarship more generally, the history of particular institutions such as the Royal Society, even, as in the case of Renaudot, the history of journalism and social welfare services and, in the case of Naudé, librarianship. I suggest that there is yet another important narrative which their lives might help to structure and enrich. It is relevant to those interested in the history of information, in the history of how societies, in times of violent and far-reaching social and political change, struggle to manage the information on which their security and identity to a large extent depend.

My four characters were ordinary members of what its contemporaries called the 'Republic of Letters' at a critical period in the development of the intellectual life of Europe. England was experiencing the upheavals of Civil War, followed by the relative calm of the Commonwealth and Protectorate. France was wracked by wars of religion and of succession. Europe was coming to the end of one of the most bloody and divisive conflicts it had experienced. The Thirty Years' War had originated as a religious struggle between Protestant and Catholic German and middle European territories, but had gradually drawn all the European states and powers onto its battle fields. Set

against these deeply-rooted political and social disturbances of monarchical
and to some extent still semi-feudal states was a vigorous, virtual, cosmopolitan
intellectual community that transcended formal political boundaries. Their
relationships were ordered by reputation and maintained by correspondence.
It was a self-declared republic of 'virtuosi' that was becoming sceptical of the
continuing value of modes of learning based on Aristotle and the scholastic
philosophers. It was energized by the new approaches, especially of Francis
Bacon and Jan Comenius amongst others, to the study of natural phenomena
and to discovering and organizing information about the world. Its members
were experimenting with the use of new physical and intellectual technologies
of investigation such as telescopes, microscopes, logic and mathematics. They
were among those who were soon to usher in the scientific revolution.[1]

My characters have a particular interest because their lives and work illustrate the characteristic social mechanisms of the Republic of Letters, the scope
of the interactions that it sustained, but also its communicative inefficiencies
and the inadequacies of the techniques it had evolved for reporting and establishing the integrity or authority of observations. They speculated about or
introduced, or eventually became caught up in, new arrangements for managing various kinds information to help deal with the social, political and
intellectual problems that engrossed them. But what their efforts revealed, at
least in hindsight, was the need for new institutional arrangements and social
practices for managing information. Some of these institutional arrangements, such as academies and learned societies, after a long pre-history were
to emerge in their recognizably modern form in the latter part of the seventeenth century. They would become major centres for mediating the development of the beliefs and practices that would constitute what would be called
'science' and for reporting, critiquing and cumulating the result of systematic
observations of the natural world.[2] A rudimentary scientific and periodical
press began to emerge for witnessing, reporting and publicizing to a diversi-
fying audience observations and discoveries about nature and society. It was
also deployed for political purposes. Less obvious but no less important was
the beginning of changes to our understanding of what was required of libraries, museums and bibliographic services more generally (indexing and bibliographic listings, for example).[3] Other institutional arrangements would wait,
despite the experiments I discuss, until the creation in the mid-nineteenth
century of public libraries and a plethora of reference and bibliographical
resources and services.

In this chapter I confine myself to the period immediately prior to the advent
of what is commonly called the scientific revolution, that is to say the middle
years of the seventeenth century.[4] Though I discuss Renaudot at some length,

my purpose is limited to attempting to catch glimpses of how aspects of the work and ideas of my four characters throw glints of light on more fundamental, overarching issues and to suggest possible approaches to a larger, perhaps more persuasive narrative about information history.

THÉOPHRASTE RENAUDOT, 1586–1653

Of the four men who are the subject of this chapter, Théophraste Renaudot is perhaps the most fascinating and enigmatic. He is difficult to place and to understand. He is perhaps best described as an opportunistic information entrepreneur whose extraordinary Bureau d'Adresse became publishing house, academy or learned society, outpatient clinic (in association with which he invented an innovative information tool for differential diagnosis), research laboratory and pawn shop.[5]

Born at Loudun in the Protestant south of France in 1586, at the age of 19 Renaudot earned a medical degree at Montpellier. This Protestant establishment was 'a bastion of novel medical ideas', with a strong emphasis on experimentation, anatomical studies and innovative chemical remedies.[6] Renaudot's interest in the problems of poverty, leprosy and unemployment in a nation torn by internal strife and imperilled by war led, in 1612, to his *Traité des Pauvres*. His work attracted interest at court and he was eventually designated Commissioner General for the Poor, and by royal decree was given authority to create what at first were called enquiry offices and registers (Bureaux et registres d'adresses) in a programme which was designed to assist the sick and unemployed poor. A convert to Catholicism and a protégé of Cardinal Richelieu, he followed his master to Paris upon the latter's rise to the summit of political power in 1624 as chief minister to Louis XIII. Now nearly 40 years old, Renaudot set out to create the 'innocent inventions' or innovations that have so beguiled his biographers.[7]

Bureau d'Adresse

Some time in the late 1620s, Renaudot opened his 'Bureau d'adresse et rencontres' in premises at the sign of 'the Great Rooster, rue de Calandre, leading to the New Market near the Palace' on the Ile de la Cité.[8] Initially the aim of the bureau was to bring the unemployed into contact with potential employers. As the problems of unemployment increased and the numbers of deserters from the army flocking to the city became an ever more serious problem for the authorities, in 1639 the unemployed were actually required to register at the Bureau d'Adresse. Those who failed to register and were caught could be designated vagabonds and vagrants and could be sent to the galleys.[9] In this way, the Bureau d'Adresse became one of the instruments of surveillance of the state. Renaudot claimed that it had made referrals for employment for over 80,000 people in the period from 1630 to 1642,[10] although how much reliance one can place on such a statistic is difficult to say.

Nevertheless, the Bureau d'Adresse's functions very soon broadened and it came to serve as a kind of clearing house for all sorts of information – of positions available or wanted, of goods and services for sale, of property lost and found. In order to publicize the bureau, Renaudot had placards put up throughout the city to advertise his wares. He also printed and widely distributed regular excerpts from the bureau's registers listing the prices of the goods and services for sale at the bureau. The fifteenth 'Feuille du Bureau d'Adresse' for September 1633, for example, lists a 'seigneurial estate' for sale with a 'lovely comfortable chateau' and income from various sources of 2,000 livres. It was to be had for 60,000 livres.[11] There was a similar glowing entry for 'a Parisian House for sale' that could be out of any property advertisement of today! Perhaps the most amusing item advertised for sale through this 'feuille' was a young dromedary camel 'at a reasonable price'.[12]

A procedure about which we know very little was devised for recording, discharging and, for those with the means, paying for submitting contributions to or receiving information from the registers in the bureau. In order to pay for the numerous personnel that he had to engage to run the bureau, he announced a charge of three sou for every entry placed in, or extract taken from, the registers of the bureau. Surely a bargain! 'For three sou anyone could be informed about or make known what he wished', though 'all was free to the unfortunate'.[13]

Outpatient Clinic and Medical laboratory

Almost from the initial setting up of the Bureau d'Adresse, it seems that Renaudot himself, together with colleagues he had gathered round him, offered medical consultations to the sick poor in what could only be called a free outpatient clinic. Solomon suggests that these consultations began as early as 1632. In 1640, letters patent recognized the extent to which at the Bureau d'Adresse the poor had 'freely received counsel and assistance for their sicknesses and infirmities through the charity of the physicians, surgeons and apothecaries brought together there for this purpose'. The letters patent gave Renaudot authority to create a laboratory, to install the necessary equipment and to carry out the experiments that would 'benefit the health and welfare of the poor whether healthy or sick and infirm'. But there seems to be no record of what these experiments were, or of their results.[14]

One of Renaudot's innovations was designed to enable those with 'shameful' diseases, or those living physically beyond the reach of the Bureau d'Adresse, to take advantage of its medical services without having to attend in person. This was a manual that enabled patients to identify on diagrams of their bodies the location of their condition, to describe its major characteristics in detail, to state the length of time during which the problem had been experienced and so on – in effect to provide such a formal and systematic description of the condition that it permitted a kind of differential diagnosis to be made by the physicians and apothecaries at the bureau. It was called intriguingly 'The Presence of the Absent' (*La Présence des Absens*).[15] And of course, using *La Présence des Absens*, the upper ranks of society would not be forced into contact with the masses of starving poor, riddled with disease and deformities, who were clamouring for free medical attention at the bureau itself and whose 'illnesses brought on by their deprivations', said Renaudot, 'infect the purity of our air'.[16]

Pawn Shop and Low-interest loans

Renudot went a step further from providing information for buyers and sellers of goods. He arranged for the goods to be brought to the bureau itself, where buyer and seller could 'encounter' one another. If a sale were successfully concluded, the bureau would be paid a fee. This idea was further developed so that the bureau could become in effect a sales bureau where goods, for a small percentage of their value, could be deposited on consignment with the option of sale either on credit or to the highest bidder, or could eventually be returned after an agreed period, the transactions being mediated by bureau staff for a small percentage fee based on the value of the goods or their sale price. His positive spin on what was in fact a pawn shop was that by means of charging low interest rates and fees for its services, the bureau would enable both the poor and others to avoid the usurious rates of other lenders.

Newspaper and Other Periodical Publications

In 1631 Renaudot embarked on another 'information' venture. Following the example of what he understood to be happening in neighbouring countries, he began publication of a periodical, the *Gazette*, later called the *Gazette de France*.[17] For a long time considered to be the first French periodical, the *Gazette* in fact had a substantial pre-history. Nevertheless, even while acknowledging precursors, more recent commentators are expansive. For Bellanger and his colleagues, for example, the *Gazette* marked 'the birth of the periodical press in France'.[18] Why Renaudot undertook its publication is unclear, though he did so with the support of his patron, Cardinal Richelieu. The *Gazette* appeared every week. Supplements soon proved necessary, and these sometimes increased the length of the weekly *Gazette* to as many as 20 or 24 pages. Renaudot collected the issues of the *Gazette* into annual volumes to create an unparalleled documentation of the events of his day. He claimed in 1638 that he was publishing 1,200 copies of the *Gazette* each week.[19]

The *Gazette* was essentially a political instrument used by Richelieu and the king for official propaganda. Personally and through functionaries attached to their bureaux, they carefully oversaw its contents. As Hatin observes: 'It is well known that Richelieu took a particular interest in the *Gazette*, which he regarded as a powerful instrument of government. He sent whole articles to it and had inserted in it what he wanted to be known throughout Europe.' As for the King, 'when he had a political upheaval in the Royal establishment, he counted on the *Gazette* to express his complaints; he wrote what he dare not say'.[20] Because of his contacts at court, Renaudot was able to have dispatches sent to the *Gazette* from embassies and offices around the world. When France became involved in the Thirty Years' War, the '*Gazette* became an integral organ of government at war'.[21] Renaudot also published in its supplements royal decrees, laws, treaties and other official documents (sometimes documents about his own establishments).

Renaudot set up his own print shop at the Bureau d'Adresse. It operated four presses. Solomon suggests that 'in sheer volume Renaudot was the most important publisher in Paris during the period 1631–44'.[22]

Conférences du Bureau d'Adresse

The last of the information innovations of the Bureau d'Adresse that I want to mention was its *conférences*. From 1633 until 1642 a public discussion group assembled in the great hall of the Maison du Grand Coq to debate the interesting questions of the day. Anyone could be present and take part in the discussion. The subjects to be discussed were agreed on by the audience, and an anonymous summary account was kept of the arguments advanced in the form: 'the first said ...', 'the second said ...', and so on. The only provisos were that French not Latin was the language to be employed, and that religious and political subjects were to be avoided (but of course they were not).[23] Selections and collections of these reports, the 'Centuries des Conférences', were issued regularly in the period 1634–41 in substantial volumes which were widely disseminated and translated. The last collection, for the years 1641–42, was issued in 1655 after Renaudot's death, by his son Eusèbe. Sutton estimates that there were at least 20 selected or collected editions all told.[24]

The range of subjects covered was enormously varied. Here is an arbitrary selection from the 1665 English translation of the 'Centuries'[25] that suggests their curiously heterogeneous mixture:

Whether it be good to use Chymical Remedies
Whether the reading of romances be profitable
What bodily exercise is the most healthful
Whether virtue consists in mediocrity
Of amulets, and whether diseases are curable by words, tickets or other things hang'd at the neck
Whether 'twere better to know all that men know or all that they ignore
Why ice being harder than water is yet lighter
Of conjuration, natural magick, auguries and auspices

Commentators like Wellman, recognizing the variety and topical inclusiveness of the conferences, acknowledge that, because they were anonymous and public, 'with publication, every bizarre idea, every inclusive discussion, every uncritical use of evidence, is laid bare'. But she goes on to suggest that 'although the mind-boggling eclecticism of Renaudot's conferences certainly makes it difficult to include them in a narrative of scientific progress, the process of competition and accommodation of gatherings like these tells us a great deal about the evolution of scientific ideas'.[26]

In full swing, the Bureau d'Adresse must have presented its contemporaries with a remarkable spectacle of 'rambunctious bustle'.[27] According to an unidentified account that Hattin cites, the Maison du Grand Coq, was

always full of those coming and going; the sick waiting for a consultation, students, apothecaries, public criers, people of all sorts coming to bring or to request information; the down at heel, secondhand clothes dealers, peddlers; in the courtyards and the rooms a mass of bizarre and disparate objects: phials, retorts and stills, all the apparatus of a great printery, heaps of objects of all sorts, arranged and classified by a mass of employees; and, in the middle of all of this, a single man watching over all, responding to all, assigning each his task, teaching, distilling, buying or selling, reading the political news, drafting successively an opinion, a newspaper article, a memorandum, and still finding time to visit the sick outside and to perform his duties as a courtier and man of the world.

This was 'the Gazetteer', Théopraste Renaudot.[28]

A Denouement

Renaudot's medical practice and practices outraged the medical establishment of Paris. His qualifications were from Montpellier, not Paris, and so in the eyes of the Faculty of Medicine he was not qualified to practise in Paris. He espoused the novel treatments that relied on chemicals such as antimony that were recommended in Montpellier. While he had the patronage of Richelieu and the king, though attracting much opposition from Guy Patin, the dean of the medical faculty and close friend of Gabriel Naudé, and others who eventually were to bring about his downfall, Renaudot was able to resist all efforts to halt his medical and other work.[29] But Richelieu died in 1642 and Louis XIII followed him barely six months later. A war of pamphlets and law suits that had been opened a little earlier against Renaudot by Patin and others now reached a climax.[30] The culmination in the Paris Parlement (a law court) in March 1644 was described gleefully a week later, in a letter from Patin to a colleague:

> The court ordered the Gazetteer to cease all his conferences, his charitable consultations, all the loans and his other a villainous business practices and even his chemistry for fear that this man who had such a desire to have them legally or illegally at last would want to commit forgery. ... Talon is the name of the Chief Prosecutor who made these tough statements against Renaudot and all his adherents, so-called medical doctors from the Faculty at Montpellier and other famous universities. M. Talon said that degrees were conferred so easily outside Paris that all of these foreign universities needed reform on this matter and that the specious title of Montpellier doctor in Paris was only a pretext that usually hid a charlatan or ignoramus.[31]

All that was left to Renaudot was the *Gazette* which he continued to publish until he died, greatly impoverished, in 1653. (It was continued by his sons and, in one form or another, its history extends to 1915.)

What the Bureau d'Adresse Was and Was Not

Renaudot's extraordinary Bureau d'Adresse was part labour exchange, part learned academy and part chemical laboratory, though we seem to have no accounts of experiments or even of regular use of the equipment Renaudot was licenced to own. It was a huge, multifaceted printing house. It was in part what today we would call a citizens' advice bureau or reference and referral service, and also undertook a function similar to that of the advertising section of modern newspapers. An outpatient clinic, it was also a pawn shop. It was a centre of state propaganda for the king and his chief minister. But it also constituted an open, public forum for the discussion and dissemination of ideas. It became, if only briefly and irregularly, a forum for the public examination of inventions and new ideas that was to be a central feature of the great academies of the latter part of the century, the Royal Society of London and the Académie des Sciences of Paris. It was set up to enable new kinds of information to be gathered and managed for new kinds of social purposes. Its registers were designed to provide information about the goods and services it advertised in a new kind of publicity vehicle, ephemeral news-sheets and posters. It was supposed to maintain lists of the names and addresses of the unemployed and others potentially subject to the vagrancy laws of the period, and to provide them with evidence of their registration. Its *Gazette*, and the *Gazette*'s related publications, represented a new approach to propaganda and the management of public opinion in the interests of the ruling elite, but also carried out a more general informative function in enabling the wide dissemination of public documents such as laws, treaties and decrees. But the *Gazette* also catered to, and perhaps helped to create in the relatively small literate population of the time, an appetite for scandal and gossip and for eyewitness reports that make the important events of the day vivid and personal, in the style of so much news reporting today. It was just this that led Gabriel Naudé to break with Renaudot at the time of the Fronde when they were both in the employ of Cardinal Mazarin. Naudé objected to Renaudot's insistence on publishing all the news he could get: 'it makes the population too knowledgeable in their own affairs as well as their neighbors", he said. 'It does not seem appropriate to me for the least of the population to have so much news of the revolts in Naples, the seditions in Turkey, of the horrible crime in England [presumably the execution of Charles I].'[32]

It is also interesting to try to understand what the Bureau d'Adresse was not. There seems to have been no attempt to impose a general philosophy on the disparate information and social service activities it embraced. Renaudot seems not to have had any particular interest in systematically turning the pages of the Book of Nature, though what might have been in that book was vigorously if unsystematically explored from the various points of view of the discussants in the conferences. As Sutton notes: 'Renaudot's Conferences on science, like everything else associated with him, proved a collection of the new and the old, the orthodox and the heterodox and the outrageous.'[33] In this respect the conferences of the bureau had the character more of a general debating society following essentially medieval practices of disputation than a highly select body of men, who, belonging to the upper levels of society and sharing special interests and expertise, were concerned with the discovery and the accreditation of new information and were to usher in the scientific revolution. Analysed from an information point of view, the Bureau d'Adresse represented a fascinating forum for the merger of, or at least an oscillation between, oral and printed cultures, the formal and informal in communication, the scholarly and the popular, 'the virtuosi', as the gentleman amateurs of learning were then called, and the lower orders.

But there may well be other circumstances that should not be neglected in attempting to explain the ultimate failure of Reanudot's initiatives, the intensity of the opposition that he attracted and the lack of intellectual coherence in what he attempted. Renaudot may be considered to have been an outsider for reasons that, though associated with his Montpellier medical background, went beyond this. It seems that he was never able to join the socially exclusive and overlapping scholarly circles his critics inhabited in the highly stratified society of the time. Despite his titles (to his earlier titles was added that of Historiographe de France in 1646) and *privilèges* from the king, it is possible that Renaudot was regarded as a social inferior, mired in the semi-commercial operations of the bureau. A Huguenot born in Loudon, before coming to Paris he had been a friend of Urbain Grandier who was executed for demonic possession in 1634. Renaudot's conversion to Catholicism, despite the example of the king's father Henri IV, may also have appeared discreditably opportunistic, especially given the Huguenot rebellions that were a constant feature of Louis XIII's reign. Renaudot was never admitted to the charmed networks that were centred, for example, on Marin Mersenne,[34] the brothers Du Puy and Peirsesc – and perhaps too, as facilitated by Naudé, on the library of Cardinal Mazarin.

This attitude to Renaudot comes out vividly, for example, in some of the letters of the aristocratic Nicolas-Claude Fabri de Peiresc who had established himself in Aix-en-Provence, after lengthy travels as a young man in Italy, Paris, London and the Low Countries. He may be considered to have been one of the most active nodes in the network that constituted the Republic of Letters at this time.[35] He belonged to the circle that was associated with Mersenne as well as to that associated with the brothers Dupuy, who presided over the great library of the de Thou family and later the Bibliothèque du Roi.[36] The friends and acquaintances whom they gathered around them constituted one of the most learned and exclusive groups in Paris. Peiresc's house was a way station for those visiting Italy and he maintained an indefatigable correspondence with scholars throughout France and Europe. Peiresc seemed to think that on occasion, such as the publication in the *Gazette* of Galileo's condemnation, Renaudot deliberately withheld circulating the *Gazette* to him in order to make him contact Renaudot. But Peisresc noted that there was nothing in the world 'that would make him descend to write to this personage', that it was worth having news late rather than submitting 'to the tyranny that he wanted to impose on them [himself and the brothers DuPuy] of writing to him'. Renaudot was a 'paltry printer' overselling his wares, the value of which he himself called into question 'because of his contacts with low persons'. Renaudot's opinions, declared Peiresc, were 'every day becoming more detestable and worthless to the extent that that there are few people willing to take the pains of reading him'.[37] But of course for Peiresc as for so many, the *Gazette* remained a major source of news that they could not really do without, and their letters and regular complaints about Renaudot testify to its value for them.

GABRIEL NAUDÉ, 1600–53

In March of 1642, Gabriel Naudé had at long last returned to Paris from Italy after 11 years as librarian and Latin secretary to Cardinal Bagno.[38] He had been summoned to Paris by Cardinal Richelieu to become his librarian. The Cardinal however died within the year and Naudé, like Renaudot, entered the service of his successor, Cardinal Mazarin, for whom he was to build one of the most splendid 'public' libraries in Europe. And through Mazarin, Naudé was to be associated with Renaudot, though he became critical of his work not long after the outbreak of the Fronde as mentioned above.

As a young man, Naudé had entered the medical faculty of the University of Paris. There he met and became friendly with Guy Patin. This friendship with a man who, 20 years later as dean of the medical faculty was one of the most passionate of Renaudot's calumniators, every aspect of whose life and work he seems to have detested, was to be lifelong. Naudé's principal professor in the faculty was René Moreau, another of those who were later violently to attack Renaudot.[39] Thus, unlike Renaudot's, Naudé's medical credentials, gained in Paris and later Padua, were for the Paris medical faculty above reproach. While at the university Naudé was invited by Henri II de Mesmes, one of the presidents of the Paris *Parlement*, to become his librarian. De Mesmes continued a tradition initiated by his grandfather, who had begun the library, of opening it to scholars. As a result the young librarian began to meet some of the most important figures in the intellectual life of the capital.

Avis Pour Dresser une Bibiotheque

In 1627, reflecting his experience in the de Mesmes library and elsewhere, Naudé published his *Avis pour Dresser une Bibiotheque*, in which he set forth the 'advice a man might regulate himself concerning the choice of Books, the means of procuring them, and how they should be dispos'd of, that they might appear with profit and honour in a fair and Sumptuous Bibliothèque'.[40] While the *Avis* has been considered the first French treatise on librarianship, Delatour points out that it had a number of predecessors. Ironically it received a rather cool reception from the brothers Dupuy, perhaps because they were not included in it, and from Peiresc. Naudé's little book was for him 'an intellectual game' (*divertissement de l'esprit*) and its author 'a novice in what he writes'.[41]

The year following the appearance of his *Avis pour Dresser une Bibiothèque*, however, under the patronage of De Mesmes, Naudé was admitted to the charmed circle of the cabinet of the brothers Dupuy, where he made many lasting friendships. Though he was only a young man, his learning attracted the admiration of the members of this group. In 1630 Pierre Dupuy recommended him to Cardinal Guido di Bagno, papal nuncio in Paris, who employed Naudé as librarian and Latin secretary, taking him back to Rome when he returned there in 1631. On their journey the travelling party visited Peiresc in Aix-en-Provence for three days, where 'the grave Piereskius' embraced the young librarian and congratulated 'his patron in that he had chosen such a man to assist him in his studies'. Peiresc himself at the time wrote to Dupuy that he had given Naudé some advice about what to expect at the court in Rome 'which he seemed to take in good part'.[42]

Italy

In these Italian years Naudé showed himself to be an active citizen of the Republic of Letters who played a complex and important networking role in the circulation both of information and the artifacts of learning and scholarship. He epitomized that 'factor and trader for helps to learning' that, a few years later, John Dury in England was to suggest should be the role of the 'reformed Librarie-Keeper' (1650). Clark gives a fascinating account of Naudé's activities during these 'Italian' years:

> To Guy Patin and Rene Moreau he sent notices of the latest publications on medicine, often the works themselves. The Dupuy brothers were deluged with inside information (sometimes in code) on ecclesiastical politics at Rome in gossipy letters that sometimes ran to thirty pages. Drawing on his intimate knowledge of French and Italian libraries, Naudé supplied the historian André Duchesne with bibliographical leads to source materials and even located several rare items for him. The mathematician Marin

Mersenne received news of the comets sighted in Italy as well as detailed descriptions of instruments that astronomers had invented to observe them. Knowing this gentle friar's interest in the theory of music and ancient musical instruments, Naudé also sent along an exquisite Greek drawing of Orpheus playing his lyre in a sylvan glade. ... Naudé's correspondence with Periesc reads like an annotated catalog of contemporary Italian literature, replete with biographical anecdotes ... Still another service Naudé rendered his friends was to search out and transcribe rare old manuscripts for their research projects ... Whenever Naudé found an item that might interest the Dupuy brothers, Gassendi, Mersenne, or his other correspondents, he hired a library copyist and had it reproduced.

... Typically, Naudé's correspondence with Jacques and Pierre Dupuy, which was meant to be read aloud to the membership of their academy as a sort of literary gazette, abounds in descriptive comments on Italian books and their authors.[43]

Bibliothèque Mazarine

Back in Paris in 1642, Naudé resumed his friendships with the many virtuosi with whom he had so long corresponded, among whom Patin and Gassendi were perhaps the two to whom he was closest. But his major task was to build for Cardinal Mazarin 'a library that would rank from its very beginning among the richest and most complete in Europe'.[44] In it he would put into practice the precepts elaborated 15 years before in his *Avis pour Dresser une Bibiothèque*. Here he had asserted that a great library should be integrated into the intellectual traditions of the past; it should embrace all fields of modern learning; it should be impartial in its selections; and it should be open to the public. 'For certainly there is nothing which renders a Library more recommendable, then when every man finds in it that which he is in search of, and could no where else encounter; this being a perfect Maxime, That there is no Book whatsoever, be it never so bad or decried, but may in time be sought for by some person or other.'[45]

The library was quickly built up, in part by extensive bulk purchases. 'In the last months of this year [1642], he [Naudé] went to the Rue Saint-Jacques, to a bookseller named Fouet, and beginning the system of acquisition from which he never departed, he bought en bloc and by weight twenty-three reams of books in sheets, without losing time by examining each volume. The price for each ream was fixed at three livres and ten sou.'[46] The cardinal himself was no less eager than Naudé for the success of his library and he solicited the dispatch of books and manuscripts from his generals in the field in Germany, as the Thirty Years' War came to its agonizingly slow end.

In January of 1644 the library was opened to the public and Renaudot reported in the *Gazette* that the Cardinal 'had made his grand establishment into an academy for the learned and curious, who every Thursday from morning to evening come in crowds to peruse his beautiful library'. Naudé himself remembered that as many as 80 to 100 persons would be there on those open days.[47]

Already one of the largest libraries in Paris, and now only the fourth great library open to the learned public in Europe,[48] it continued to expand rapidly. In part this was through Mazarin's own efforts to secure material through his agents abroad and from the gifts of books, manuscripts, paintings and other valuable works that he received from those seeking influence and favour. But it was also in large part through the continuation of Naudé's programme of bulk acquisition. Having exhausted the resources of the Parisian book trade, he made a number of collecting trips abroad in the period 1644–48. He visited London in 1647. Nothing seems to have been written about this visit. It is, however, of particular interest given what was happening there with the rise of puritanism and the outbreak of civil war. It was a time of great intellectual ferment, much of which was centered on Samuel Hartlib and his circle of colleagues and friends. This ferment was expressed in a massive increase in the numbers of books being published and in what might seem a deluge of pamphlets by – at least for the moment – an unregulated press.[49] Did Naudé collect these publications? Whom did he meet and what did they talk about?

For Nelles, Naudé's *Avis* proposed 'a practical methodology which sought the universalization of the library as an institution of learning on a Baconian model'.[50] So successful was the process of 'augmentation' or collection development that Naudé had instituted for Mazarin's library that in 1646, Mazarin enlarged his palace to provide quarters for the library in a new building along the Rue Richelieu. Here he created the edifice which until the advent of the Bibliothèque de France, Tolbiac, housed the Bibliothèque Nationale's *department* of printed books. Naudé's absences from and returns to Paris on his book acquisition trips were noted in the Renaudot's *Gazette*, because the library was sometimes closed while he was away and readers complained about the lack of his services.[51]

One may now hasten over the rest of Naudé's rather sad story. The great library fell victim to the political events of the Fronde. Comprising some 40,000 volumes, it was sold off in February 1652 despite Naudé's protests and the ploys he and others used to try to stop the sale.[52] Naudé described the extraordinary events surrounding the sale in a number of long letters to Mazarin.[53] Cardinal

Mazarin returned in triumph to Paris in 1653, and let it be known that he would reassemble his library. Naudé, who had accepted the post of librarian to Queen Christina of Sweden, made haste to rejoin him, but on the return journey died suddenly. He was 53 years old. Mazarin, anxious to re-establish his own library, thereupon bought the contents of his librarian's library.

Naudé was an important figure in the Republic of Letters of his day. In Paris he articulated a new vision of what a research or scholarly library might be, one that would be almost uniquely open to anyone among the scholarly public of the day. He established such a library for Cardinal Mazarin, and it became a feature of the intellectual life of Paris during the relatively short period that it was publicly available before the onset of the Fronde.

But it is important to note that it had at that time no institutional base. Like many of the important libraries of the time, including the de Mesmes library in which Naudé served his apprenticeship, it was a personal possession that served to establish an aspect of the identity of its owner as well as his reputation in the world of learning. Both Richelieu and Mazarin wanted their libraries to become permanent testaments to their vision and benevolence, and for this purpose to become centrepieces of a formally established educational institution. Richelieu died before he could create such an institution for his library, and despite the wishes he expressed in his will, it languished in neglect for almost twenty years before being attached to the library of the College of the Sorbonne. Mazarin, however, was much clearer and more direct, and provided in his will for the foundation of the College des Quatre Nations of which what was soon called the Mazarine Library would be a central feature. He provided huge sums of money, including continuing revenues from various properties as bequests to support the college and library, and to ensure their continuity. He even ordered in his will that the library should be 'open to all men of letters two times a week'.[54] The new institution was given legal standing as a royal institution by letters patent of Louis XIV in 1665. The library was to have an official life from that time forward. Housed in the Palace of the College of Four Nations in which the Institut de France was placed in 1805, the library was formally attached to the Institut in 1945. Unlike the Institut's own library, The Bibliothèque Mazarine remains a public library.[55]

SAMUEL HARTLIB, 1600–62, AND JOHN DURY, 1596–1680[56]

Samuel Hartlib was born in Elbing in what was then Polish Prussia. As a young man he studied at Cambridge, and after some travel in Europe, then in the grip of the Thirty Years' War, settled in England. His major claim to fame is that he gathered around him an important circle of social and religious reformers and mediated communications among them. Milton dedicated his pamphlet on education to him. He was acquainted with Boyle. One of his close friends was John Dury, a Scottish clergyman much of whose life was spent in travels abroad attempting to secure reconciliation between the Protestant churches of Europe. In 1650 Dury became briefly a librarian having been appointed deputy to Bulstrode Whitelocke, who had been given charge of the king's library when it had become the possession of the state with the execution of the king in 1649.

As the political situation deteriorated and the struggles between king and parliament led to civil war, the execution of the king and the Protectorate of Oliver Cromwell, it seemed to Hartlib and his group of Puritan friends that a new kind of world was in the making. At last it seemed that society, religion and knowledge itself might all be reformed and renewed. Hartlib's interests and the contacts that they engendered at home and throughout Europe and North America became so extensive that he was known to his contemporaries as 'the State Agent for the Advancement of Universal Learning'.[57] The network of which he was so important a part expressed itself in various kinds and levels of social relationships, in a veritable spate of pamphlets, in widely circulated manuscripts and in a seemingly interminable correspondence which was itself sometimes copied for circulation, sometimes hastily and crudely printed for this purpose.[58]

The Office of Publick Addresse

Much of the discussion by Hartlib and his colleagues turned to creating a new kind of agency for learning and for the reform and welfare of society. They called this the Office of Publicke Addresse, and it seemed to be modelled in substantial part on Renaudot's Bureau d'Adresse.[59] Discussed informally in 1646 by Hartlib and his friends, the first sustained public account of the Office of Publick Addresse was a pamphlet issued by Dury in the following year.[60] In the Hartlib papers is a draft act of parliament and other reports in which the creation of the office is foreshadowed, and which allocate responsibility for its management to Hartlib and others in his circle. In the same papers are copies of documents related to Renaudot's Bureau of Adresse, which had by this time been suppressed for several years, except for the publication of the *Gazette*.[61] Replying to Hartlib's 13-point query in early July 1648 for information about the Bureau d'Adresse, Arnold Boate reported disparagingly from Paris of usury and 'unconscionable dealings' by Renaudot and declared that the Bureau d'Adresse 'was no such magnificent business as you seemed to have imagined'.[62] Nevertheless, much of the language of the documents by Hartlib, Dury and Sir William Petty and others about the Office of Publicke Adresse reflects that of Renaudot. In what follows I conflate to some extent the various accounts of the Office of Publicke Addresse in these documents. They form an extended discussion centred in part on what might be done if Hartlib and Dury were to be allowed to put the ideas they contain into effect.

The Office of Publicke Addresse was to be a special kind of information bureau that should be created under the supervision, and with the support, of the state. Its purpose would be to achieve a 'well-ordered Society' by 'providing information for the relief of human necessities.' Dury suggested the office would have two parts. One would be called the Addresse of Accommodations and would be concerned with all the matters of daily living, which owes most to Renaudot in its formulation. The second, the Addresse of Communications, would be concerned with intellectual and spiritual matters and represents something new that goes far beyond anything the pragmatic and opportunistic Renaudot contemplated. The functions of the Addresse of Communications were to provide to all who might benefit from its work 'adresses and informations in matters of religion, of learning, and all ingenuities which are objects of contemplation and delight unto the mind for their strangenesse and usefullnesse unto the life of Man'. Most important for Dury was the way in which the office would 'facilitate the meanes of rectifying mistakes' and reduce disputes about matters of religious opinion and practice.[63] Disputes would no longer be necessary because truth would in this way be incontrovertibly established.

Libraries and their keepers were to be a central part of this great movement for reforming and advancing learning. At this time Dury was himself acting as a librarian. In his *Reformed Librarie-Keeper*, he spelled out in much greater detail what he thought libraries should be and do.[64] For Dury the role of the new librarian, as mentioned above, was that of a 'factor and trader for helps to learning' whose work required the maintenance of an extensive correspondence on the one hand and an extraordinary set of professional activities on the other. These tasks would help 'reduce' what he called the 'whole variety and diversity of matters useful unto this present life, as they come within the sphere of learning' to a useful form that would help achieve basic social and religious ideals.

William Petty, later surveyor of Ireland and one of the founders of the Royal Society, speculated about how the office might work. For him, like Dury, one of its tasks would be to allow men 'to see what is well and sufficiently done already, exploding whatsoever is nice, contentious, and merely fantastical'. To achieve this he believed, like Dury, that a survey of the current state of knowledge was necessary. 'This survey', he said,

> may be made by perusing all books, and taking notice of all mechanical inventions. In this perusal, all the experimentall learning may be sifted and collected out of the said books. There must be appointed able readers of all such books, with certain well-limited directions what to collect out of them. Every book must be so read by two several persons a-part to prevent mistakes and failings from the said directions. The directions for reading must be such that the readers observing them may exactly agree in their collections. Out of all of these books one book or great work may be made though consisting of many volumes. The most artificial indices, tables, or other helps for the ready finding, remembering, and well-understanding all things contained in these books must be contrived and put into practice.[65]

Hartlib explained in some detail how the Office of Accommodations would function. What is needed he says is 'a place of common resort appointed like unto an exchange where they [men] should receive information of all that they desire to know'. The office's standing or permanent registers would contain 'a catalogue of all catalogues of books'. This would allow an enquirer to find anything that had been written on the subject of his enquiry. At the office one would find geographic information on all the localities and a directory of officials throughout the kingdom; importation details of foreign and local commodities, including transportation and marketing data; and a biographic directory of important persons and families – in effect a *Who's Who*.[66]

The changeable registers or 'Occasional Registers' would provide information on 'matters of daily occurrence'. There were essentially four:

> one for the accommodation of the poor; another for the accommodation of trade, commerce and bargains for profit; a third for the accommodation of all actions which proceed from all relations of persons to each other in all estates and conditions of life; a fourth for ingenuities and matters unto the delight of the mind in all virtues and rare objects. These four registers may be distinguished and intituled, from the properties of their subjects thus: the first should be called the register of necessities or of charity; the second, of usefulness of profit; the third, of performance or of duties; and the fourth of delights and honour.

Effectively, what Hartlib was describing was, like Renaudot's Bureau d'Adresse, an agency that combined the functions located today in citizen's advice bureaux or neighbourhood information centres, labour exchanges, tourist information offices and also in classified advertising of the kind found in newspapers. Again modelled on Renaudot, the advertising of items was specified in great detail by Hartlib and others: real estate for sale or rent, the sale of commodities and services of various kinds and employment. Information about shipping movements, what we would call courier services, money lending and interest rates and currency exchange rates would also be provided. And of course the office would disseminate the kinds of information now found in a range of yearbooks and directories (including *Who's Who*) that are the staple of ready-reference sections in modern public libraries. All the information involved was to be collected, recorded and managed by a staff under the supervision of a warden. Given the importance of the work of the office, Hartlib thought that 'there should be one in every place of resort' and, further, that the offices should be networked 'by the correspondency of one office to another in every principal city'.

The one great practical consequence of the developments of the Interregnum was the creation of the Royal Society in 1660, and through it a continuing and increasingly formalized approach to the discovery and verification of 'scientific' information. Some of Hartlib's friends and acquaintances, such as Petty and Boyle, were closely involved with its foundation and development. But Hartlib's connections with the previous regime were too close for him to be allowed to participate in the work of the new body, and in any case he was becoming old and infirm. John Dury, who had been sent abroad in 1654 as a special agent for Oliver Cromwell, was unable to return to England with the Restoration and died in Kassel in Germany in 1681.

CONCLUSION

Regarding information history in the period under discussion here, one should notice that there was a clear recognition that books were of ever-increasing importance in the world of learning, a world that, even with the rise of publishing in the vernacular languages, embraced whatever was of a serious nature being produced anywhere in Europe. But finding out about these books and acquiring them were understood to present problems of the greatest difficulty. The subject of books filled the letters of the members of the Republic of Letters. There was much speculation on the part of Hartlib and his colleagues about how to collect and organize them. 'We have reason to fear that the multitude of books which grows every day in a prodigious fashion will make the following centuries fall into a state as barbarous as that of the centuries that followed the fall of the Roman Empire unless we try to prevent this danger by separating those books which we must throw out or leave in oblivion from those which one should save and within the latter between what is useful and what is not,' declared Adrien Baillet a few years later in France.[67] One must recognize, however, that various bibliographic initiatives were undertaken in the period, not the least being the influential catalogues of the German book fairs that had begun to appear in the middle of the sixteenth century, which became the basis of a number of European and English bibliographic compilations. At the end of the period under review there appeared one of the first major English trade bibliographies, William London's *Catalogue of the Most Vendible Books in England* covering the period of the death of Oliver Cromwell to the Restoration, that is from 1657 to 1660.[68] But Naudé also showed the way towards the idea of a publicly accessible research library in which anything published could find a place and attain potential value. Blair mentions Naudé's defence of the use of the 'reference' works of the time; increasing systematization in the preparation of book indexes; and new practices of summarizing and annotating what was read, as among the responses to the 'crisis'.[69]

In England there was speculation about how to inventory, index and excerpt the mass of books that had to be found and brought into the country in order to assemble from them scholarly information sufficiently comprehensive and reliable to be used to defuse disagreements, especially religious disputes. In both France and England there was also a recognition by a few far-sighted men of affairs that new modes of acquiring and disseminating more practical kinds of information were desperately needed to allow the various ranks of the populace to deal with the impacts on their lives of the social, religious and political upheavals they were living through. This led to the experiments initiated at the Bureau d'Adresse in Paris, and to the discussions of the Bureau of Publicke Addresse in London.

What ultimately was to be relied upon, however, was, to use Dury's term, 'a correspondency', that system of personal communication that had created and sustained the Republic of Letters as it then was. The Republic of Letters, with its networks of correspondence which were so important for the circulation of information in the early and middle years of the seventeenth century, was, it seems to me, an extension of the oral culture of what essentially were closed elite social groups. This is to say that there were limits with respect to who could visit and write to whom. Lux and Cook's open networks of weak ties were open only within certain conditions of civility that in part depended on social status, the degrees of intimacy that this would permit and the mastery of an elaborate code of etiquette for managing these complex relationships.[70] That is to say, what were to some extent open networks were also closed circles. Renaudot, for example, was beyond the pale, so to speak, of permissible network connections, beyond even the possibility of the weakest of weak ties. Peiresc, for example, as I have indicated, could not be induced to lower himself to correspond with such a person, important as he was in his own distinctive way in the Republic of Letters.

Three hundred years later, in the 1960s and 1970s, we find emerging once again a deep-seated anxiety about the growing volume and fragmentation of scientific literature. The highly elaborated modern print-based system of formal scientific communication, the first elements of which had been introduced towards the end of the seventeenth century, seemed to be becoming increasingly inefficient and ineffective. As a result, the system became the subject of sustained and continuing multidisciplinary research by scientists, sociologists and scholars of library and information science, among others.[71] One of the discoveries that emerged from their studies was not only the existence but the central importance of invisible colleges of informally communicating colleagues. These groups, it became clear, had not come into existence simply to provide 'work-arounds' for the problems that were being experienced in the system. They were an essential feature of the system itself. More recently, with the advent of the internet and e-mail, and of computer-mediated communication more generally, the idea of a 'republic of letters' consisting of innumerable and ever-changing invisible colleges based on a 'correspondency' – with all that this involves in determining who can communicate with whom, how and when, and the emergent etiquettes that govern these interactions – is as pertinent as ever in contributing to our understanding of scientific communication. Indeed the invisible college, Derek de Solla Price suggests, is 'a mechanism thrown up automatically by the scientific community, just as was the first historic Invisible College that became the Royal Society of mid-Seventeenth century London'.[72] If this is so, what becomes of central importance for the research of the historian of information are (to avoid too mechanistic a reference) the cultural and social dynamics of these groups as they create and modify distinctive information-handling infrastructures for their own disciplinary and political purposes. It can never be quite the case, surely, that *plus ça change, plus c'est la même chose*?

NOTES

1. There are large literatures on all the general topics I mention in this introduction, and I provide only selected examples. For discussions of the concept and a survey of the relevant literatures on the Republic of Letters, though emphasizing the later period, see A. Goldgar (1995), *Impolite Learning: Conduct and Community in the Republic of Letters, 1680–1750* (New Haven: Yale University Press) and D. Goodman (1994), *The Republic of Letters: A Cultural History of the French Enlightenment* (Ithaca:

Cornell University Press). A useful survey is M. Ultee (1987), 'The Republic of Letters: Learned Correspondence, 1680–1720', *Seventeenth Century*, 2, pp. 95–112. The article, M. Biagioli (1996), 'Etiquette, Interdependence, and Sociability in Seventeenth-Century Science', *Critical Inquiry*, 22 (2), 193–238, concentrating on the early years of scientific academies, refers to much of the literature that touches on the norms and social practices that governed behaviour of their members. See also R. Mayhew (2005), 'Mapping Science's Imagined Community: Geography As a Republic of Letters, 1600–1800', *British Journal for the History of Science*, 38, pp. 73–92.

2. See, for instance, H. Brown (1967/1930), *Scientific Organizations in Seventeenth-century France, 1620–1680* (New York: Russell & Russell); M. Ornstein (1938), *The Role of Scientific Societies in the Seventeenth Century* (Chicago: University of Chicago Press) and F. Yates (1947), *The French Academies of the Sixteenth Century* (London: Warburg Institute, University of London) and the discussions reported in S. Schaffer and S. Shapin (1985), *Leviathan and the Air-Pump: Hobbes, Boyle, and the Experimental Life* (Princeton: Princeton University Press). Also, for example, S. Shapin (1994), *A Social History of Truth: Civility and Science in Seventeenth-century England* (Chicago: University of Chicago Press); M. Hall (1991), *Promoting Experimental Learning: Experiment and the Royal Society 1660–1727* (Cambridge: Cambridge University Press); M. Hunter (1989), *Establishing the New Science: The Experience of the Early Royal Society* (Suffolk: Boydell Press); M. Purver (1967), *The Royal Society: Concept and Creation* (Cambridge: MIT Press).

3. See, for example, H. Linder (1959), *The Rise of Current Complete National Bibliography* (New York: Scarecrow Press); B. Manzer (1977), *The Abstract Journal, 1790–1920: Origin, Development, and Diffusion* (New Jersey: Scarecrow Press); D. A. Kronick (1976), *A History of Scientific and Technical Periodicals: The Origins and Development of the Scientific and Technical Press, 1665–1790* (New Jersey: Scarecrow Press); B. Houghton (1975), *Scientific Periodicals: Their Historical Development, Characteristics, and Control* (Hamden: Linnet Books); R. Wiles (1957), *Serial Publication in England before 1750* (Cambridge: Cambridge University Press); A. Growoll (1964), *Three Centuries of English Booktrade Bibliography: An Essay on the Beginnings of Booktrade Bibliography Since the Introduction of Printing and in England since 1595* (London: Holland Press); T. Besterman (1968), *The Beginnings of Systematic Bibliography* (New York: B. Franklin); R. Blum, (1980), *Bibliographia, an Inquiry into its Definition and Designations* (Chicago: American Library Association).

4. For my purposes I assume that there was a scientific revolution whose origins can be found towards the end of the seventeenth century in the work of Boyle, Newton and their colleagues, and which was marked in England by the founding of the Royal Society and in Paris by the Founding of the Académie des Sciences. See, for example, S. Shapin (1996), *The Scientific Revolution* (Chicago: University of Chicago Press); S. Lindberg and S. Westman (eds) (1990), *Reappraisals of the Scientific Revolution* (Cambridge: Cambridge University Press); M. Osler (ed.) (2000), *Rethinking the Scientific Revolution* (Cambridge: Cambridge University Press); P. Dear (1995), *Discipline and Experience: The Mathematical Way in the Scientific Revolution* (Chicago: University of Chicago Press); and W. Eamon (1994), 'From the Secrets of Nature to Public Knowledge', in Eamon, *Science and the Secrets of Nature: Books of Secrets in Medieval and Early Modern Culture* (Princeton: Princeton University Press), pp. 319–50.

5. The standard and indispensable work in English is H. Solomon (1972), *Public Welfare, Science, and Propaganda in Seventeenth-century France: The Innovations of Théophraste Renaudot* (Princeton: Princeton University Press), on which I have drawn heavily. I have also relied on G. De la Tourette (1884), *Théophraste Renaudot d'après des Documents Inédits* (Paris: Librairie Plon), for much of the information I present about Renaudot, because he quotes extensively the primary sources.

6. Tourette, *Théophraste Renaudot*, pp. 5, 7–11.

7. His biographers include Tourette, *Théophraste Renaudot*; Solomon, *Public Welfare*; E. Hattin (1883), *Théophraste Renaudot et ses 'Innocents Inventions'* (Poitiers: Imprimerie Oudin); C. Bailly (1987), *Théophraste Renaudot, un Homme d'Influence au Temps de Louis XIII et de La Fronde* (Paris: Le Pré aux clercs); and P. Gouhot (1974), *Théophraste Renaudot ou Médecin, Philanthrope et Gazetier* (Paris: Pierre Gouhot and La Pensee Universelle). K. Wellman (2003), *Making Science Social: The Conferences of Théophraste Renaudot, 1633–1642* (Nebraska: University of Nebraska Press); S. Mazauric (1997), *Savoir et Philosophie à Paris dans la Première Moitié du XVIIe siècle: Les Conférences du Bureau d'Adresse de Théophraste Renaudot, 1633–1642* (Paris: Publications de la Sorbonne); and G. Sutton (1995), 'Pawning off the New Science: Theophraste Renaudot and the Conferences of the Bureau d'Adresse', in G. Sutton, *Science for a Polite Society: Gender Culture and the Demonstration of Enlightenment* (Colorado: Westview Press), pp. 19–52, provide overviews of Renaudot's life and work before concentrating on an analysis of the discussions represented by the conferences of the Bureau d'Adresse. They will be called conferences in English in this chapter.

8. This is how it is described in the sixth issue of Renaudot's *Gazette*, 4 July 1641, the first to give the location of the publisher of the *Gazette*; see E. Hattin (1859), *Historie Politique et Littéraire de la Presse en France avec une Introduction Historique sur les Origines du Journal et la Bilibliographie Générale des Journaux*; tome 1 (Paris: Poulet-Malassis et de Broise), p. 75.

9. Tourette gives the text of the regulation specifying this requirement and the penalty in Tourette, *Théophraste Renaudot*, pp. 57–9.

10. Solomon, *Public Welfare*, pp. 56–7.

11. *Conferences of the Bureau d'Adresse*, V.3f252 to 3-v.

12. *Conferences of the Bureau d'Adresse*, V.3f253 to11.v; Solomon, *Public Welfare*, p. 54; Tourette, *Théophraste Renaudot*, p. 49.

13. Tourette, *Théophraste Renaudot*, p. 54.

14. Tourette gives the text of this and related documents.

15. Solomon gives an excerpt of this Appendix C, pp. 237–8, that deals with tumours.

16. Tourette, *Théophraste Renaudot*, p. 50.

17. For a good summary of information about Renaudot and the Gazette see C. Bellanger et al. (1969), *Historie Générale de la Presse Françaises*; tome 1: des origines à 1814 (Paris: Presses Universitaires de France); F. Dahl (1951), *Les Débuts de la Presse Française: Nouveaux Apreçus* (Paris: Librairie Raymann); R. Chartier (1989), 'Pamphlets et Gazettes', in R. Chartier and H. Martin (eds) *Histoire de L'Edition Françaises: Le Livre Conquérant du Moyen Age au Milieu du XVIIe Siècle* (Paris: Rayard); Solomon, *Public Welfare*, chs 4 and 5

18. Bellanger et al., *Historie Générale*, p. 8.

19. Solomon, *Public Welfare*, p. 120.

20. Hattin, *Historie Politique*, p. 105.
21. Solomon, *Public Welfare*, p. 133.
22. Solomon, *Public Welfare*, pp. 239–51, gives a full bibliography of Reanudot's many publications.
23. Tourette, *Théophraste Renaudot*, 97–103, excerpts Renaudot's preface to *the Recueil Général des Questions Traité ès Conférences du Bureau d'Adresse, par les plus Beax Esprits de ce Temps*, 2e edn, 1650; to Solomon, *Public Welfare*, chs 3 and appendices A and B must be added the more recent studies of Sutton, 'Pawning off the New Science', pp.19–52; Mazauric, *Savoir et Philosophie*; and Wellman, *Making Science Social*.
24. Sutton, 'Pawning off the New Science', p. 23.
25. *Another Collection of Philosophical Conferences of the French Virtuosi, upon Question of all Sorts; for the Improving of Natural Knowledge Made in the Assembly of the Beaux Esprits at Paris, by the Most Ingenious Persons of that Nation. Rendered into English by G. Havers and J. Davies* (1665) (London: Thomas Dring and John Starkey).
26. Wellman, *Making Science Social*, pp. 63, 65.
27. Sutton, 'Pawning off the New Science', p. 41.
28. Hattin, *Historie Politique*, pp. 68–9.
29. See Solomon, *Public Welfare*, chapter on the Faculty of Medicine.
30. Solomon, *Public Welfare*, recounts in detail the 'war' of pamphlets and law suits that was waged against Renaudot in the chapter on the Faculty of Medicine.
31. P. Triaire (ed.) (1907), *Lettres de Gui Patin, 1630–1672* (Paris), pp. 376–8. Lettre 103 à Monsieur Spon de Paris, ce 8 mars 1644.
32. Solomon, *Public Welfare*, pp. 153–4.
33. Sutton, 'Pawning off the New Science', p. 41.
34. The twelve volumes of Mersenne correspondence are indexed in the ARTFL-FranText database; see: http://www.lib.uchicago.edu/efts/ARTFL/databases/TLF/, in which there are numerous letters addressed to Peiresc. For Mersenne see P. Dear (1998), *Mersenne and the Learning of the Schools* (New York: Cornell University Press).
35. Arnoult, 1988, p. 128
36. A. Coron (1988), '"Ut Prosint Aliis": Jaques-Auguste Thou et sa Bibliothèque', in C. Jolly (ed.) *Histoire des Bibliothèques Françaises: les Bibliothèques sous l'Ancien Régime, 1530–1798* (Paris: Promodis), p. 125.
37. N. de Peiresc (1982), *Lettres de Peiresc. Tome Troisième, Janvier 1634 – Juin 1637* (Paris: Imprimerie Nationale), pp. 13, 15, 43. Peiresc's correspondence is indexed in the Artfl-Frantext database http://www.lib.uchicago.edu/efts/ARTFL/databases/TLF.
38. The standard English source is J. Clarke (1970), *Gabriel Naudé, 1600–1653* (Hamden: Archon Books). I have also drawn extensively on A. Franklin (1901), *Historie de la Bibliothèque Mazarine* (Paris: Welter), who quotes extensively from many of the original documents concerning Naudé and the Mazarin Library.
39. Clark, *Gabriel Naudé*, p. 7. See also Tourette, *Théophraste Renaudot*, pp. 170–1, and Tourette, *Théophraste Renaudot*, p. 138 for Moreau.
40. G. Naudeus (1661), *Instructions Concerning Erecting of a Library Presented to My Lord, the President De Mesme*, interpreted by J. Evelyn (London), p. 2.
41. A. Coron (1988), '"Ut Prosint Aliis": Jaques-Auguste Thou et sa Bibliothèque', in Jolly (1998), *Histoire des Bibliothèques*, p. 123.

42. Clarke, *Gabriel Naudé*, p. 35.
43. Clarke, *Gabriel Naudé*, pp. 43–4. For his correspondence specifically with Naudé, see N. de Peiresc (1983), *Lettres à Naudé (1629–1637): Éditées et Commentées par Phillip Wolfe* (Paris and Seattle: Papers on French Seventeenth Century Literature). Naudé's name crops up throughout Peiresc's general correspondence (see 'Peiresc' in the ARTFL-Frantext database at http://artfl-project.uchicago.edu/).
44. Clarke, *Gabriel Naudé*, p. 63.
45. Naudeus, *Instructions Concerning*, p. 20.
46. Franklin, *Historie*, p. 9.
47. Franklin, *Historie*, pp. 13–17, 25–6; P. Gasnault (1998), 'de la Bibliothèque de Mazarin à la Bibliothèque Mazarine', in C. Jolly (ed.), *Histoire des Bibliothèques Françaises: Les Bibliothèques sous l'Ancien Régime, 1530–1798* (Paris: Promodis), pp. 139, 145.
48. Franklin, *Historie*, pp. 17–18, for the comparisons; pp. 20–21 for details of the three libraries: the Ambrosian in Milan (1608), the Angelica in Rome (1620) and the Bodleian (about 1612) in Oxford; also Gasnault, 'de la Bibliothèque', p. 138.
49. C. Webster (1975), *The Great Instauration: Science, Medicine, and Reform, 1626–1660* (London: Duckworth), pp. 489–90, charts the enormous increase in book production in the period just before the outbreak of the Civil War and the acceleration in publication in the Interregnum. George Thomason's contemporary collection of Civil War pamphlets, known as the Thomason Tracts, consists of over 22,000 items produced between 1640 and 1661. For a description of the collection see the British Library site: http://www.bl.uk/reshelp/findhelprestype/prbooks/thomason/thomasoncivilwar.html. [Date accessed 26 November 2009].
50. P. Nelles (1997), 'The Library As an Instrument of Discovery: Gabriel Naudé and the Uses of History', in D. Kelly (ed.) *History and the Disciplines: The Reclassification of Knowledge in Early Modern Europe* (New York: University of Rochester Press), p. 45.
51. Franklin, *Historie*, pp. 23, 37, 30.
52. Franklin, *Historie*, reprints two pamphlets by Naudé: 'Advis a nos seigneurs de Parlement sur la vente de la Biliothèque de M.le Cardinal Mazarin', 7, pp. 2–76; and 'Remise de la Bibliothèque de Mgr le Cardinal Mazarin', 65–8; see also these translated in G. Naudé (1907), *News from France or a Description of the Library of Cardinal Mazarin Preceded by the Surrender of the Library now Newly Translated: Two Tracts by Gabriel Naudé* (New York: McCLurg).
53. Franklin, *Historie*, pp. 78–98.
54. Franklin, *Historie*, p. 127.
55. See website for the library, http://www.bibliotheque-mazarine.fr/. [Date accessed 26 November 2009].
56. A version of some of the material presented in this section has appeared in W. Boyd Rayward (1994), 'Some Schemes for Restructuring and Mobilising Information in Documents: A Historical Perspective', *Information Processing and Management*, 30, pp. 163–75.
57. Webster, *The Great Instauration*, p. 71.
58. Sheffield University Library has produced a CDROM database of the Hartlib Papers which comprises 'The papers and correspondence of Samuel Hartlib, educationalist, natural philosopher and polymath of the seventeenth century' and states 'The archive, which includes copies of his own letters as well as those sent

to him by others, represents the greater part of extant Hartlib material.' For a good example of the apparently hasty and crude printing of correspondence see the original publication of J. Dury (1972/1650), 'The Reformed Librarie-Keeper' in J. Dury, *The Reformed School and the Reformed Library Keeper 1651* (Menston: Scolar Press).

59. The standard work on the matters dealt with in this section is Webster, *The Great Instauration*, pp. 67–76.

60. J. Dury (1647), 'Considerations Tending to the Happy Accomplishment of England Reformation', in C. Wenster (ed.) (1970), *Samuel Hartlib and the Advancement of Learning* (Cambridge: Cambridge University Press), pp. 119–39.

61. A broadside format of 'Choses dont on peut Recuior auis au Bureau d'Addreffe', Hartlib Papers (item 48/B), Sheffield University.

62. Arnold Boate to Samuel Hartlib, Paris 16/26 July 1648, Hartlib Papers, (58/3A-4A), Sheffield University.

63. J. Dury (1653), 'Some Proposals towards the Advancement of Learning', in C. Wenster (ed.) (1970), *Samuel Hartlib and the Advancement of Learning* (Cambridge: Cambridge University Press), pp. 165–92.

64. Dury, 'The Reformed Librarie-Keeper'.

65. W. Petty (1648), 'The Advice of W. P. to Mr. Samuel Hartlib, for the Advancement of Some Particular Parts of Learning', *Harleian Miscellany* (1810), 6, pp. 1–14.

66. S. Hartlib (1648), 'A Further Discovery of the Office of Publick Addresse for Accommodations', *Harleian Miscellany*, 6, pp. 4–17.

67. A. Blair (2000), 'Annotating and Indexing Natural Philosophy', in M. Spada and N. Jardine (eds), *Books and the Sciences in History* (Cambridge: Cambridge University Press), p. 70.

68. M. Schotte (2008), ' "Books for the Use of the Learned and Studious": William London's Catalogue of Most Vendible Books', *Book History*, 11, pp. 33–57.

69. Blair, 'Annotating and Indexing', p. 70.

70. D. Lux and H. Cook (1998), 'Closed Circles or Open Networks: Communicating at a Distance During the Scientific Revolution', *History of Science*, 36, pp. 182–202.

71. See, for example, the classic studies reported in W. Garvey and B. Griffith (1964), 'Structure, Objectives, and Findings of a Study of Scientific Information Exchange in Psychology', *American Documentation*, 15, 258–67; D. Crane (1972), *Invisible Colleges: Diffusion of Knowledge in Scientific Communities* (Chicago: University of Chicago Press); S. Crawford (1971), 'Informal Communication among Scientists in Sleep Research', *Journal of the American Society for Information Science*, 22, pp. 301–10; D. Price (1971), 'Some Remarks on Elitism in Information and the Invisible College Phenomenon in Science', *Journal of the American Society for Information Science*, 22 (2), pp. 74–5; J. Ziman (1968), *Public Knowledge: An Essay Concerning the Social Dimension of Science* (Cambridge, Cambridge University Press); and the papers by Menzel, Crane, Garvey and Griffith in B. Griffith (ed.) (1980), *Key Papers in Information Science* (New York: published for the American Society for Information Science by Knowledge Industry Publications).

72. Price, 'Some Remarks on Elitism', p. 75.

4

DESIGNING AND GATHERING INFORMATION: PERSPECTIVES ON NINETEENTH-CENTURY FORMS

Paul Stiff, Paul Dobraszczyk and Mike Esbester

In this chapter we introduce information design and the insights it offers into the use of some ubiquitous documents of everyday life.[1] We then explore one document genre which in nineteenth-century Britain marked the growth of a national information-gathering economy: the administrative form, a medium for the conduct of dialogues and interrogations between regulators and citizens. We consider the design and use of early census schedules and tax forms, describing interactions of language, layout and handwritten responses. The result is a picture of people's engagement with the state mediated through forms, and also of the demands made on their reading, writing and numerical skills.

INFORMATION DESIGN AND FORMS

Designing 'Information'

'Information design' is an orphan: unrecognized in Library of Congress subject headings,[2] ignored by Dewey decimal classifiers, absent from Yellow Pages, and saddled with a weak name for a good idea. Add to that problem of name recognition the obvious weakness: is there anything which cannot be conceived of as 'information'?[3] The good idea – design for reading, elsewhere known as user-centred designing – is so simple that a string of qualifiers follows. First, design decisions should be evidence-based, as far as possible. Second, the right kind of evidence is in short supply, and building an information-base for practice is slow. Third, design practice rests not on science, on technology, or on theory, but on an accumulated body of experiential know-how, of trial-and-error, and in this sense is a craft.

There is plenty of evidence about reading, but little that designers can use. They need design-relevant models of reading acts and of readers' purposes and strategies. And because the socially situated acts of reading described in this chapter are usually followed by other kinds of act – selecting, calculating, figuring, answering questions – our interest is in 'reading for action'.[4] Information design supports readers in deciding how to act when using documents which suggest, invite, or require actions from them.

As designing, however cross-disciplinary, may seem an interloper in this book, it may be worth reminding readers of some characteristics of design work. There is always a brief, however ill-founded; usually negotiation over costs and fees; a deadline, a budget and finite resources; technologies of socially organized production; several interests to satisfy; the work of modelling, prototyping and specifying for production; and, with luck, feedback from clients if rarely from users, and even the chance of future revisions. But this account is too rosy, as designers are still often commissioned late in the development process, after the main decisions have been made, when structural defects have been built into the project. This is a reason why combining writing and designing, shaping content and form together – one simple explanation of information design – remains a radical proposition. Another reason is that even professional writers – journalists who are capable of stylistic shifts, or mandarins like Sir Ernest Gowers, author in 1948 of *Plain words* – write in just one form: linear prose.[5] They are all at sea if asked to write ordinary language algorithms, compound lists, look-up tables, bar charts, scatter graphs, or to manage the sequence of injunctions, questions and interpolations that characterize 'forms', let alone to reconcile the often conflicting requirements of all those who have interests in the planned publication.

There is as yet no history of information design, and only a sketch can be supplied here.[6] An idea of the late twentieth century, its germs can be seen in the late nineteenth century's psychology of reading, notions of 'reading hygiene',[7] and in legibility research of the 1930s. Designers aspiring to evidence-based practice must trawl widely: in pragmatics and discourse analysis, for insight into language at work; applied psychology and ergonomics, for functional reading and writing; librarianship and information science; technical documentation, consumer advocacy and plain language campaigns; even in that branch of economic theory which holds that a 'perfect market' calls for perfect information, such that all buyers and sellers have equal access to complete information on which to base their decisions. But designers, driven by the urgency of practical demands, tire of talk, wanting evidence that can guide their decisions in the often messy and never wholly predictable circumstances of production, delivery and projected use.

What are the proximate sources of this mongrel discipline? It is a commonplace that war drives innovation. For example, operational diagrams were almost entirely developed within the idea of a 'technology of training' in the US armed forces after the Second World War.[8] One of the biggest customers for design, and sponsors of research about it, has been the US Department of Defense. A gathering in the Netherlands in 1978 could be a marker for the beginning of modern information design: from it grew *Information Design Journal*, in 1979, and later *Information Design* the book.[9] Its title page reminds us of the military habit of sponsoring such events, and the genesis of this one: a 'NATO conference on the visual presentation of information'. But there was no military monopoly: in 1979 the British Library set up a working group to report on 'the problems of characterizing the domain of information design'.[10] In the decades before that report two informing strands can be traced. First, information theory, its source in the United States but in this tributary flowing briefly through Europe and embracing semiotics. The second strand, empirical research into people's behaviour with documents, was and remains largely Anglo-American.

Information theory emerged from telecommunications and bequeathed a metaphor – 'signal-channel-noise' – of questionable value to students of human interactions.[11] But the idea that communicating information could be subject to standards of accuracy, efficiency and effectiveness was attractive, if forbidding, to designers. In his 1957 book, *On Human Communication*, the engineer Colin Cherry provided a rich context for Claude Shannon's mathematical model and added a semantic dimension. This appeared to offer designers solid support for their decision-making. So, unusually for the time, Ken Garland gave space in his *Graphics Handbook* of 1966 to the challenge of 'organizing information', used jargon like 'originating source', 'channel', 'data', 'transmission', 'redundancy', and turned on its head a favoured term: 'the graphic designer may be in for some shocks. Some of his favourite devices may turn out to be quite incomprehensible. Feedback is a double-edged weapon.' In the 1950s there had been attempts in Europe to marry information theory to aesthetics: at the *Hochschule für Gestaltung*, Ulm, the philosopher Max Bense developed an aesthetic theory of information and semiotics, while in Strasbourg the French engineer-philosopher Abraham Moles explored musical perception in *Information Theory and Esthetic Perception*.[12] But in the year of that book's appearance in English, an intervention from psychology suggested why information theory was unable to provide convincing insight into figure perception.[13] After five decades it is still hard to discern any fruitful impact of that theory on information design practice.

More productive strands emerged in Britain, where the Presentation of Technical Information Group was founded in London in 1948 and the Ergonomics Research Society in 1949; the journals *Ergonomics* and *Human Factors* first appeared in 1958. At the Communications Research Centre established at University College London in 1952, work on algorithms by Peter Wason in the early 1960s[14] led to practical guidance published, appropriately, by the Civil Service College 'to show how, by a change of format, rules and regulations can be made intelligible to almost everyone'.[15] This was the context from which emerged Patricia Wright's work on language and comprehension, graphic formats and decision-making. In a paper of 1971, she formatted a brief instructional text with embedded conditionals as a list of short sentences, as a table, and as a logical tree, implicitly asking a fundamental question: which graphic configuration is most appropriate in which situation of use? The first answer was: there is no optimal format for all situations – it depends on the reader's questions and task. The second answer appears in the following sentence. When the information is at hand to be read as needed, use a table if readers will know what to look up, but use a logical tree if readers need help in finding relevant parts of the information; if the information must be remembered, use lists of short sentences, with appropriate headings. That last sentence was articulated only by punctuation. Here is the same information reconfigured to support memory:

- *when the information is at hand to be read as needed*
  - use a table if readers will know what to look up
  - use a logical tree if readers will need help in finding relevant parts of the information
- *when information must be remembered*
  - use lists of short sentences, with appropriate headings

Observing that logical trees with the same information content can be designed in various ways, Wright added a challenge to designers: 'At the moment, almost nothing is known about the factors which determine the optimal design of these types of presentation.' Little has changed since then.

Information design practice, largely untouched by theory or empirical research, derived in large measure from European modernist design of the 1920s and 1930s: 'new typography', and Isotype. This, the 'Vienna method' of pictorial statistics and process visualization, should be better known for its praxis of the 'transformer':

> It is the responsibility of the 'transformer' to understand the data, to get all necessary information from the expert, to decide what is worth transmitting to the public, how to make it understandable, how to link it with general knowledge or with information already given ... In this sense, the transformer is the trustee of the public.[16]

The work of émigrés such as the Czech Ladislav Sutnar in the USA from the 1940s, and the Austrian Ernest Hoch in Britain from the 1950s, was exemplary.[17] Also notable was the research done in London, from 1966 to 1982, into graphic formats in 'information printing' and visual displays, by designers at the Graphic Information Research Unit.[18]

Understanding and Designing Forms

Given the challenges facing Whitehall in 1945 – economic remobilization, establishing the mechanisms of a welfare state – it may be surprising to find in that year of transition from total war to economic crisis the Organization and Methods Division of H. M. Treasury making time to compile an aid to civil servants entitled *The Design of Forms in Government Departments*.[19] The book, in its subsequent editions, is rarely consulted today; it gives little insight into the ways people read and use those 'formulary documents with blanks for the insertion of particulars'. Forms are more interesting than those words from the OED's bleak description may suggest.[20] As standardized instruments to manage information-gathering, they enable questioners to control the manner and pace of interaction with those whom they question. For example, in an early study of these attributes, Patricia Wright identified on one form six ways of asking questions and constraining answers.[21] By definition, forms are impersonal, not tailored to individual needs. They broadcast all necessary questions to all possible respondents, but only some will be relevant to any one respondent. It follows that forms pack in conditionals of the type: 'if x applies, then y; if not, then z'. So 'routing' is a challenge: writers and designers must help readers to navigate and select the routes relevant to them. Forms are among the few types of document that need to be read in a linear manner. In the view of a contemporary innovator in forms design: 'It's the only way that routing instructions work. You have to read them on rails.'[22] And research confirms experience: people skip headings and instructions, consulting them only *in extremis*. David

Frohlich summarized form-reading and -filling behaviour in terms of a handful of principles such as:

- *linear progression*: work through the questions in the order in which they appear on the form;
- *least reading effort*: only read what seems to be necessary to maintain form-filling progress;
- *question routing*: jump directly to a new question if the form tells you to;
- *question omission*: miss out questions which don't seem to apply to you.[23]

In 1974 a sociolinguistic model emerged to account for the organization of turn-taking in conversation, one signal characteristic of which is sensitivity to 'recipient design'. By this its authors meant several dimensions of reciprocity in conversation, finding it in

> word selection, topic selection, admissibility and ordering of sequences, optionsandobligationsforstartingandterminatingconversations...Recipient design is a major basis for that variability of actual conversations glossed by the notion 'context-sensitive'.[24]

By extension a static printed text can, especially if typographically articulated, be envisaged as a medium for dialogue between writer and reader, in which control of the 'conversation' is passed back and forth. The nineteenth-century documents which we describe below are called 'returns'. But with forms this is 'dialogue' in the most neutral sense, entailing no assumption of equality between participants. Public forms issued by the state are more likely to be experienced as an interview (the passport form, say) or as an interrogation (welfare benefits forms).

Modelling textual discourse, however illuminating, is not designing, and has a limited direct bearing upon it. For public forms, politics drove practice: the usability of public documents became a matter of policy when in 1978 President Carter ordered that US federal regulations should be 'clearer, less burdensome, and more cost-effective'. The Document Design Project, from 1978 to 1981 – involving the American Institutes for Research (AIR) in Washington DC, Carnegie Mellon University (English and Psychology departments) and the New York design business Siegel & Gale (slogan: 'simple is smart') – worked on simplifying instructions in Internal Revenue tax forms, and evaluating people's understanding of linguistically complex instructions. From this project emerged the Document Design Center (later Information Design Center) at AIR and, from 1979 to 1990, the Communications Design Center at Carnegie Mellon.

The pioneering analytical work done in Britain in the 1960s and 1970s waited a decade for practice to catch up, again driven politically. With public forms subject to increasingly vocal complaints,[25] a business-friendly government included forms reform in its plan to cut rules and 'red tape'. A review by Derek Rayner, then chairman of Marks & Spencer and Prime Minister Thatcher's adviser, led in 1982 to the white paper *Administrative Forms in Government.*[26] It estimated that over 2,000 million government forms and leaflets were used by the public each year, averaging 36 for every man, woman and child in the country.[27]

Few if any designers were then aware of, let alone exploring, how the conduct of the remote interactions embodied in forms could be supported by design. One who did was Ernest Hoch, having reported in July 1979 to the Post Office on 'Forms in the Postal Business: a Survey of the Scale of the Problem'. Like most large organizations which published vast numbers of documents, the Post Office lacked a coherent policy for their management. In one of his case studies, 'Saying "yes" and signing for "no" ', Hoch showed how, because of a form's design, 'responsible and experienced staff can be tricked into first stating that an item has been delivered and immediately afterwards confirm by their signature that it has been lost'. In another he analysed a form which counter clerks frequently misinterpreted, and of which a high proportion was returned by the public either wrongly or incompletely filled in. He identified a single facet of its design as a probable cause of difficulty, modified it in isolation, showed that improved performance was due to this modification – suggesting the cumulative effect of such improvements. In the wake of the white paper, Hoch was consulted by the Department of Health and Social Security – producer of 12,000 different forms, of which half were publicly issued in annual runs of up to 30 million.[28] He was instrumental in setting up the DHSS's Forms Design Unit in 1982, the first such professional group within a government department. That impetus has since faded. But what happened before forms were rigorously designed?

Forms before Designers

Printed forms probably become widespread around the mid eighteenth century. And although the *OED* definition cited above offers Charles Dickens[29] as its first authority for such usage, we find a census document of 1821 declaring itself as 'A form to be filled up by every housekeeper in this parish'. Michael Twyman shows, earlier still, a 'Catalogue of blank forms' issued by the Worcester printer J. Tymbs in 1780, listing by name the 85 different forms which he supplied, and referring to other generic types: 'burial affidavits, exchequer writs, land tax receipts, orders of removal, parish certificates, petitions for insolvents'.[30] Twyman also points to J. Soulby jnr, printer in Ulverston 1819–26, who offered a range of legal forms for use by local attorneys, typically printed and reprinted in runs of 50.

In his survey of the state's collection of information about citizens Edward Higgs observed of forms that 'there has been little attempt to understand how and why this generic bureaucratic device was developed'.[31] Here we make such an attempt, using the perspectives of information design – taking the position of readers, required by law to read questions and to answer them in writing, as much as that of those sanctioned by authority to ask such questions – in order to examine the interactions conducted through forms in nineteenth-century Britain. We investigate two kinds of major public form, instruments for counting people and for taxing them, and embodying both data enquiry and trans-actions between state and individual. We more or less cover the century, with census forms from early decades and tax forms from later ones.

In those early nineteenth-century forms printed in short runs by intaglio or by lithography – six or more by the latter could be cheaper than manuscript – the appearance if not the reality of handwriting persisted, as that means of mark-making on printing surfaces was supported by these technologies. But for runs in the thousands, setting type and printing letterpress offered not only economy but also the advantage of easier correction and revision. This technology, in common use until the 1960s, may also have contributed to the changing aspect of forms – most saliently, a clearer demarcation between the questioner's standard texts and the responses of those questioned.

We observe that early forms followed book conventions – their standard texts set out like a page of linear prose, with gaps for handwritten responses (subject to printers' imperfect guesses), and simple language cues to flag switches of turn-taking: 'I,   , of   , do state that   ' (and so on). We have found no evidence to suggest that the shift from such constrained turn spaces, to the questionnaire within regularized grid formats, delimited by a rectilinear net of printed rules, which gradually emerged throughout the century, was prompted by any incipient concern for readers, or what today is called 'usability'. To speculate, a better bet is that such standardization aimed to filter out irrelevant responses, to limit the respondent's options to what was strictly required by the questioner. In short, the operational needs of efficient data-handling had priority. By the time of the reintroduction of income tax in 1842 the 'form' – its language, shape and style, its 'look and feel' – had stabilized into a set of lin-guistic and graphic conventions which would be recognizable today. The form had already begun to solidify, in metal type, into a genre which would remain more or less fixed for over a century.

COUNTING THE PEOPLE: CENSUS FORMS, 1801–41

The British census, initially carried out in 1801 and thereafter every ten years, is a good starting point for our consideration of forms design and reception in the nineteenth century. With the census came the first public forms disseminated on a national scale, as well as the earliest and most significant attempt by the British state to gather information on its citizens at the level of the individual. Census historians, particularly Edward Higgs, have examined its impact in detail, including the production and dissemination of the forms, or household schedules, by which the state gathered the information it desired.[32] Yet, one aspect of the census has remained unexplored: the willingness or otherwise of the public to divulge the information requested, and their ability to do this through the medium of the printed form. By examining the census at its point of contact with its subjects, we can learn much about the relationship between state and citizens in its everyday contexts – in this case, the imposition of census forms and their reception by users.

The organization of the first nationwide census in Britain in 1801 drew upon the precedents set by numerous local population surveys carried out in the eighteenth century, such as that in Westmorland in 1787 – the first at county level.[33] In this case local officials, known as constables, carried out the census, going from house to house and drawing up a list of names of inhabitants, their occupations and sex, and their relationships to their respective families.[34] The returns themselves were probably similar to many in the eighteenth century: they were handwritten forms, the constables organizing the format as they saw fit, resulting in a wide variety of different layouts. The enumeration papers used for the 1801 census attempted to standardize these existing practices by issuing a prescribed schedule (Figure 4.1) with the 1800 Census Act, overseen by John Rickman (1771–1840), a prominent statistician and government official who supervised the first four decennial censuses.[35] The questions asked by the schedule were all but identical to those seen in previous local population surveys (on the number of houses, people and their occupations). What was new was the standardized format: a tabular layout that departed from the existing conventions of form design. As we have said, late-eighteenth-century forms, such as warrants, marriage certificates and licences, looked like pages from books with spaces left blank for the insertion of handwritten words and a signature at the bottom of the sheet (Figure 4.2). However, the tabular format was not completely unprecedented: when the national duty on hair powder was introduced on 5 May 1795, a tabular form was prescribed (Figure 4.3). Yet only after its introduction in the 1801 census schedule was this format widely disseminated, and it went on to be employed for a wide range

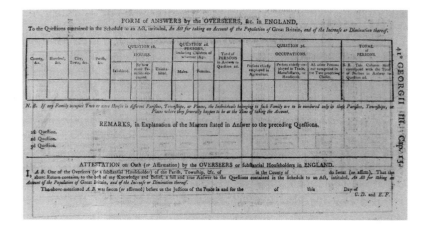

Figure 4.1   The first prescribed enumeration form in 'An Act for taking an account' 1800.

of statistical enquiry in the nineteenth century, most notably civil registration, which adopted standardized tabular forms when a centralized repository was set up in 1836.[36]

Despite the fact that the 1801 census prescribed a standard form, some local governments adapted its design to meet the needs of their residents. Whilst all of the official returns were destroyed by the Public Record Office before the First World War, some local returns still exist in county archives, notably those held by the City of London.[37] In 1801, the City parish of St Nicholas Acons printed its own schedules, with other districts adopting a similar practice.[38] The parish of St Nicholas Acons was one of 118 in the City and consisted of only a few streets: in this case, Nicholas Lane, Abchurch Lane, Boot Alley and Fox Ordinary Court, situated between Cornhill and Cannon Street. Unlike most census schedules before 1841, this and many others in the City were filled in by householders themselves rather than by overseers: the latter would have copied the information given by householders into the schedules prescribed by Rickman before forwarding them to the census offices in London. However, the layout of the 46 surviving householder schedules from 1801 differs significantly from the prescribed schedule. Instead of a tabular format, the questions are arranged as continuous text, in the manner of other types of forms that would have been familiar to at least some City residents, such as registration and legal documents or tax returns. The alterations display a

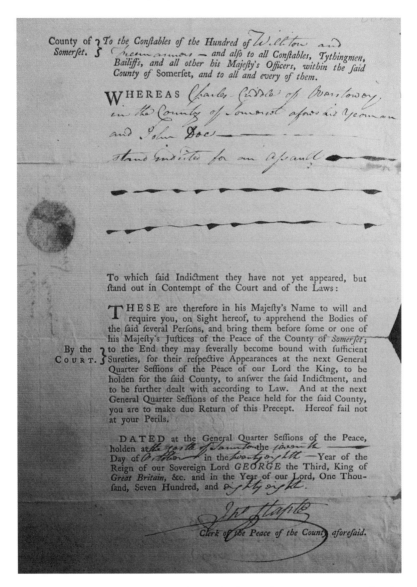

Figure 4.2 Conventional form design in the late 18th century: a warrant for the arrest of Charles Criddle to appear before the Justices of the Peace on the charge of assault, Taunton, 7 October 1788, 317 × 195mm (Rickards Collection, University of Reading, sheet 79).

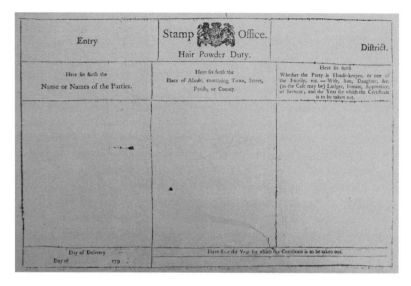

The table depicted:

Entry	Stamp Office. Hair Powder Duty.	Diſtrict.
Here ſet forth the Name or Names of the Parties.	Here ſet forth the Place of Abode, containing Town, Street, Parish, or County.	Here ſet forth Whether the Party is Houſe-keeper, or one of the Family, viz. — Wife, Son, Daughter, &c. (as the Caſe may be) Lodger, Inmate, Apprentice, or Servant ; and the Year for which the Certificate is to be taken out.
Day of Delivery Day of 179	Here ſtate the Year for which the Certificate is to be taken out.	

Figure 4.3   An early example of the tabular layout in forms: a license issued to users of hair powder, *c.*1795, 155 × 197mm (Rickards Collection, University of Reading, Hair Powder 2).

concern with aiding residents' comprehension of the form: the terse questions on the prescribed schedule are expanded into seven proper sentences; basic navigation tools are included, such as broken rules to guide the reader's eye to the spaces corresponding to the questions; and instructions are printed in a smaller typeface ('insert the proper number in answer to each question', or for the 'Party making the return' to sign at the bottom right of the sheet in the space provided). Also included, in the substantial area of text below the questions, is a clear warning to householders of the five-pound penalty that would be imposed on any person refusing to fill in the form or for deliberately giving wrong answers – a warning that would appear on every subsequent census schedule in the nineteenth century. Finally, there are detailed instructions on procedure, a reiteration of the order to insert proper numbers in the spaces provided, and further commands to sign with a proper name, to include an address and to have the completed and correct return ready on the morning of 10 March for the enumerator to collect.

This schedule would have been authorized by parish officials in St Nicholas Acons, but probably designed by the local printer, in this case J. Abraham, who was based in Clement's Lane and printed all the St Nicholas Acons' schedules from 1801 to 1831.[39] To invest both time and money in the production of

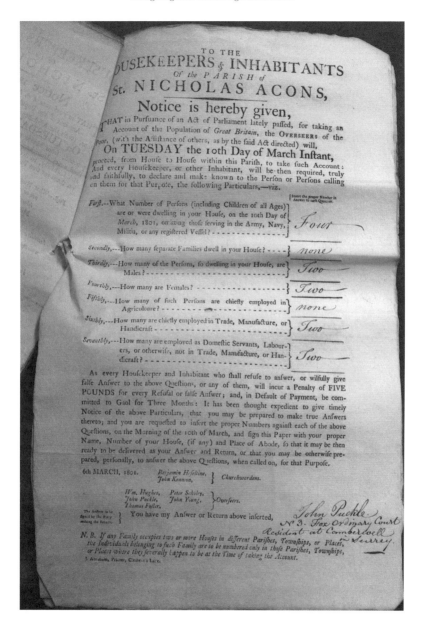

Figure 4.4 The 1801 census schedule as adapted for the householders of the parish of St Nicholas Acons, City of London, 1801, 325 × 208mm. The handwritten annotations are by John Puckle and the form was printed by J. Abraham (Guildhall Library, London (GL), MS 4306).

their own schedules indicates that parish officials either had remarkable faith in the reading and writing skills of their residents, or that they viewed form-filling by householders as more efficient than that carried out by enumerators. Either view stood in stark contrast to Rickman, who was adamantly opposed to householders filling in the schedules themselves, and even doubted the abilities of enumerators to provide accurate returns.[40] Yet, taken as a whole, the 46 returns from St Nicholas Acons seem to confirm the confidence of the parish officers. John Puckle, who filled in the example shown in Figure 4.4, was one of only two parish residents who completed schedules for all four censuses from 1801; the other was William Bond, a wine merchant who lived at 31 Nicholas Lane. In 1801, Puckle was both householder and overseer; not only would he have completed his own schedule, but he would also have transcribed those of his fellow householders into the prescribed format. We would therefore expect Puckle to be an exemplary form-filler; yet like most other residents, he spelled out numbers rather than writing numerals, despite the repeated instructions to the contrary.[41] Here, Puckle was following existing conventions in forms that generally consisted of continuous text interrupted by word-length spaces – much too large for numerals alone. Convention also governed another feature of Puckle's form: his inscription of an extended line at the end of each number that fills the remaining space; this cancel was a common device used in legal forms – and seen clearly in the blank space in Figure 4.2 – for ensuring that no other hand could tamper with the answers (and is still used when writing cheques today). Finally, Puckle's writing was confident and careful like the majority of his fellow parishioners, who demonstrate a remarkable level of competence in reading, writing and numeracy – only seven of the 46 forms display any crossings-out or overwriting. Despite the obvious drawbacks of such a small sample, these census forms raise questions about historians' assessment of literacy in this period, which tend to evaluate literacy through an analysis of book reading, although literacy rates have been assessed throughout this period on the basis of people's ability to sign the marriage register – in effect a type of form.[42]

In 1811, the parish officials in St Nicholas Acons introduced a new tabular format to its residents (Figure 4.5). The new layout was essentially a simplified version of the prescribed schedule, while the questions – identical to those in 1801 bar the omission of the seventh – were shortened to statements as in the prescribed schedule. But compared with the 1801 schedule, this one was remarkably free of explanatory text, leaving a large amount of space in the table beneath the column headings. Presumably, the parish officers felt confident that their residents would cope with this new tabular format. The years between the 1801 and 1811 censuses had seen the widespread dissemination

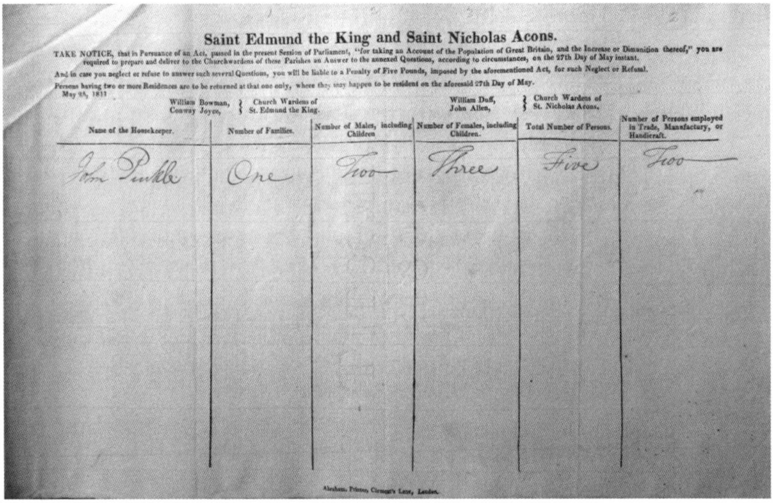

Saint Edmund the King and Saint Nicholas Acons.

TAKE NOTICE, that in Pursuance of an Act, passed in the present Session of Parliament, "for taking an Account of the Population of Great Britain, and the Increase or Diminution thereof," you are required to prepare and deliver to the Churchwardens of these Parishes an Answer to the annexed Questions, according to circumstances, on the 27th Day of May instant.

And in case you neglect or refuse to answer such several Questions, you will be liable to a Penalty of Five Pounds, imposed by the aforementioned Act, for such Neglect or Refusal.

Persons having two or more Residences are to be returned at that one only, where they may happen to be resident on the aforesaid 27th Day of May.

May 25, 1811

William Bowman, Conway Joyce, } Church Wardens of St. Edmund the King.

William Duff, John Allen, } Church Wardens of St. Nicholas Acons.

Name of the Housekeeper.	Number of Families.	Number of Males, including Children	Number of Females, including Children.	Total Number of Persons.	Number of Persons employed in Trade, Manufactory, or Handicraft.
John Puckle	One	Two	Three	Five	Two

Abraham, Printer, Clement's Lane, London.

Figure 4.5 The 1811 household schedule filled in by John Puckle of St Nicholas Acons, 204 × 325mm. Printed by Abraham (GL, MS 4306).

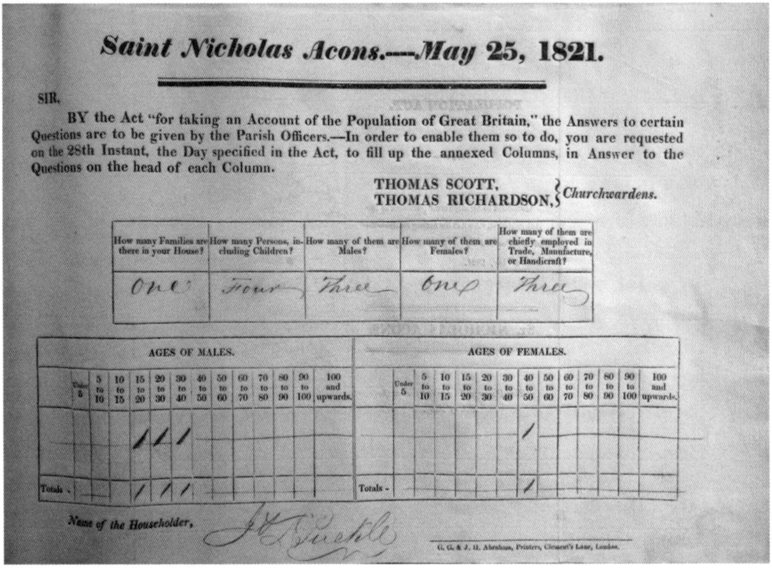

Saint Nicholas Acons.—May 25, 1821.

SIR,

BY the Act "for taking an Account of the Population of Great Britain," the Answers to certain Questions are to be given by the Parish Officers.—In order to enable them so to do, you are requested on the 28th Instant, the Day specified in the Act, to fill up the annexed Columns, in Answer to the Questions on the head of each Column.

THOMAS SCOTT, THOMAS RICHARDSON, } *Churchwardens.*

How many Families are there in your House?	How many Persons, including Children?	How many of them are Males?	How many of them are Females?	How many of them are chiefly employed in Trade, Manufacture, or Handicraft?
One	Four	Three	One	Three

AGES OF MALES.

	Under 5	5 to 10	10 to 15	15 to 20	20 to 30	30 to 40	40 to 50	50 to 60	60 to 70	70 to 80	80 to 90	90 to 100	100 and upwards.
				/	/	/							
Totals -				/	/	/							

AGES OF FEMALES.

	Under 5	5 to 10	10 to 15	15 to 20	20 to 30	30 to 40	40 to 50	50 to 60	60 to 70	70 to 80	80 to 90	90 to 100	100 and upwards.
							/						
Totals -							/						

Name of the Householder, J. Puckle

G. G. & J. H. Abraham, Printers, Clement's Lane, London.

Figure 4.6 The 1821 household schedule filled in by John Puckle of St Nicholas Acons, 204 × 325mm. Printed by G. G. & J. H. Abraham (GL, MS 4306).

of tabular forms, more specifically after the Invasion Act of 1803. Fearing an imminent attack by Napoleon, the government issued a plethora of forms to be completed by parish officials nationwide and by specific groups in their communities: bakers and millers (for ensuring a regular supply of bread); the nobility, gentry and yeomanry (for provision of wagons for the transport of troops and supplies).[43] However, not all members of the community would have been exposed to these new forms and it seems that, in 1811, some residents struggled with the new tabular format. Compared with the 1801 schedules, more householders made corrections to their answers – 12 of the forms show crossings-out or overwriting of the numbers. Puckle himself seems to have been as careful as he was in 1801; on this schedule, in faint pencil written at the top of the sheet above the respective columns, he made a trial count in numerals before committing his answers to the permanence of ink.

The 1821 schedule included a new question on age ranges, resulting in a second table being included beneath the now standard questions (Figure 4.6). Rickman introduced this feature into his 1821 schedules for enumerators, who were asked to group persons in five year bands up to the age of 20 and 10 thereafter. This clearly caused problems for enumerators, for this feature was not reintroduced again until 1921. A new task was required of householders in St Nicholas Acons: to tally the age ranges of their families and to articulate these in a new format. We know from his 1831 return (Figure 4.7) that Puckle was a trader by profession. Although his exact trade is unspecified, that he would have had extensive experience of calculating figures, in ledger books or invoices and price lists, is indicated in this schedule by his confident recording of ages and their totals, where he employed slanted lines instead of numerals and scored the blank spaces in between to secure his answers. Of the 35 other householders in St Nicholas Acons, many were not so adept as Puckle: seven tried to fit spelled-out numbers into the spaces, one resorting to writing them vertically in the columns; eight failed to enter totals into the spaces provided, while two wrote the totals in the wrong place (one immediately to the right of the word 'totals', the other in the blank space above). In all, 14 of the schedules are defaced by crossings-out or overwriting, suggesting that many residents were confused by this new format, or were not as numerically agile as Puckle, or both.

Although the 1831 schedule used in St Nicholas Acons (Figure 4.7) dispensed with the age tallies, it increased its complexity in other ways, namely, by expanding the number of questions to nine, with four on occupations alone and three subdivided into further categories. The form followed the layout and content of Rickman's prescribed schedule more closely than in previous censuses, adopting a similar tabular arrangement and wording of the questions;[44]

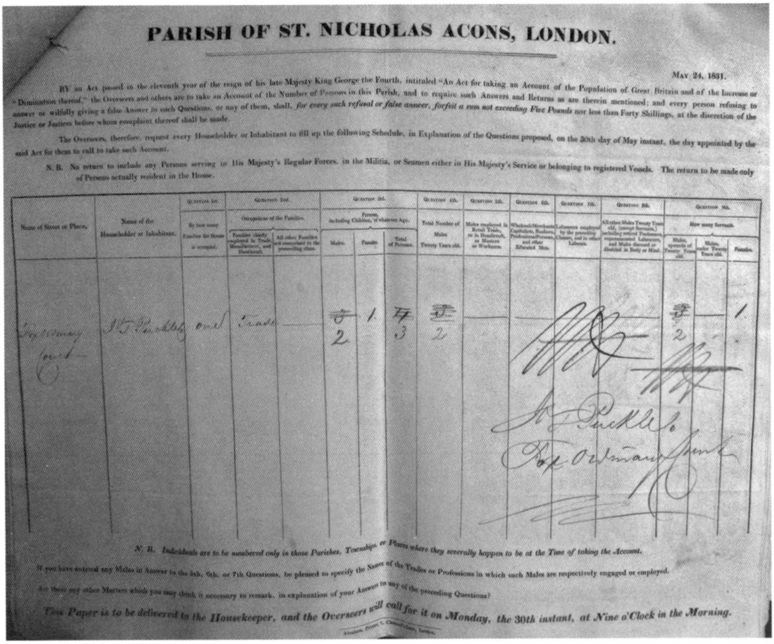

PARISH OF ST. NICHOLAS ACONS, LONDON.

May 24, 1831.

BY an Act passed in the eleventh year of the reign of his late Majesty King George the Fourth, intituled "An Act for taking an Account of the Population of Great Britain and of the Increase or "Diminution thereof," the Overseers and others are to take an Account of the Number of Persons in this Parish, and to require such Answers and Returns as are therein mentioned; and every person refusing to answer or wilfully giving a false Answer to such Questions, or any of them, shall, *for every such refusal or false answer, forfeit a sum not exceeding Five Pounds* nor less than Forty Shillings, at the discretion of the Justice or Justices before whom complaint thereof shall be made.

The Overseers, therefore, request every Householder or Inhabitant to fill up the following Schedule, in Explanation of the Questions proposed, on the 30th day of May instant, the day appointed by the said Act for them to call to take such Account.

N. B. No return to include any Persons serving in His Majesty's Regular Forces, in the Militia, or Seamen either in His Majesty's Service or belonging to registered Vessels. The return to be made only of Persons actually resident in the House.

Name of Street or Place.	Name of the Householder or Inhabitant.	Question 1st. By how many Families the House is occupied.	Question 2nd. Occupations of the Families. Families chiefly employed in Trade, Manufacture, and Handicraft.	All other Families not comprised in the preceding class.	Question 3rd. Persons, including Children, of whatever Age. Males.	Females.	Total of Persons.	Question 4th. Total Number of Males Twenty Years old.	Question 5th. Males employed in Retail Trade, or in Handicraft, as Masters or Workmen.	Question 6th. Wholesale Merchants, Capitalists, Bankers, Professional Persons, and other Educated Men.	Question 7th. Labourers employed by the preceding Classes, and in other Labour.	Question 8th. All other Males Twenty Years old, (except Servants,) including retired Tradesmen, superannuated Labourers, and Males diseased or disabled in Body or Mind.	Question 9th. How many Servants. Males, upwards of Twenty Years old.	Males, under Twenty Years old.	Females.
[illegible]	[illegible]	one	Trade		3 / 2	1	4 / 3	3 / 2					3 / 2		1

N. B. *Individuals are to be numbered only in those Parishes, Townships, or Places where they severally happen to be at the Time of taking the Account.*

If you have entered any Males in Answer to the 5th, 6th, or 7th Questions, be pleased to specify the Names of the Trades or Professions in which such Males are respectively engaged or employed.

Are there any other Matters which you may think it necessary to remark, in explanation of your Answers to any of the preceding Questions?

This Paper is to be delivered to the Housekeeper, and the Overseers will call for it on Monday, the 30th instant, at Nine o'Clock in the Morning.

Figure 4.7 The 1831 household schedule filled in by John Puckle of St Nicholas Acons, with corrections by the unnamed enumerator, 333 × 417mm. Printed by Abraham (GL, MS 4306).

perhaps the parish officers of St Nicholas Acons considered their residents now adept enough to cope with its complexity, or they wanted to facilitate the transcribing of the information from household to prescribed schedules. For the first time Puckle's form displayed crossings-out: he mistakenly counted one extra male servant, crossing out four of the entries and writing the correct numbers below. Puckle did not count himself – presumably he owned the property but did not live there, returning at the time of the census to perform the enumeration of the servants. Puckle's mistake was probably not the result of confusion caused by the form's intricacy. Yet, of the other 38 returns in the parish, 14 exhibit crossings-out, overwriting in pen, or additions in pencil, while the enumerator made corrections on six, mainly filling in answers that had been left blank, and confirmed his important role by signing each of the forms in duplicate.

In 1841, householder schedules were introduced for the entire population of Britain, a practice that continues to this day. From them on, all schedules (and many other types of forms associated with the census) were specified in advance and printed by the government stationery office in ever-increasing numbers. It is ironic that the majority of extant householder schedules date from the period before their official sanction and standardization in 1841. They survive because they fell outside of the official process; none of the pre-1841 London schedules were sent back to the census offices, thus evading the destruction of all household schedules by the Public Record Office before the First World War. These rare survivals illustrate, albeit within a narrow geographical and demographic range, an urban population coming to terms with the demands the census – and the changing layout of its forms – made on their skills of reading, writing and numeracy. They are also some of the earliest surviving examples of public forms and, in the case of John Puckle, give some indication of the nature of form-filling behaviour of the 'common man' at the dawn of state-controlled national information-gathering.

TAXING THE PEOPLE: TAX FORMS, 1842–1910

Taxation was not an invention of the nineteenth century: the British state, in its various incarnations, has taxed its citizens for over 1000 years.[45] However, the development of the state's administrative capability in the nineteenth century made possible a system of centrally administered taxation, contributing to the creation of the Inland Revenue in 1849. Whereas previously tax had been levied either by an arbitrary charge or by an inspection and assessment of property, the income tax between 1799 and 1816 required individuals to complete a tax return, a form on the details of which an assessment was made. Abolished in 1816, the tax was reintroduced in 1842, and was again charged on the basis of information supplied on returns. Historians have not yet considered these forms as worth examination in their own right; instead, they have attended to the facts and figures contained within forms.[46] Tax forms, like those for the census, represented the growth of state information-gathering in the nineteenth century, posing challenges to people required to complete them. They help us to assess relationships between state and citizens, mediated by the design and use of information.

Tax forms were completed annually, by people believed by tax officials to have earned more than the minimum threshold. After 1842 this varied between £100 and £160, effectively excluding the working classes from the tax.[47] Nevertheless the number of tax forms issued was large: for just two of the five income tax schedules, numbers rose from around 200,000 forms in 1848, to around 960,000 forms in 1905.[48] In addition, several other taxes were levied, including inheritance tax, assessed taxes and land tax – all of which involved forms. The growing numbers of forms circulating after 1800 reflect the ways in which the state increasingly attempted to 'know' its citizens.[49] Taxation was resented by many taxpayers: in 1904 the Clerk and Counsel to the Commissioners of the Taxes for the City of London observed that '[t]here are always people prepared to make an attack upon any system of taxation'.[50] Forms were part of the problem.

We can envisage these tax forms as turn-taking dialogue, often involving several exchanges in several different forms.[51] In the broadest terms, we see the following pattern of exchanges:

- the state's agent (the Inland Revenue from 1849) demanded an individual's financial information, through the medium of a form which it had devised and had printed;
- the person responded by providing information – completing the form in some way, having attended more or less to the instructions and guidance printed on the form;
- based on information provided by the person, the Inland Revenue assessed the tax they should pay and delivered the assessment, with a demand for payment, to the person;
- the person paid the tax due;
- the state's agent completed the exchange by issuing a receipt to the person, verifying that payment had been made.

By 1842 many people who received tax forms would be familiar with the forms genre, which had become increasingly widespread since the start of the century. Tax officials – assessors – delivered income tax forms to the addresses of those deemed liable to be assessed. These forms demanded various details, depending on the schedule of assessment. Questions typically required details of the person's amount and sources of income (for example professional earnings, Figure 4.9), and the amount and nature of expenses (for example rent, Figure 4.11). And by signing in the requisite place – indicated by the cue-word 'signed' and a ruled space (Figure 4.13) – the person could give notice of their intention to claim full or partial exemption from taxation. The legal act in the form-filling process was a declaration of the truth of the details which had been provided, attested by a signature (Figure 4.12).

There were many different tax forms. Each was designed to apply to as many circumstances as possible, in effect an 'all-purposes' approach

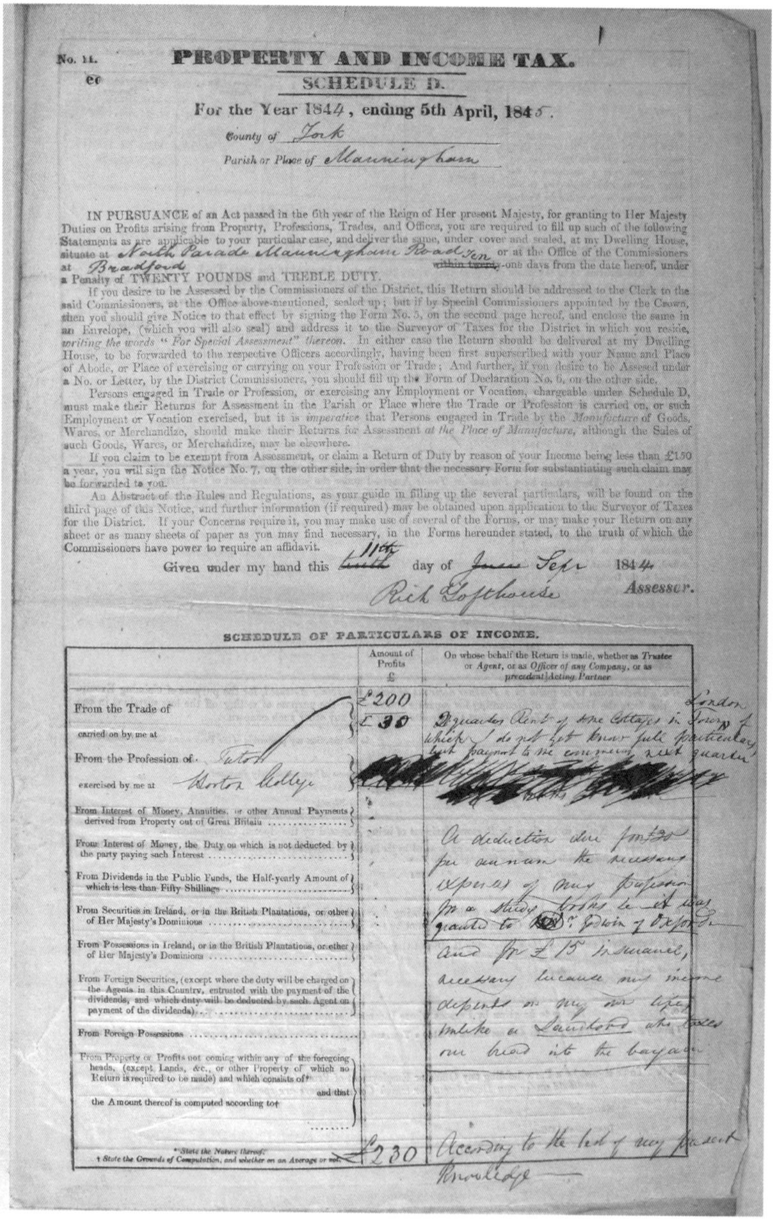

No. 11.

PROPERTY AND INCOME TAX.

SCHEDULE D.

For the Year 1844, ending 5th April, 1845.

County of York

Parish or Place of Manningham

IN PURSUANCE of an Act passed in the 6th year of the Reign of Her present Majesty, for granting to Her Majesty Duties on Profits arising from Property, Professions, Trades, and Offices, you are required to fill up such of the following Statements as are applicable to your particular case, and deliver the same, under cover and sealed, at my Dwelling House, situate at North Parade Manningham Road or at the Office of the Commissioners at Bradford Ten ~~within twenty~~-one days from the date hereof, under a Penalty of TWENTY POUNDS and TREBLE DUTY.

If you desire to be Assessed by the Commissioners of the District, this Return should be addressed to the Clerk to the said Commissioners, at the Office above-mentioned, sealed up; but if by Special Commissioners appointed by the Crown, then you should give Notice to that effect by signing the Form No. 5, on the second page hereof, and enclose the same in an Envelope, (which you will also seal) and address it to the Surveyor of Taxes for the District in which you reside, *writing the words "For Special Assessment" thereon.* In either case the Return should be delivered at my Dwelling House, to be forwarded to the respective Officers accordingly, having been first superscribed with your Name and Place of Abode, or Place of exercising or carrying on your Profession or Trade; And further, if you desire to be Assesed under a No. or Letter, by the District Commissioners, you should fill up the Form of Declaration No. 6, on the other side.

Persons engaged in Trade or Profession, or exercising any Employment or Vocation, chargeable under Schedule D, must make their Returns for Assessment in the Parish or Place where the Trade or Profession is carried on, or such Employment or Vocation exercised, but it is *imperative* that Persons engaged in Trade by the *Manufacture* of Goods, Wares, or Merchandize, should make their Returns for Assessment *at the Place of Manufacture*, although the Sales of such Goods, Wares, or Merchandize, may be elsewhere.

If you claim to be exempt from Assessment, or claim a Return of Duty by reason of your Income being less than £150 a year, you will sign the Notice No. 7, on the other side, in order that the necessary Form for substantiating such claim may be forwarded to you.

An Abstract of the Rules and Regulations, as your guide in filling up the several particulars, will be found on the third page of this Notice, and further information (if required) may be obtained upon application to the Surveyor of Taxes for the District. If your Concerns require it, you may make use of several of the Forms, or may make your Return on any sheet or as many sheets of paper as you may find necessary, in the Forms hereunder stated, to the truth of which the Commissioners have power to require an affidavit.

Given under my hand this 11th day of ~~June~~ Sept 1844.

Rich Lofthouse Assessor.

SCHEDULE OF PARTICULARS OF INCOME.

	Amount of Profits £	On whose behalf the Return is made, whether as *Trustee* or *Agent*, or as *Officer of any Company*, or as *precedent Acting Partner*
From the Trade of / carried on by me at / From the Profession of Tutor / exercised by me at Horton College	£200 £30	
From Interest of Money, Annuities, or other Annual Payments derived from Property out of Great Britain		
From Interest of Money, the Duty on which is not deducted by the party paying such Interest		
From Dividends in the Public Funds, the Half-yearly Amount of which is less than Fifty Shillings		
From Securities in Ireland, or in the British Plantations, or other of Her Majesty's Dominions		
From Possessions in Ireland, or in the British Plantations, or other of Her Majesty's Dominions		
From Foreign Securities, (except where the duty will be charged on the Agents in this Country, entrusted with the payment of the dividends, and which duty will be deducted by such Agent on payment of the dividends)		
From Foreign Possessions		
From Property or Profits not coming within any of the foregoing heads, (except Lands, &c., or other Property of which no Return is required to be made) and which consists of* and that the Amount thereof is computed according to†		
* State the Nature thereof. † State the Grounds of Computation, and whether on an Average or not.	£230	According to the best of my present knowledge

Figure 4.8 First page of Income Tax Form 11, 1844. 399 × 252mm.

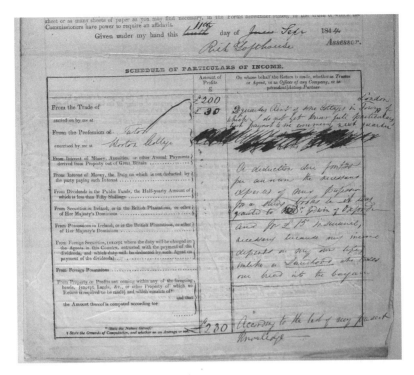

Figure 4.9 Detail of Form 11 (1844), showing details of income under the column headed 'Amount of Profits'. 232 × 252mm. Reproduced by permission of The National Archives: IR 9/1, Form 11 (1844).

to information-gathering. As a result, people might be confronted with a lengthy document: as much as a four-page 'voluminous return'.[52] In 1905 the Departmental Committee on Income Tax considered form 11, one of the commonest forms. Of page two (Figures 4.12 and 4.13) they noted that it 'is applied to a number of different cases with which a great number of people are not concerned'.[53] Consequently, on many tax forms the respondent had to supply only minimal details. This could be as little as a statement of total income and signing the declaration at the end of the form, a total of two marks on the page.

In order to respond to the state's demand for information, people had to negotiate the language and layout of forms. For example, tax forms regularly contained tables. Individual units of information could be distinguished from each other by horizontal bold rules (seen in Figure 4.10), or by numbers to

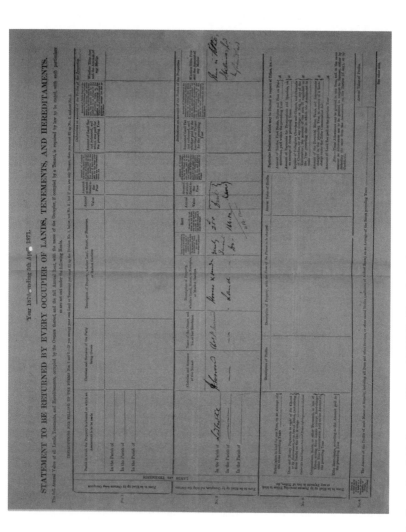

Figure 4.10 Second and third pages of Form 10 (1870). Note the horizontal rules, printed in bold and dividing discrete sections of the form from each other. Double-page spread 388 × 472mm. Reproduced by permission of The National Archives: IR 9/1, Form 10 (1870).

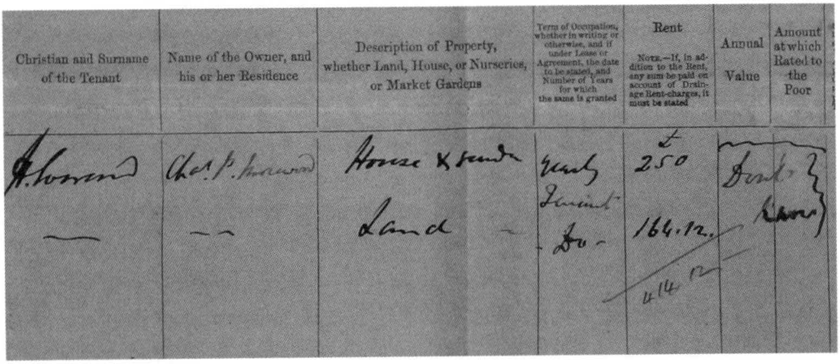

Figure 4.11   Detail of Form 10 (1870), showing expenditure under the column headed 'Rent'. Note also the form-filler's disregard for the constraints imposed by the rules bounding each answer, shown by the response 'Don't know' given across the 'Annual value' and 'amount at which rated to the poor' columns. 93 × 207mm. Reproduced by permission of The National Archives: IR 9/1, Form 10 (1870).

the left of the row (Figure 4.14). Such numbers formed a sequence to guide form-fillers through the form. People had to read each section and answer questions if required. Within the table shown here, the rows contained a number of sub-questions, divided from each other by vertical rules. By providing only a limited amount of space for answers, the Inland Revenue intended that information would be given in a standardized format. This would make it easier to process. However there was no guarantee that respondents would co-operate, as Figures 4.9 and 4.11 show: form-fillers ignored the ruled spaces of the table and included the details they wished to give. The information provided in Figure 4.9 was probably not wanted by the assessor. Presumably the respondent felt that it explained their situation more accurately than the simple facts and figures requested. If the form-filler did not have the details necessary to complete the form, they might not have returned it, or might have returned it blank. Alternatively, as in Figure 4.11, they might have stated that they 'don't know'. Simply providing the form did not guarantee that the state obtained the information it wanted.

A purge of Inland Revenue records before the First World War means that very few completed tax forms remain. To gain a better impression of how forms were perceived, we can combine surviving forms with contemporary testimony. The evidence suggests that many taxpayers had difficulty in understanding and completing them. One Glaswegian noted in 1886 that there were 'no documents with which I have had to do which are harder to understand than this income tax schedule'.[54] When asked whether income tax forms

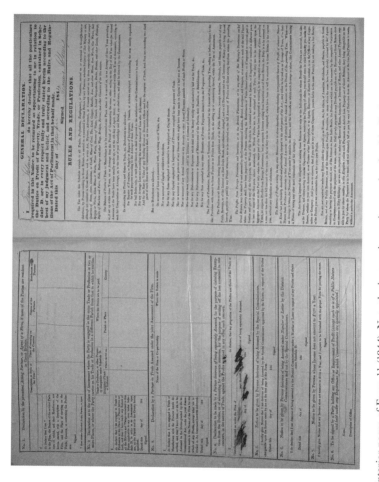

Figure 4.12 Interior pages of Form 11 (1844). Note the instructions, given under the title 'Rules and Regulations', on the right-hand page of the form (p. 3). Double-page spread 399 × 504mm. Reproduced by permission of The National Archives: IR 9/1, Form 11 (1844).

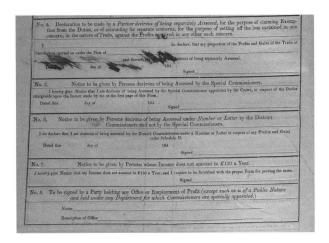

Figure 4.13 Detail of Form 11 (1844), showing the points at which an individual had to sign their name in the various sections of the complex tax form. 167 × 224mm. Reproduced by permission of The National Archives: IR 9/1, Form 11 (1844).

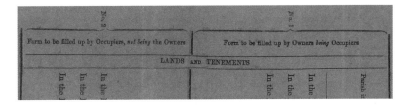

Figure 4.14 Detail of Form 10 (1870), showing the numbering of individual sections of the form. 217 × 60 mm. Reproduced by permission of The National Archives: IR 9/1, Form 10 (1870).

Figure 4.15 Detail of Form 10 (1870), with instructions above the questions to which they refer (see Figure 4.10): 'Instructions for filling up the forms Nos. 1 and 2. – If you occupy your own Land or Tenement you must fill up the Division No. 1, below, not No. 2; but if you are only Tenant, then you must fill up No. 2, and not No. 1'. Reproduced by permission of The National Archives: IR 9/1, Form 10\(1870).

should be simplified, a chartered accountant replied: 'Yes, but no doubt to an expert it is all right.'[55] While experts might have understood tax forms, lay people had greater difficulty. Surviving returns contain a number of errors by form-fillers, including crossings out (Figure 4.8), correct information added in the wrong location, and incorrect information given in the correct location.

We do not know how many tax forms were returned with errors, but given contemporary testimony and errors found on surviving forms it is likely to have been a relatively large number. Yet most people filling in forms could be expected to have had a relatively high degree of literacy. So tax forms still tested reading, writing and numeracy skills. Errors stemmed from two difficulties of understanding: what kind of information the form required, and where on the form to provide that information, and how.

The laws that set down what financial information the state required were extremely complex, and this complexity was reflected in tax forms. So the producers of forms included instructions and guidance to form-fillers. Generalized guidance was found on most forms. Often it detailed how the respondent should calculate the financial figures that were demanded (for example, what items were to be included, or excluded, as part of an individual's income). Such guidance is seen in Figure 4.12. Other kinds of localized instruction explained which parts of the form should be completed, and how. They were usually found alongside or near individual questions. They could be explicit, as in Figure 4.15, which, above the table, gave 'Instructions for filling up the forms' in detail. On some forms the instructions were given as marginal notes, again close to the point at which they would be useful to the reader. However, such instructions were not always understood. Many people were 'confused when they receive a paper with four pages of rules'.[56] Present-day research into forms design has shown that many people simply ignore instructions,[57] and this must have been the case before 1914: of rules and instructions, most people had 'neither the time nor the inclination to read them all'.[58]

Non-compliance was due, in part, to official language. Tax forms replicated the characteristically dense, legalistic, vocabulary and syntax found in the acts of parliament governing taxation. This caused problems for some form-fillers. 'A victim' informed readers of the *Daily News* in 1887 that he complied with 'the very elaborate instructions (so far as, not being a lawyer, I can possibly understand them) in the exasperatingly complicated paper'. Clearly this 'victim' felt that the language used on the form was difficult to understand, even for those who were well educated. The perceived brusqueness of the form's language also gave rise to complaint. The same correspondent to the *Daily*

News objected that the tax form 'demands 3¼ per cent. of my income in the most offensive way'.[59] Similarly, in 1895 the *Glasgow Herald* complained that the 'statutory phraseology of the municipal notification is brutal'.[60]

The language and design of income tax forms remained relatively consistent between 1842 and 1914, and the examples shown in the figures are typical of this period. There were minor changes, such as repositioning of content. For example, the instructions on form 11A were moved from page 3 to page 2 at some point between 1855 and 1881. This may have been done in the hope that more people would pay attention to the instructions if they were located before the part of the form that required completion.[61] In 1866 the request for details of profits arising from industrial possessions was transferred from form 10 to form 11. The text announcing the change was printed in red on the front page of form 11, so drawing it to readers' attention.[62] Aside from such local modifications, the questions which taxpayers had to answer, and their organization on forms, changed relatively little before the First World War.

The Inland Revenue was aware of deficiencies in the system of annual tax returns. It tried an alternative method, by which tax was deducted at source. The trial was conducted on the Lancashire and Yorkshire Railway Company in the early 1860s, so pre-dating the Pay-As-You-Earn system by around 80 years. However, the Court of Exchequer ruled that the Inland Revenue was not justified in requiring tax to be deducted in this way, and the experiment was dropped.[63] So forms, completed annually by taxpaying individuals, were retained with all their faults as the instruments of assessment and deduction, continuing the disjunction between form-producers and form-fillers. In 1910 a self-help guide to completing tax forms observed: 'First, that the subject is not an attractive one; next, that the papers issued officially are to many minds complicated and confusing.'[64] Form-fillers coped as best they could: pre-filling in pencil before overwriting in pen,[65] seeking help from friends, accountants, or the Inland Revenue itself.[66] If taxpayers felt that they were incorrectly taxed, or if communication between individual and Inland Revenue broke down for other reasons, they were entitled to a face-to-face hearing with officials.

To be able to survey large populations, the state required information gathered, sorted and ordered in standardized forms. The form was key to this. But the use of forms to extract information from citizens was problematic. This was an erratic medium for interaction, and people responded in varied and not always predictable ways. The abilities of some respondents in literacy, numeracy and comprehension were challenged by tax forms. For some, they were an 'abominable inquisition' and represented the extension of an increasingly bureaucratic, intrusive state.[67] People challenged the state's demand for information, whether accidentally, in their mistakes, or deliberately, by withholding details or by making incorrect replies. The results can be seen in surviving forms – conscientiously and clearly filled for the most part, but with unforced errors here, crossings-out there, miscalculations, omissions – all witness to frustrated acts of reading, calculating and writing by almost-anonymous citizens.

WHAT FORMS OFFER TO HISTORIES OF INFORMATION

The official form, site of mediated exchange between interrogator and respond-ent, intricate in its linguistic and graphic representations of state and subjects, authority and readers, remains a disregarded class of document and a void in design history. There exists barely any account of the development of this neglected genre of information artefact. We have sketched what can be discov-ered by analysing two kinds of major public form which served the British state in the nineteenth century, and suggested ways in which such documents may be read by design historians – drawing upon commentary in the periodical press and from written responses within the objects themselves – for people's interactions with these often unwelcome proxies for dialogue.

Why should this work be of interest to historians of both design and infor-mation? Because forms instantiate the earliest type of what came in the late twentieth century to be called interaction design. They give concrete shape and particularity to the abstractions of 'discourse'. They offer the prospect of insight into modes of anonymous designing before designers. And they prom-ise the possibility of richer conceptions of historic users of design than are usu-ally available – in this case citizens who as readers and writers were required to respond with acts of compliance but who misunderstood, committed errors, stubbornly made refusals, and routinely transgressed the boundaries of the question field inscribed by the official mind.

NOTES

1. The work reported here arises from a research project at the Department of Typography & Graphic Communication, University of Reading – 'Designing Information for Everyday Life, 1815–1914' – funded by the Arts and Humanities Research Council. Paul Stiff is principal investigator, Paul Dobraszczyk and Mike Esbester are post-doctoral research fellows. The authors thank the Centre for Ephemera Studies at the University of Reading for permission to reproduce items from the Rickards Collection.
2. See, for example, the Library of Congress CIP entry for Karen Schriver's *Dynamics in Document Design* (1997): '1. Technical writing. 2. Graphic design. 3. English-language – rhetoric. 4. Reading, psychology of. 5. Printing – layout.' Not a bad try

at summarizing some constituents of information design practice while avoiding the term.

3. The International Institute for Information Design (www.iiid.net/Definitions. htm) has for years tried to define its subject, most recently as anything-and-nothing: 'the defining, planning, and shaping of the contents of a message and the environments it is presented in with the intention of achieving particular objectives in relation to the needs of users'. Liz Orna gathers a few more tries, returning to a question which she first addressed in 1980: 'Information science and information design: have they anything to communicate to one another?' L. Orna (2007), 'Collaboration between Library and Information Science and Information Design Disciplines. On what? Why? Potential benefits?', *Information Research*, 12 (4), http://informationr.net/ir/12–4/colis/colis02.html

4. See, for example, P. Dobraszczyk (2008), 'Useful Reading? Designing Information for London's Victorian Cab Passengers', *Journal of Design History*, 21 (2), pp. 121–41; M. Esbester (2009), 'Designing Time: The Design and Use of Nineteenth-century Transport Timetables', *Journal of Design History*, 22 (2), pp. 91–113; P. Dobraszczyk (2009), ' "Give in your Account": Using and Abusing Victorian Census Forms', *Journal of Victorian Culture*, 14, pp. 1–25; M. Esbester (2009), 'Nineteenth-Century Timetables and the History of Reading', *Book History*, 12, pp. 156–85.

5. Gowers warmly endorsed a 'golden rule' passed down by the Board of Inland Revenue to its staff, that 'we should try to put ourselves in the position of our correspondent', because this would enable officials 'to speedily detect how much we may be taking for granted'. But this was about correspondence with taxpayers, not the language of forms.

6. For more, see P. Stiff (2005), 'Some Documents for a History of Information Design', *Information Design Journal*, 13 (3), pp. 216–28. 'Information design' is a construction of the 1970s, but something describable as 'information' has long been planned, produced as documents, and those documents published and disseminated. While there is no comprehensive overview of these processes, there are several episodic contributions to such an account, of which only a handful can be selected here: for example, A. Biderman (1990), 'The Playfair Enigma: The Development of the Schematic Representation of Statistics', *Information Design Journal*, 6 (1), pp. 3–25; P. Costigan-Eaves (1990), 'Some Observations on the Design of William Playfair's Line Graphics', *Information Design Journal*, 6 (1), pp. 27–44; M. Twyman (1986), 'Articulating Graphic Language: A Historical Perspective', in M. Wrolstad and D. E. Fisher (eds), *Toward a New Understanding of Literacy* (New York: Praeger), pp. 188–251; E. Tufte (1983), *The Visual Display of Quantitative Information* (Cheshire: Graphics Press); M. Macdonald-Ross (1977), 'How Numbers Are Shown: A Review of Research on the Presentation of Quantitative Data in Texts', *AV Communication Review*, 25 (4), pp. 359–409.

7. E. Huey (1908/1968), *The Psychology and Pedagogy of Reading; With a Review of the History of Reading and Writing and of Methods, Texts, and Hygiene in Reading* (Cambridge, MA: MIT Press).

8. M. Macdonald-Ross (1977), *Graphics in Text*, IET Monograph no. 6 (Milton Keynes: The Open University), p. 34.

9. R. Easterby and H. Zwaga (eds) (1984), *Information Design: The Design and Evaluation of Signs and Printed Material* (Chichester: John Wiley).

10. P. Wright (1979), *Designing Information: Some Approaches, Some Problems, and Some Suggestions*, BL Report 5509 (London: British Library Research and Development Department), p. 3.

11. Claude Shannon (1948), 'A Mathematical Theory of Communication', *The Bell System Technical Journal*, 27 (July and October), pp. 379–423, 623–56.

12. A. Moles (1966), *Information Theory and Esthetic Perception* (Urbana: University of Illinois Press).

13. R. Green and M. Courtis (1966), 'Information Theory and Figure Perception: The Metaphor That Failed', *Acta psychologica*, 25 (1), pp. 12–35.

14. P. Wason (1962), *Psychological Aspects of Negation* (London: Communications Research Centre, University College London).

15. B. Lewis, I. Horrabin, and C. Gane (1967), *Flow Charts, Logical Trees and Algorithms for Rules and Regulations*, Civil Service College Occasional Paper 2 (London: HMSO), p. 3.

16. M. Neurath (1974), 'Isotype', *Instructional Science*, 3, pp. 127–150. The best introduction to these ideas is the recently published collection of essays by M. Neurath and R. Kinross (2009), *The Transformer: Principles of Making Isotype Charts* (London: Hyphen Press). At the time of writing there is a research project at the University of Reading, 'Isotype Revisted', one objective of which is to track the changing dimensions and contexts of Isotype work.

17. L. Sutnar and K. Löndberg-Holm (1950), *Catalog Design Progress: Advancing Standards in Visual Communication* (New York: Sweet's Catalog Service); L. Sutnar (1961), *Visual Design in Action* (New York: Hastings House); P. Stiff and P. Cerne Oven (2009), 'Ernest Hoch and Reasoning in Typography', *Typography Papers*, 8, pp. 187–208.

18. L. Reynolds (2007), 'The Graphic Information Research Unit: Pioneer of Typographic Research', *Typography Papers*, 7, pp. 115–37.

19. Published in revised editions in 1962 and 1972.

20. *Oxford English Dictionary* (1989).

21. P. Wright (1984), 'Informed Design for Forms', in Easterby and Zwaga (1984), *Information Design*, p. 547.

22. Robert Waller, founder-principal of Information Design Unit, now returned to academic work as Professor of Information Design at the University of Reading and director of its Simplification Centre.

23. D. Frohlich (1986), 'On the Organization of Form-Filling Behaviour', *Information Design Journal*, 5 (1), p. 56.

24. H. Sacks, E. Schegloff and G. Jefferson (1974), 'A Simplest Systematics for the Organization of Turn-Taking for Conversation', *Language*, 50 (4), p. 727.

25. For example, T. Vernon (1980), *Gobbledegook* (London: National Consumer Council).

26. *Administrative Forms in Government*, Command Paper 8504.

27. *Parliamentary Affairs* (1982), 'Parliamentary Developments February–April 1982', 35, pp. 238–9.

28. Coopers and Lybrand Associates (1984), *Forms Effectiveness Study* 1, Report for Department of Health and Social Security.

29. Charles Dickens (1855), *Little Dorrit* (London: Hurd and Houghton).

30. M. Twyman (2008), 'The Long-Term Significance of Printed Ephemera', *RBM: A Journal of Rare Books, Manuscripts, and Cultural Heritage*, 9 (1), p. 40, www.ala.org/ala/mgrps/divs/acrl/publications/rbm/9–1/twyman08.pdf. [Date accessed 26 November 2009].

31. E. Higgs (2004), *The Information State in England* (Basingstoke: Palgrave Macmillan), p. 164.

32. E. Higgs (2005), *Making Sense of the Census – Revisited* (London: Institute of Historical Research and The National Archives).

33. On eighteenth-century population surveys in Britain see C. Law (1969), 'Local Censuses in the Eighteenth Century', *Population Studies*, 23 (1), pp. 87–100; D. Glass (1973), *Numbering the People: The Eighteenth-century Population Controversy and the Development of Census and Vital Statistics in Britain* (Farnborough: Saxon House), pp. 1–90; and C. Chapman (1994), *Pre-1841 Censuses and Population Listings in the British Isles* (Dursley: Lochin), pp. 38–60.

34. L. Ashcroft (1992), *Vital Statistics: The Westmoreland 'Census' of 1787* (Kendal: Curwen Archive Texts).

35. 'An Act for taking an account of the population' 1800. A separate form was issued to clergymen asking for the numbers of baptisms and burials from 1700 to 1780 in decades, and then every year from 1780 to 1800, and for the numbers of marriages from 1754 to 1800.

36. J. Burn (1836), *The Marriage and Registration Acts (6&7 Will. IV. Cap.85 and 86) with Instructions, Forms, and Practical Directions for the Use of Officiating Ministers, Superintendent Registrars, &c* (London: Henry Butterworth), pp. 125–7.

37. For listings of local census returns see R. Wall, M. Woollard and B. Moring (2004), *Census Schedules and Listings, 1801–1831: An Introduction and Guide* (Colchester: University of Essex).

38. For other schedules see Guildhall Library, MS 6852: Parish of St Helen, 1801 (102 returns); MS 7627: St Stephen and St Bennett, Sherehog, 1821 (26 returns); MS 4620: St Margaret, Lothbury, 1821 (67 returns) and 1831 (57 returns); MS 8935: St Bennett, Paul's Wharf, 1831 (85 returns); and MS 7697: Saint Catherine Cree Church, 1831 (223 returns).

39. S. Bailey, at 50 Bishopsgate Within, printed the 1801 schedules for the Parish of St Helen; Bryan & Co, at 9 Poultry, printed the 1821 schedules for St Stephen and St Bennett, Sherehog; and Cox, at 27 Old Change, printed the 1831 returns for St Bennett, Paul's Wharf.

40. Minutes of Evidence Taken (Session 1830) before the Select Committee on the Population Bill, *Parliamentary Papers*, 1840 XV, pp. 396, 29.

41. Of the 41 inhabited houses in the parish, only 15 used numerals, even then often in combination with spelled-out numbers.

42. D. Vincent (1989), *Literacy and Popular Culture, England 1750–1914* (Cambridge: Cambridge University Press).

43. Eleven of these forms are held by the Essex Record Office, Chelmsford, D/P 129/17/1: 'forms in relation to Invasion Act of 1803 for parish of Rochford'.

44. 'An Act for Taking an Account of the Population of *Great Britain*, and the Increase or Diminution Thereof' (1830), 11 Geo. IV, c.30, pp. 14–15.

45. Higgs, *The Information State*, pp. 4, 35, 44–5.

46. M. Turner and D. Mills (eds) (1986), *Land and Property: The English Land Tax 1692–1832* (Gloucester: Alan Sutton); E. Baigent (1988), 'Assessed Taxes as Sources for the Study of Urban Wealth: Bristol in the Later Eighteenth Century', *Urban History Yearbook*, pp. 31–48; J. Tiley (2004), 'Aspects of Schedule A', in J. Tiley (ed.) *Studies in the History of Tax Law* (Oxford: Hart), pp. 81–97.

47. C. Stebbings (2001), 'Popular Perceptions of Income Tax Law in the Nineteenth Century: A Local Tax Rebellion', *Journal of Legal History*, 22 (2), pp. 46, 48, 66; M. Jubb (1987), 'Income, Class and the Taxman: A Note on the Distribution of Wealth in Nineteenth-century Britain', *Historical Research*, 60 (141), p. 122.

48. 1848 figures abstracted from a return made to Parliament, as reported in *Glasgow Herald*, 25 June 1849, 4; 1905 figures from *Return of the Number of Assessments to the Income Tax, pt II – Year Ending 5 April 1905* (HMSO: London, 1906).

49. O. Frankel (2006), *States of Inquiry: Social Investigations and Print Culture in Nineteenth-century Britain and the United States* (Baltimore: Johns Hopkins).

50. Departmental Committee (1905): q. 1193. See also W. Blanch (1891), *Shall I Appeal Against My Income Tax Assessment?* (London: P. S. King and Sons), p. 3; G. Bauer (1946), 'The Mystery of the Income Tax', in C. Madge (ed.), *Pilot Papers*, 1 (4), pp. 60, 73.

51. Frohlich (1986), 'On the Organization'; Wright, 'Informed Design for Forms'.

52. Anon (1909), 'Income-Tax Returns', *The Times*, 10 August, p. 9.

53. Departmental Committee (1905), q. 2270.

54. Anon (1886), 'Income Tax', *Glasgow Herald*, 20 March, p. 6.

55. Departmental Committee (1905), q. 501.

56. Departmental Committee (1905), q. 500. See also Blanch (1891), *Shall I Appeal*, 5; Anon (1904), *How to Deal with your Taxes* (London: Grant Richards), p. 81.

57. D. Sless (1999), 'Designing and Evaluating Forms in Large Organizations', in H. Zwaga, T. Boersema and H. Hoonhout (eds), *Visual Information for Everyday Use: Design and Research Perspectives* (London: Taylor and Francis), p. 138; P. Wright (1980), 'Strategy and Tactics in the Design of Forms', *Visible Language*, 14 (2), p. 161; P. Barnard, P. Wright and P. Wilcox (1979), 'Effects of Response Instructions and Question Style on the Ease of Completing Forms', *Journal of Occupational Psychology*, 52, pp. 209–26.

58. Departmental Committee (1905), pp. 500, 2267.

59. Anon (1887), 'How the Income Tax is Collected', *Daily News*, 15 February, p. 2.

60. Anon (1895), 'Editorial', *Glasgow Herald*, 5 November, p. 6.

61. Examples are found in The National Archives of the UK (TNA), IR 9/1, Form 11A (1855 and 1881).

62. Examples are found in TNA, IR 9/16A, Form 11 (1866).

63. B. Sabine (1966), *A History of Income Tax* (London: George Allen & Unwin), p. 96.

64. F. Leeming (1910), *Income-Tax* (London: Effingham Wilson), p. v.

65. For example, see TNA, IR 9/1, Form 9A (1878).

66. Anon (1842), 'Income Tax', *The Times*, 22 November, 5; Blanch (1891), *Shall I Appeal*, p. 5.

67. Anon (1887), 'How the Income Tax is Collected', p. 2.

5

BROADSIDE BALLADS, ALMANACS AND THE *ILLUSTRATED NEWS*: GENRES AND RHETORIC IN THE COMMUNICATION OF INFORMATION IN DENMARK 1800–1925

Laura Skouvig

INTRODUCTION

Information history has gained success as a unique perspective on past societies and cultures, although as Toni Weller has shown in her introduction to information history one currently finds a British dominance within the discipline.[1] In Denmark, much information history research can be found within related areas such as library history, media history, history of technology and communication, or book history, for example.[2] Book history offers, for instance, aspects on how information was distributed in the various written media of books and almanacs.[3] The neighbouring and joint discipline of library history has a long and strong tradition mainly focusing on the construction period of the public library system in Denmark, from 1880 to 1920.[4] The strong concentration on public library history has therefore in many respects led to scholars neglecting the research libraries, other kinds of libraries and more broadly library functions. In short, traditional library history in Denmark is a typical example of the focus on the library as an institution, and not on the library as a function. From my point of view, information history comprises the history of the library and reframes it by rethinking its history as a question of the library function of dispersing and distributing information, of gathering and preserving information in many other areas than just within the frames of the library. Libraries have to a large extent monopolized these functions – a position that library historians (including the author of this chapter) have reproduced when concentrating alone on public libraries.

It is important to stress from the start that information history is just as culturally embedded as library history. For this author, information history is interesting for two reasons. First, information history has a strong potential of defining a research field within history with the legitimacy of studying history for its own sake from all possible perspectives: institutional, social, political, technological, cultural and many more. Weller has discussed the possible explanations for the interest in information from a historical perspective, concluding that the normal definition of the present society as an information society directs an interest in historical awareness of information in general.[5] According to Weller, information history is not just related to the academic disciplines that have information as their object. As such, information history as a broader term opens the possibility for studying other aspects such as libraries – and hopefully giving new perspectives on an institution that still puzzles.

However, as a second point of departure, information history has a strong heritage within the field of Library and Information Science (LIS). In many respects, information history has been affected by a predominant LIS understanding of information as a question of computerized information storage.[6] Even though research by Alistair Black has contributed to a much wider understanding of the relation between information and information systems,[7] the LIS understanding of information seems to narrow it to a question of data transmission in the age of the computer. In light of this, communication of information is reduced to a question of interaction with databases through the computer, without considering the context of the information user. Students presented with a module on information history tend to dismiss it as the history of the computer. This conceptual confusion is well known in the debate on information history, and should as such not be reproduced here.[8] But it explains that one of my prime interests in the field of information history is to use history as a constant reminder that information is a multifaceted concept, interacting with people in different cultural, historical and sociological contexts. It is in this respect (and within the LIS field) essential to constantly repeat the historical, cultural and social influence on information in order to stress its character of contingency. This is in fact the exact same reason that motivated my own research on the history of the Danish public libraries: a critical look at this institution should provoke students and others within the field to reconsider the traditional story that designates the library as transcendent and unchangeable. In this respect, this kind of library history is heavily influenced by the

French theorist, Michel Foucault (and many other historians), who define the role of history as a constant reflection on the present. For me (information) history has a crucial role within the LIS world as enabling an immanent self-critique within an academic discipline that strives to get rid of the associations of professional library training as opposed to academic research.[9]

Thus information history combines many traditional research fields: book history, media history, library history, to name but a few. But information history also introduces a unique look at historical study. It asks the central questions of how information has been understood, dispersed and communicated in past societies. It is thus essential to state (with influence from Charles Bazerman) that information is influenced by the period in which it exists. This statement may seem self-evident to historians, but is at the same time crucial because it is often forgotten in the current information-overloaded society. This society ascribes an almost unhistorical position to itself as the only information society where communication and texts of all kinds are at the center of attention. Following this it seems relevant to focus on information historically in order to contest the present understanding of information.

GENRES AND RHETORIC IN THE COMMUNICATION OF INFORMATION, 1800–1925

This article explores aspects of a bigger project entitled 'Genres and Rhetoric in the Communication of Information 1800–1925'.[10] The overall aim of the project is to investigate how the communication of information developed in different genres in the period from 1800 to 1925. Three different media – broadside ballads, almanacs and the *Illustrated News* (a Danish imitation of the *Illustrated London News*) – are analysed in detail, focusing on how the genres adopted different rhetoric tools and how they were situated differently rhetorically. Consequently it is important to examine texts from the three media in order to characterize the rhetorical situation by asking what the text intended, what kind of audience was construed by the rhetoric of the text, and what were the actual rhetorical conditions? Information can be seen as a form of communication where the sender wants to persuade the receiver. However, this is always embedded in specific moments and contexts. This reinforces the understanding of information as a social act created by humans with a human purpose, and situated in a specific historical situation.[11]

The intention (as explained at the start of the chapter) is to broaden the understanding of information and of how information is communicated, by implementing a methodology based on genre and rhetoric. The inspiration for this approach comes from Charles Bazerman, professor in the Department of Education at the University of California, Santa Barbara, USA, whose research field (among others) is the history of (scientific) writing. His use of socially-oriented theories on genre and rhetoric is particularly relevant, and has inspired this theoretical and methodological approach. Bazerman has done research within a broad range of historical periods from the seventeenth century and the transactions of the Scientific Academy through to post-war newsletters on nuclear information in an American context.[12] Although he focuses on the manifestations of writing, his use of rhetoric has also lead him to look at what was written and how it was presented to the reading public. His research also emphasizes the historicity of information. As a consequence he challenges the general understanding of information as 'an abstract universal, like atoms and electrons'.[13] Contrary to this, Bazerman argues that information 'is a human creation for human purposes'.[14]

It is not possible to cover all aspects of the project in this chapter. The focus here is therefore to draw a picture of Denmark in the period from 1800 to 1925, focusing on several key questions. What did the media landscape look like, and how did it work as the channel for dispersing information? How was the need for information defined? How was information dispersed through the medium of the broadside ballad, how was information understood in these broadside ballads and, finally, how was this information ultimately communicated?

PRESENTING THE PERIOD: DENMARK, 1800–1925

It is not, of course, possible to give a full history of Danish society in the period from 1800 to 1925 in such a short space as one has here. However, it is important to provide some sense of context in order to situate the discourses that are, according to the methodological approach, essential for uncovering the genres.

Generally, this period in Danish history was characterized by a society in transition. One could describe this transition as the modernization of the old, traditional society governed by an absolute king and structured in three hierarchical ranks. Through the nineteenth century, new classes emerged: first and foremost the independent peasant, and later in the century the worker. It is important to stress that Denmark remained a peasant society throughout the period. What uniquely defined the nineteenth century was the rise of the peasants economically and politically. The bourgeoisie, though largely a phenomenon in Copenhagen, was a powerful factor.[15] The emancipation of the peasants started in 1788 with the Danish equivalent of the enclosure movement, and most importantly the abolition of the adscription. From the mid-nineteenth century the folk school movement gave the peasants an educational and almost spiritual belief in advocating their political participation in government.[16] The economic basis was created through the co-operative movement in the late nineteenth century. Industrialization in Denmark took off between 1870 and 1890.[17] This led to a society characterized by different social classes and the latter part of the period, from around 1900 onwards, witnessed the first small signs of the Danish welfare state. In this very early period it was primarily the local communities that carried such developments.[18] On the national scale, however, the First World War resulted in a government that was far more interested in expanding its power over society, and particularly in controlling the market forces.[19]

The Napoleonic wars devastated Danish self-confidence following the English destruction of the Danish fleet in the 1801 Battle of Copenhagen, and once more in 1807 with the bombing of the capital. The sensational news of these events was reflected in the broadside ballads, and later on the chapter deals with the ballads and how they depicted these events. The consequence of Danish foreign policy was eventually state bankruptcy and a diminishing of the kingdom's territory (the loss of Norway). The bankruptcy had an especially large impact across the social strata in Danish society.[20] At the same time it is worth noting that these events not only increased the general loyalty towards the monarchy, but also gave rise to the concept of a national identity.[21] This national awakening continued after other wars throughout the nineteenth century, most notably after the lost war to Prussia in 1864 where true Danish soil (the southern part of Jutland) was surrendered to Prussia.[22] Denmark was suddenly reduced to a small state, and the traditional cultural exchange with German states was complicated by a general antipathy against Prussia.[23] It is interesting to see if and how this is reflected in the *Illustrated News* communication of information on Germany and Prussia.

Equally important on a political level were the changes in the systems of government. The path from absolutism to democracy was, however, a process that took half a century (at least to get to the fundamentals of what we would now consider to be a representative democracy).[24] In the 1830s a pre-democratic process was inaugurated with the Assembly for the Ranks. The first constitution was passed in 1849, transforming the government from an absolute monarchy to a constitutional monarchy. The 1890s were heavily affected by a conflict between on the one side the landed interest and bourgeoisie, and on the other side the different representations of the peasants obstructing more or less all legislation. At the beginning of the twentieth century the peasant's representatives were finally able to take over government, followed in 1924 by the first government led by the Social Democratic Party.[25]

The revolution in reading at the end of the eighteenth century was a general European phenomenon which also had an impact in Denmark.[26] Though the fashion for reading was primarily reserved to the upper classes, it has been widely discussed how literate the general Danish population was at the beginning of the nineteenth century.[27] In 1814 a national School Law was passed, with compulsory education as the most important component. This obviously had a major impact on literacy rates in Denmark and even though it might still be argued to what extent the population was literate, the major part of the population was able to read by the middle of the century.[28]

The growth in the proportion of the population which was literate had a significant effect upon the media. The nineteenth century thus also gave rise to a new variety in the media for communicating information.[29] The major change was that nineteenth-century media, to a large extent, was aimed at the general population: a mass media. This does not mean however that there was no written communication to the general public before the nineteenth century. As Horstbøll and Appel show, the period from the sixteenth century to the nineteenth century introduced a wide range of media appealing to the perhaps not so illiterate Danish population, embracing very different literary genres such as broadsheets, folk books (popular tales), newspapers and devotional books, to mention just a few.[30] In the nineteenth century the media situation changed into the more familiar media types of today, including weekly magazines, and newspapers and journals also developed the characteristics that one associates with them today.[31]

The highly interesting study that Weller and Bawden made on four Victorians' understanding of information shows that information was not a well-defined and stable concept.[32] The many transitions in Danish society throughout the nineteenth century would have influenced the need for information – and even perceptions of information would reflect changes and different discourses. It is thus a basic assumption in choosing the different types of media that they reflected different perceptions of information and that they communicated different understandings of information. Finally, it is possible that they also reflected changing perceptions of information within the media.

Enlightened thinking in Denmark encouraged the peasants to have some access to information so that they would fulfil their place in society in a prosperous way.[33] The rhetorical intention would therefore be to disperse methods for farming and relevant legal information. Perhaps even this represented information that the central authorities wanted to pass on for their own purposes? Both kinds of information were apparently communicated through the vicar who was the local representative for the central administration.[34] However, information was not only related to this kind of necessity. Information on political events, trade and people, to name but a few, was presented in the newspapers (although mainly for the minority), but the number of newspapers and their growing size indicate an increasing interest in this kind of information.[35] This interest was also reflected in the popularity of the broadside ballad. It is a central assumption that how information on news was understood changed dramatically during the nineteenth century.

The following paragraphs will present and discuss the three types of empirical material – the almanac, the broadside ballads and the *Illustrated News* – and their relation to communication of information. One could choose a chronological point of departure that would begin with the broadside ballads, continue with the almanacs and end with the *Illustrated News*. This would surely represent the central development of media into the well-known forms of the media situation in the late twentieth century. Although chronology is not chosen as the decisive frame, reflections on broadside ballads from the year 1801 are presented first, followed by a general discussion on the relation between information and the ballads. Before the concluding remarks the ballads are placed into the perspective established by the almanac and the *Illustrated News*. In so doing, it is possible to gain a more general understanding of information that seems to emerge in the period from 1800 to 1925.

SKETCHING OUT SOME EMPIRICAL CONDITIONS: THE YEAR 1801 IN BROADSIDE BALLADS

This section narrows the focus and concentrates on ballads, dating from 1801, which informed the inhabitants of Copenhagen about the Battle of Copenhagen which took place in early April. The aim of this paragraph is to discuss some of the characteristics of these ballads, with the aim of reflecting on some issues that will be analysed more thoroughly in the aforementioned bigger project.

A general presentation of the ballads points to some general features. A headline typically gave a thorough presentation of the ballad's theme (with an illustration on the first page) and was often followed by a prose description of the specific event giving factual information.[36] Finally, the ballad and instructions on choice of melody appeared – sometimes more ballads would be in the same issue. Most of the ballads included here have the same author, J. C. Brestrup, who wrote for the printing office of Matthias Seest. He gathered the material for all his ballads from a daily walk through Copenhagen.

In many ballads Brestrup portrayed the more picturesque aspects of everyday life in Copenhagen.[37] In his memoirs he depicted the conditions for
the authors of the ballads, comparing the work with a prostitute's job; as
a poet he saw himself selling his intellect and spirit in just the same way.
Furthermore, Brestrup uses the metaphor of a factory to describe the production of the commercial news ballads.[38] In this respect he kept his own professional work at arm's length, as he also did by reproducing contemporary
critiques of the ballads.

Andersen has thoroughly examined ballads about the battle originating
from the printing office of Matthias Seest in Copenhagen, paying particular
attention to the reliability and credibility of the ballads compared to the actual
events.[39] It seems to be a central issue for her research to examine whether the
ballads gave the inhabitants access to reliable information on the battle. In
Andersen's estimation the ballads were not reliable purveyors of information –
which is hardly surprising – in terms of describing what actually happened
according to academic or journalistic standards.[40] This questions to what
extent the ballads were providers of factual information. I am not convinced
that Andersen believes they were – it is more likely a question of two different
positions that run together: the traditional historical use of empirical material
(where such considerations would be valuable and necessary), and the ballads'
role as providers of news which speaks to people's feelings.

The ballads were not expressing high-level poetry: it was not their poetic
value but their news value that was pivotal for their popularity. And news
flourished during the days of the battle, just waiting to be communicated in
the ballads. As far as this chapter is concerned, the ballads represent a unique
medium for communicating information. Still, one basic condition must be
remembered: the ballads were commodities and were meant to be sold, and
this is crucial to keep in mind. It does not, however, make them worthless
as evidence since studying information also illuminates how information was
commodified, distributed and sold.[41] This is fundamental when devising a
map of the ballads' rhetorical situation, since they had to capture the interest
and imagination of the audience.

Through the ballads, one is able to follow the course of events in early spring
1801: before the battle, during the battle and its aftermath. In this specific
example of the Battle of Copenhagen, information was clearly interpreted as
news (and the need for news was there), but the ballads were obviously not the
only providers of news. On the other hand, when we look at the content of the
ballads, it seems as if they often speak to the emotions of the readers: patriotism
or national feeling was roused by praising the brave Danish sailors and naval
officers, and by focusing on Danish creativity. Another element here was to

ridicule the English. This indicates that information would not just be news in the factual sense as described above. A question for further research would be to what extent the information in the ballads suggested an intention of locating the battle in a mythological frame. A more prosaic feature is that the ballads were often relying on earlier ballads. In this case there is a sequel of at least four ballads about two deserters.

The main questions to follow are not just about the different rhetorical tools, but also how they affected the communication of information. Did different genres emerge within the ballads, differing between types of information? Was it necessary to use prose to communicate a specific kind of information, as was the case in the presentation of the background of the battle, where Brestrup relied on a classic mythological scheme for sketching out the historical reasons for the dispute?[42] And furthermore, when were imaginary dialogues in prose, and when in verse? One example gives a dialogue between a farmer and a citizen in prose, and another example describes a dialogue between prisoners-of-war – also pure fiction.

THE (IN)CREDIBLE INFORMATION: SOME GENERAL REFLECTIONS ON BROADSIDE BALLADS

This section highlights some general characteristics about the broadsheets as a medium. As in the case of the almanac the broadsheets have a long history, dating more or less from the first printing press in Denmark in the 1530s.

The term 'broadsheets' covers many different types of print media: posters, pamphlets and broadside ballads. In the context of this chapter, the focus is on the broadside ballads. The broadside ballads have to a large degree been considered as curiosities, and therefore as of lesser value for historical research. It is important to stress however that research since the 1960s has focused on the simple fact that the ballads existed as part of contemporary popular life, and that they consequently had an importance.[43] One major reason for narrowing the focus is that the ballads combined the print medium with the oral culture in the prime characteristic of the ballads: the ballad-monger who sold them and advertised their content by singing them to the audience. This provoked the authorities to prohibit the selling by loud, overt advertising of the ballads.[44] Their simple form and often sensational content indicate that the audience of the ballads would be found among the poorest inhabitants in Copenhagen.[45] As printed information, the ballads were the preferred reading for those without education beyond the village school.[46] Men of culture and education were greatly concerned with what they considered to be an urge for sensation that the ballads provoked in ordinary people.[47] The critics' main objective was not so much to prohibit the distribution and selling of the ballads, but to promote ballads that would educate and elevate the lower classes.[48] Though the prohibition against the selling of the ballads was clearly caused by the level of noise involved, it should not be forgotten that many ballads were libellous, as pamphlets often more broadly criticized the established structures in society.[49]

Existing Danish research on broadside ballads have had many remits: tracking down ballads from one specific printing office;[50] their relation to general media history;[51] and analysing their content in the light of contemporary commentators' opinion of the medium.[52] An important outcome of such research is different typologies of the ballads, distinguishing first of all between commercial ballads, and traditional ballads that were primarily oral and with a lyrical content. The commercial broadside ballads are different from the old folk songs.[53]

The construction of typologies for the broadside ballads has a starting point in either the production or the content. From these two points some of the typologies seem to coincide, for instance in the class named 'news ballads', which is without doubt the largest. From the perspective of the production, the class 'news' would include lyrical ballads on the eternal topics of (un)happy love affairs.[54] Taking the content as a starting point, news ballads and lyrical ballads would be two different classes, differentiated by the degree of (eternal) topicality. It is instructive however to consider that the lyrical ballads represent communication of information – for example, on how to handle love affairs or to promote a general understanding of the importance of sustaining the general moral code of the time. Taking this as a starting point, a rhetorical analysis would concentrate on defining the necessity for communicating even these kinds of information, and identifying the intended audience for that communication.

Piø discusses the commercial ballads based on two terms: topicality and credibility. *Topicality* is a question of either using real events, or making fiction real.[55] In terms of communicating information understood as news, the ballads therefore reflected the change from a medieval understanding of topicality as being always factual to the understanding of topicality as 'new'.[56] In the discussion of *credibility*, Piø stresses that the producer's intention was that the ballad was true in the sense that the listening or reading audience would accept and feel the message as a reality.[57] Andersen considers the credibility of most of the ballads that form her empirical material to be low. From the point of view of a historian who is trained to value empirical material as 'trustworthy information' about events that actually took place, it is obvious that broadside ballads are not necessarily to be trusted. Yet, this is exactly what is interesting when aiming to identify the understanding of information in Danish society around 1800, and how this understanding had changed. In terms of this, the broadside ballads can be seen as so fundamentally different from the present understanding of information that they represent unique empirical material. Information was not solely considered as rational and factual. The ballads reflected thus an understanding of information as highly dependent on experience and sentiments.

Piø's definition of credibility is closely related to the commercial ballad that was not necessarily based on real events. The eighteenth century was a formative century for the broadside ballads because they still to a large degree concentrated on finding and communicating news which in the context of this article is seen as a specific kind of information.[58] Thus the actual news ballads were based on real and often sensational events.[59] The news ballad would not necessarily reflect only crucial political events, but to a larger extent events closely related to everyday life of the more sensational kind such as murders, robberies, suicides and especially the plight of the 'fallen woman'. The broadside ballads have been described as an early version of the tabloid papers.[60] From time to time in them, large-scale political events and everyday events merged.

Contemporary men of letters saw the broadside ballads as having low quality, which suggests (and this is obviously a hypothesis of perhaps even a larger scale than that of the intended project) that it was acceptable to communicate information by addressing something other than the rational intellect of (the enlightened) man. In this respect the broadside ballads reflect a rupture between two discourses, where the emerging discourse defined information in relation to facts and what could be termed 'productive information'. Productive information would be that which enabled the individual to fulfil his duties towards society, fit into society and perform better in every day life.[61] This implies that information had to be communicated by using specific rhetorical tools that produce a particular genre within e.g. news articles. Ultimately, this implies the need for an institution (the public library) that could provide useful information under the eye of trained professionals. However, the same discourse can be seen as characterizing information as too difficult for ordinary readers to understand. The chapter briefly returns to this point under the theme of the *Illustrated News*. This assumption leads to two further assumptions. First, the audience is construed as unwilling to spend time and effort on serious information communication, thus making it necessary to make the communication entertaining and easy to grasp; and second, at the same time the entertaining aspects of the communication would be seen as highly problematic because they would clash with the discourse on productivity and information value.

THE ALMANAC, BROADSIDE BALLADS AND THE
ILLUSTRATED NEWS

Defining Danish society as a peasant society explains the interest in studying how the peasants obtained information on the various aspects of the management of a farm, its household, agriculture and so on. It was mentioned above that much information was passed on to the local population after the vicar's Sunday sermon. Another key channel was the almanac, which from 1578 was published under the authority of the university in Copenhagen that held general censorship in Denmark. The aim was to prevent prophecies of all kinds.[62] In 1633, the university's monopoly was reinforced by king's orders and it strongly forbade prophecies, though they remained part of the almanac as weather prophecies. It represented a scientific discourse, or at least reflected the increasing impact of the scientific discourse on society. In the almanac, peasants (and others) would find information on time and the seasons through the calendar, including weather forecasts, a list of kings, a list of markets and other important events. From the end of the eighteenth century the Danish Royal Society for Agriculture was using the almanac to inform on new farming methods – this practice was maintained until the university's monopoly was broken in the 1840s. From then onwards, the almanacs introduced articles on sociological themes, such as problems of nationality in the duchies with German majorities.

The major impact of the almanac was the introduction of time for the individual. From the very beginning the almanac included both the religious and the secular calendar, thus relying on the medieval notion of the connexion between the 'micro cosmos' and the 'macro cosmos'.[63] From a contemporary perspective, one of the curious elements in the almanac was the manifestation of the weather. Here the almanac reflected the general assumption that the weather could be prophesied through different omens, which made weather prophecies for the coming year one of the most important items in the almanac.

The almanac was not restricted to weather prophecies: other prophecies, including political ones, were also common. The central authorities in Copenhagen were increasingly interested in what information the almanac distributed: seeing the prophecies as an example of sustaining superstition, the authorities tried to ban them from the almanac in 1633. This was not just a question of educating the readers of the almanac, but was obviously an attempt to control the information dispersed through the almanac.[64] It is interesting to observe that a serious attempt by a responsibly-minded university professor to abandon the weather prophecies in 1779 resulted in a dramatic fall in its sale.

The weather prophecies were an essential part of the almanac tradition, and not a disposable element. The weather prophecies returned the year after, and remained a part of the almanac until the 1830s.[65]

In the period from 1816 to 1842 the almanac was widely used for informing the population, especially peasants, about new methods of cultivation on a scientific basis. This period also witnessed the increasing division between religion and science. The almanac was consequently used as a weapon in the rationalist critique of tradition initiated by enlightenment philosophers.[66] The large number of readers showed that the almanac definitely had a unique position as a mass medium, for dispersing popular stories and as a tool in the construction of a common identity. Its status as a mass medium meant that one of its prime results was to help synchronize its readers' experience of time.[67] All these features are important in enabling us to see how the almanac was a unique means for communicating different kinds of information. Consequently it is important to study the content of the almanac, and secondly to ask how the layout and arrangement of the content affected the communication of information.

With the new post-monopoly situation in the 1840s, almanacs experimented with size, content and illustrations.[68] Experiments with articles up to 30 pages in length seemed unsuccessful, however, and the later almanacs renewed the concept of articles no longer than two pages, with many woodcut illustrations between them.[69] Another experiment with quarterly supplements to the almanac was similarly unsuccessful, and perhaps heralded the coming of the weekly magazines. It is not the intention here to suggest any continuity between the almanac and the *Illustrated News*. It is, however, interesting to note that the renewal of the almanac was related to its woodcut illustrations, and the success of the *Illustrated News* was founded on its illustrations.[70]

The *Illustrated News* provides an example of the weekly magazines, partly as an extension of Weller's analysis of the *Illustrated London News* in nineteenth-century England, but more importantly as an example of how illustrations were used in order to communicate information.[71] The *Illustrated News* is important for its selection of content, which concentrated on topicality, and the mix of light entertainment and serious reporting of wars and revolutions. It was partly an exclusive magazine aimed at the cultured upper classes, especially in Copenhagen. 'The *Illustrated News* [was] ... the Sunday paper of the bourgeoisie',[72] and it is a working assumption that this specific target group had consequences for the rhetoric conditions of the text and illustrations. The main text book on Danish media history states that the content and 'themes covered by the *Illustrated News* might not be that different compared to other educating magazines after 1750 but the presentation of the material and the writing style are modern'.[73] It is unexplained what exactly defines a modern presentation and writing style, apart from the literary technique *in medias res*. This technique, it could be argued, indicates a need to stimulate the reader's imagination, and it is worth considering what this implied for the understanding of information – and of the audience. As a further consideration, it is interesting to compare this feature with the technique 'tableau vivant' of the later open-air museums. Though the open- air museums had their early phase in the late nineteenth century, their basic inspiration came from the world exhibitions with their focus on different national characteristics.[74] Through the tableaux, the open-air museums aimed at stimulating the visitor's imagination of the past, and some historians have argued that historical correctness and authenticity were lost in these reconstructions.[75] Consequently the communication of information had to present the facts to the rational mind of the reader (or the visitor), and not stimulate their imagination. Another interesting similarity is the inclusion of to an ethnographical dimension, and the cultivation of the national folk culture by contrast with primitive cultures.

Though primarily concentrating on the bourgeoisie in Copenhagen, the *Illustrated News* extended the horizons of its audience, with its reports from the borders of Denmark and abroad. The quality of the articles and the elegant distinction between public and intimate worlds in biographies of important men (and women) gave the magazine the reputation of a serious periodical of much higher status than the average weekly magazine.[76] The considerable attention given to biographies in the *Illustrated News* indicates a tremendous interest by the readers in the lives of these important people. It would be interesting to study these biographies in detail, determining how information on high-ranking men was communicated, how this communication was rhetorically formed and how it shaped biographical information as a genre – in this respect not as a literary genre, but as a medium sustaining the notion of the individual as important in his/her own right.

Still, the prime reason for studying the *Illustrated News* is the illustrations. As mentioned in the previous section, illustrations were also part of the almanac. The main difference between the almanac and the *Illustrated News* was the larger numbers printed, and the new xylographic technique that facilitated the use of illustrations. The illustrations sustained the feelings and sentiments evoked in the text, and the text explained the illustrations.[77] As a source of information the illustrations are invaluable, and therefore the motives for the selection of illustrations are as important as the motives for the use of language and the composition of text, when we ask how the audience was constructed.

CONCLUDING REMARKS

A main point to stress in my concluding remarks is that this chapter reflects the many expectations that accompany the start of a research project. Many reflections might seem – and might prove to be – mere speculations on the possible relations in which information is embedded, although existing empirical research on other countries in this period would seem to support the arguments presented here in relation to Denmark.[78] Such an approach can offer a general overview of the period, and the three media used as examples has hopefully generated interesting and useful considerations on the relations between different media and their possibilities for communicating information.

Both the almanac and the broadside ballads remained important and vital throughout the entire period. The *Illustrated News* only covers the period from 1859 to 1924, which limits the scope of empirical studies, although different criteria could be defined. Since the material is vast for the almanac and the ballads, it is necessary to set limits here too. Some temporal lines will be drawn: the study of the ballads should be restricted to the period from 1800 to 1810, and the study of the almanac to the period from 1816 to 1842. Arbitrary as it may seem, there is logic behind this relating to the specific characteristics of the two media, and the intention for the project to study the variety of information across as broad (and yet manageable) a field as possible.

The reason for studying broadside ballads in the period from 1800 to 1810 is the expectation that the ballads would to some degree reflect the importance of the major political events of the Napoleonic wars to Danish society. The treatment of the ballads is biased towards an understanding of information as news. The fundamental assumption is that this understanding of information in terms of news was dramatically different not just from our present understanding, but also from the notion of news in the later nineteenth century. The first limited studies of the ballads – and the research on them – indicate that this way of understanding information was changing. The ballads introduced the genre of sensational news, including its bad reputation. It is also assumed that the ballads represent other views on, and uses of, information that the project is intended to uncover.

The almanac is certainly worth studying in details in other periods than the chosen period between 1816 and 1842. It is especially tempting to include the period before 1800 when major changes in the almanac took place, for instance the introduction of the farm household focus in 1782. In the period from 1816 to 1842, though, it is assumed that the concept of articles on improvements of farming methods was well known, and this facilitates a rhetorical analysis of the articles' genres. The almanac represents a particular kind of medium, since it was an annual publication. This does not mean that the almanacs did not publish articles on current events, but that the rhetorical presentation might differ from that of the *Illustrated News*.

The rhetorical tools of the ballads, the almanac and the *Illustrated News* were clearly different, and it is not the aim of the project to describe these differences. It would be interesting if three rhetorically different media reflected the same discursive rupture that turned the understanding of information from one involving feeling and imagination into something that is expected to be real and factual and supporting productivity. In so doing, the project would demonstrate a change in the way information was perceived in nineteenth- and early- twentieth-century Denmark.

NOTES

1. T. Weller (2008a), *Information History: An Introduction – Exploring an Emergent Field* (Oxford: Chandos), p. 8.
2. See, for example, S. Pedersen (2000), *Ord i Sigte: Optisk Telegrafi i Danmark 1794–1862* (Denmark: Skrifter fra Post and Tele Museum) on the history of the telegraph and K. Jacobsen (2004), *Jydsk Telefon: 'Verdens bedste Telefonselskab'* (Denmark: Skrifter fra Post and Tele Museum), which deals with telephones as an aspect of communication history.
3. C. Appel (2001), *Læsning og Bogmarked i 1600-tallets Danmark* (Denmark: Det kongelige Bibliotek og Museum Tusculanums Forlag) and H. Horstbøll (1999), *Menigmands Medie. Det Folkelige Bogtryk i Danmark 1500–1840. En Kulturhistorisk Undersøgelse* (Denmark: Det kongelige Bibliotek og Museum Tusculanums Forlag) could be placed within the discipline of book history.
4. See, for example, M. Dyrbye, J. Svane-Mikkelsen, L. Lorring, and A. Orom (2005), *Det Stærke Folkebibliotek: 100 år med Danmarks Biblioteksforening* (København: Danmarks Biblioteksforening); N. Dahlkild (2006), *Åbningen af Biblioteksrummet – de Formative år i Danske Folkebibliotekers Arkitektur i det 20. Århundredes første halvdel*, http://biblis. db.dk/uhtbin/hyperion.exe/db.nandah06. [Date accessed 26 November 2009]; L. Skouvig (2004), *De Danske Folkebiblioteker 1880–1920: En Kulturhistorisk Undersøgelse ud fra Dannelses- og Mentalitetshistoriske Aspekter*, http://biblis.db.dk/uhtbin/hyperion. exe/db.lausko04 [Date accessed 26 November 2009].
5. Weller, *Information History,* pp.1–6.
6. Weller, *Information History,* pp. 11 ff. gives a thorough description of this fusion.
7. A. Black, 'Information History', in Blaise Cronin (ed.) (2006), *Annual Review of Information Science and Technology Volume 40* (New Jersey: Information Today Inc), pp. 441–74. See A. Black and R. Brunt (2001), 'Information Management in MI5 Before the Age of the Computer', *Intelligence and National Security*, 16 (2), pp. 158–65; and A. Black, D. Muddiman and H. Plant (2007), *The Early Information Society: Information Management in Britain before the Computer* (Aldershot: Ashgate) for empirical studies.
8. J. Aho and D. Davis (2001), 'Whither Library History? A Critical Essay on Black's Model for the Future of Library History with some Additional Options', *Library History*, 17, pp. 21–37 is in this respect symptomatic of the correlation of information history with the history of the computer.

9. For a discussion of this academic legitimacy see T. Weller and J. Haider (2007), 'Where Do We Go From Here? An Opinion on the Future of LIS as an Academic Discipline', *Aslib Proceedings*, 59 (4/5), pp. 475–82.

10. The project is titled 'Genres and Rhetoric in the Communication of Information 1800–1925: The Communication of Information in Broadside Ballads, Almanacs and the *Illustrated News*'. Besides the three main participants, Dr Trine Schreiber, Dr Jack Andersen and Dr Laura Skouvig (all at the Royal School of Library and Information Science in Copenhagen), the project anticipated participation to some degree from Dr Toni Weller (De Montfort University, Leicester, UK) and Professor Charles Bazerman (University of California, Santa Barbara, USA). The project application was sent to the Research Committee of the Danish Ministry of Culture in June 2009. Though the application was rejected in September 2009 it is the intention to work in more detail on the project in order to present a refined project application in 2010.

11. C. Bazerman (1988), *Shaping Written Knowledge* (Wisconsin: The University of Wisconsin Press).

12. Bazerman, *Shaping Written Knowledge*, pp. 59–79.

13. C. Bazerman (2001), 'Nuclear Information: One Rhetorical Moment in the Construction of the Information Age', *Written Communication*, 18 (3), pp. 259–95.

14. Bazerman, 'Nuclear Information'.

15. K. Hvidt (1990), 'Det Folkelige Gennembrud og dets Mænd', in O. Olsen (ed.), *Gyldendal og Politikens Danmarks Historie* (Copenhagen: Gyldendal), p. 11.

16. O. Korsgaard (1997), *Kampen om Lyset: Dansk Voksenoplysning Gennem 500 år* (København: Gyldendal).

17. Hvidt, 'Det Folkelige Gennembrud', pp. 338–353.

18. S. Kolstrup (1996), *Velfærdsstatens Rødder: Fra Kommunesocialisme til Folkepension* (Selskabet til forskning i arbejderbevægelsens historie).

19. N. Christiansen (1990), 'Klassesamfundet Organiseres 1900–1925', in O. Olsen (ed.), *Gyldendal og Politikens*, p. 204.

20. C. Bjørn (1990), 'Fra Reaktion til Grundlov', in O. Olsen (ed.), *Gyldendal og Politikens*, p. 147.

21. O. Feldbæk (1982), 'Tiden 1730–1814', in A. Christiansen, H. Clausen, S. Ellehøj and S. Mørch (eds), *København Danmarks Historie 4* (Copenhagen: Gyldendal), p. 51.

22. Hvidt, 'Det Folkelige Gennembrud', p. 160.

23. Hvidt, 'Det Folkelige Gennembrud', p. 187.

24. Feldbæk, 'Tiden 1730–1814', p. 313.

25. See Bjørn (1990), *Fra Reaktion til Grundlov*; Hvidt, 'Det Folkelige Gennembrud'; and Christiansen (1990), 'Klassesamfundet Organiseres', as general references for this paragraph.

26. On the reading revolution in Europe see J. Melton (2001), *The Rise of the Public in Enlightenment Europe* (Cambridge: Cambridge University Press), pp. 86–92.

27. See, for example, Feldbæk, 'Tiden 1730–1814' and V. Skovgaard-Petersen (1985),'Tiden 1814–1864,' in H. Clausen and S. Mørch (eds), *Danmarks Historie 5* (København: Gyldendal) on literacy.

28. Bjørn, 'Fra Reaktion til Grundlov', p. 159.

29. See K. Bruhn-Jensen (2001), *Dansk Mediehistorie. Mediernes for Historie og 1840–1880*, vol. 1 (Samfundslitteratur) in general on the development of media in the period.

30. Appel, *Læsning og Bogmarked*; Horstbøll, *Menigmands Medie*.
31. Bruhn-Jensen, *Dansk Mediehistorie*, pp. 23–4.
32. T. Weller and D. Bawden (2006), 'Individual Perceptions: A New Chapter on Victorian Information History', *Library History*, 22 (2), pp. 137–56.
33. Feldbæk, *Danmarks historie*, p. 236.
34. G. Hansen (1971),'Præsten', in A. Steensbrg (ed.), *Dagligliv i Danmark 1720–1790* (Copenhagen: Nyt nordisk forlag Arnold Busck), p. 89.
35. Bruhn-Jensen, *Dansk Mediehistorie*, p. 69.
36. Alternatively, these lines in prose would follow the ballad.
37. R. Andersen (1995), *Den Rapmundede Muse. 10 års Danmarkshistorie i Skillingsviser fra Matthias Seest Bogtrykkeri* (Odense: Odense Universitetsforlag), p. 199.
38. Bruhn-Jensen, *Dansk Mediehistorie*, p. 38.
39. Andersen, *Den Rapmundede Muse*, pp. 90–148.
40. Andersen, *Den Rapmundede Muse*, pp. 113, 118.
41. Burke discusses, for instance, the selling of knowledge known as 'printing capitalism' in P. Burke (2000), *A Social History of Knowledge: From Gutenberg to Diderot* (Cambridge: Polity Press), pp. 149–77.
42. Andersen, *Den Rapmundede Muse*, p. 118.
43. I. Piø (1969), *Produktionen af Danske Skillingsviser Mellem 1770 og 1821 og Samtidens syn På genren* (Københavns Universitets Fond til tilvejebringelse af læremidler), p. 48.
44. Skovgaard-Petersen (2006), *Fra støv til guld, brugsbøger og skillingstryk fra Det Kongelige Bibliotek* (København: Det kongelige Bibliotek), pp. 13–51.
45. It is important to stress that broadside ballads were not restricted to Copenhagen. They were distributed at market places and sold by travelling salesmen.
46. Hvidt, Det Folkelige Gennembrud, p. 205.
47. It is interesting to see that this way of arguing was picked up by public library advocates about 100 years later, and turned into a critique of detective stories and pulp literature.
48. Piø, *Produktionen af Danske*, p. 94.
49. Bruhn-Jensen, *Dansk Mediehistorie*, p. 38.
50. Andersen, *Den Rapmundede Muse*.
51. Bruhn-Jensen (2001), *Dansk Mediehistorie*.
52. Piø, *Produktionen af Danske*.
53. This is obviously an interesting discussion but is considered not to be within the scope of this chapter.
54. Piø, *Produktionen af Danske*. See also a Danish digitization project on broadside ballads: http://viser.bib.sdu.dk/. [Date accessed 28 November 2009].
55. Piø, *Produktionen af Danske*, p. 48.
56. Bruhn-Jensen, *Dansk Mediehistorie*, p. 37.
57. Piø, *Produktionen af Danske*, p. 49.
58. Bruhn-Jensen, *Dansk Mediehistorie*, p. 37.
59. Piø, *Produktionen af Danske*, p. 66.
60. Skovgaard-Petersen, 'Tiden 1814–1864'.
61. This point is well known in relation to the emergence of public libraries.
62. Horstbøll, *Menigmands Medie*, p. 570.
63. Bruhn-Jensen, *Dansk Mediehistorie*, p. 41.
64. Horstbøll, *Menigmands Medie*, p. 572.

65. Horstbøll, *Menigmands Medie*, p. 582.
66. Horstbøll, *Menigmands Medie*, p. 590.
67. Bruhn-Jensen, *Dansk Mediehistorie*, p. 40.
68. Horstbøll, *Menigmands Medie*, p. 593.
69. Horstbøll, *Menigmands Medie*, p. 599.
70. Bruhn-Jensen, *Dansk Mediehistorie*, 180.
71. T. Weller (2008b), 'Preserving Knowledge through Popular Victorian Periodicals: An Examination of the Penny Magazine and the *Illustrated London News*, 1842–1843', *Library History*, 24 (3), pp. 200–8; and T. Weller (2009), *The Victorians and Information: A Social and Cultural History* (Saarbrücken: VDM Verlag).
72. Christiansen, *Klassesamfundet Organiseres*, p. 114.
73. Bruhn-Jensen, *Dansk Mediehistorie*, p. 183 (author's translation).
74. Skougaard, 2005, p. 104.
75. S. Müller (1897), *Museum og Interiør. Tilskueren: Maanedsskrift for Litteratur, Kunst, Samfundsspørgsmaal og Almenfattelige Videnskabelige Skildringer*, pp. 683–700.
76. Bruhn-Jensen, *Dansk Mediehistorie*, p. 181.
77. Bruhn-Jensen, *Dansk Mediehistorie*, p. 181.
78. Weller, 'Preserving Knowledge', pp. 200–8; Weller, *The Victorians and Information*.

6

INFORMATION AND EMPIRE: THE INFORMATION AND INTELLIGENCE BUREAUX OF THE IMPERIAL INSTITUTE, LONDON, 1887–1949

Dave Muddiman

Empire – and its goals of control; exploitation; assimilation; 'civilization' – is perhaps inherently an informational project. Certainly, the expansion of European empires from 1600 onwards acted as a catalyst in the forging of the modern information age. By 1815, these empires had helped establish new methods of gathering, storing, transforming, displaying and communicating information: systems such as accurate maps; scientific classification; semaphore; and statistics.[1] By the later nineteenth century – the high noon of European colonialism – mechanization and industrial technologies such as shallow-hulled steamboats and electric cable enabled a 'death of distance' which some see as the beginnings of the contemporary networked world.[2] Meanwhile, in often subtle and sophisticated ways, colonized societies themselves developed new kinds of information order into which they assimilated, transformed and hybridized the project of informational and cultural dominance emanating from Europe.[3] Conversely, metropolitan societies absorbed the experience of empire; often, it is true, distorting and rejecting knowledge of the 'Other'; but ultimately, perhaps, enriching and enhancing their own institutions and national cultures.[4]

Over recent years a number of historians, including those cited above, have begun to analyse the reciprocity between a 'long' information revolution linked to the advent of modernity, and the concurrent enterprise of empire.[5] However, in Britain at least, one element largely absent from this analysis has been the imperial significance of institutions of information themselves: before 1900 especially libraries, and more latterly until the 1970s, various kinds of information, intelligence or documentation services. Of course, most former colonies of Britain have their published library histories, but the majority of these are preoccupied with narratives of education, literacy and 'development', even though more recent research sometimes adopts a critical and 'postcolonial' stance.[6] Studies of the impact of empire on United Kingdom libraries also tend to be thin on the ground, reflecting perhaps the pervasive blindness to themes of national identity in much British library history.[7] Moreover, where histories of overtly 'imperial' libraries do exist, they commonly neglect the theme of information: for example accounts such as those of the India Office Library and the British Council Library Services, focusing respectively on oriental scholarship, and culture and literacy.[8] As a result, very few histories can be found of government, commercial, technical, scientific, administrative or military *information* services within the British imperial orb. Hence, the starting point of this chapter is an attempt to redress such neglect. It comprises a case study and a re-appraisal, from an information history perspective, of a project which some late-nineteenth-century observers saw as potentially critical for the development and survival of the British Empire: the establishment of information and 'intelligence' bureaux at the Imperial Institute, London.

The general history of the Institute itself is well documented.[9] Planned as a memorial for Queen Victoria's Golden Jubilee in 1887, on a wave of high enthusiasm for empire, the Institute was constructed in six years and opened amid a blaze of Victorian celebratory kitsch in 1893, on a site now occupied by Imperial College, London. The building itself was an 'eclectic and florid' monument to late-Victorian imperial esteem, but although the Queen hoped it would serve as a 'lasting emblem of the unity and loyalty of empire' it never really attracted architectural acclaim.[10] Despite this, the fundamental rationale for the Institute was utilitarian as well as symbolic. It was hoped that it would become a centre for developing the scientific, economic and commercial resources of empire, and to this end it was equipped with permanent exhibition galleries, laboratories, a statistics unit and a library, as well as commercial and scientific 'intelligence' departments. However, plagued by insufficient funding, fluctuating political support and uncertain public demand, the Institute struggled to achieve its ambitious goals, prompting its principal historian, John Mackenzie, to claim that 'for the first forty years, its record was one of almost complete failure'.[11] Only from the late 1920s onwards, Mackenzie argues, did the Institute discover its *metier* as a kind of propagandist advocate of empire, running a cinema, lectures, exhibitions and other 'extension' activities targeted especially at school parties. As Mackenzie demonstrates, these activities flourished amid the brief renaissance of imperial sentiment in Britain between 1930 and 1945. However, as the empire was disbanded in the 1950s, the Institute was gradually wound up. Its laboratories and libraries were closed in 1949; its buildings demolished in 1957. Its cultural functions were passed on, in tune with the times, to a newly named 'Commonwealth' Institute, in 1962.

The informational functions of the Institute endured, as we shall see, throughout almost all of its life until 1949. Initially, their most important element was a pioneering Department of Commercial and Industrial Intelligence, established in 1888 even before the opening of the Institute's building. After 1903 this department was superseded by the Board of Trade Commercial Intelligence Office in the City of London, and the emphasis at the Institute shifted to scientific and technical information provision aimed at aiding the exploitation of the natural resources of empire. This work expanded significantly before 1914 and again after the amalgamation of the Institute and the Imperial Mineral Resources Bureau in 1925. By the late 1930s the Institute could boast separate 'intelligence' sections relating to both minerals and plant/animal products and these were serviced by separate statistics, indexing and publishing sections, together with a library of 75,000 volumes. In addition, the Institute's education and propaganda work at this time utilized resources such as the Empire Film Library, which it housed, and a collection of 'empire lantern slides'.[12]

Utilizing evidence from the Institute's archives and records,[13] this chapter aims to analyse this informational work in detail: in particular the history of the Commercial and Industrial Intelligence Department, between 1886 and 1902, and the Scientific and Technical Information Bureaux, which survived until 1949. In doing so, it seeks to situate the ideas about empire and information embodied in these new services within the changing context of British imperialism, as it regressed from late Victorian euphoria to the disillusionment of Empire's end. Finally, and appropriately in a volume entitled *Information History in the Modern World*, the chapter considers the Institute as a pioneering exemplar of the early information society in Britain: a material and ideological formation linking science, industrial efficiency, nationalism and information which coalesced in late-Victorian Britain and remained influential in early and mid-twentieth-century Europe until (arguably) about 1975.

A 'BRAIN CENTRE OF EMPIRE': COMMERCIAL AND INDUSTRIAL INTELLIGENCE AT THE IMPERIAL INSTITUTE, 1886–1903

Although the origins of the Imperial Institute can be traced to the Great Exhibition of 1851 and the subsequent desire for a permanent exhibition of the arts and manufactures of empire, its genesis as a feasible project effectively dates from the later 1886 Colonial and Indian Exhibition in London.[14] Delighted by the success of this 'imperial display', Edward, Prince of Wales, anxious to establish a permanent memorial for his mother's forthcoming Golden Jubilee in 1887, suggested in an open letter to the Lord Mayor of London the creation of 'an Institute which should represent the Arts, Manufactures and Commerce of Empire'.[15] Initially, for the Prince at least, an element of spectacle and prop-aganda was perhaps uppermost: his letter emphasized the potential role of an Institute as exhibition centre, museum and meeting place. However, a hastily-appointed working committee of eminent Victorians under the chairmanship of former Lord Chancellor Herschell swiftly proceeded to widen the Institute's remit. They appointed Sir Frederick Abel, a recently retired military chem-ist and director of Woolwich Arsenal, as Organizing Secretary Designate.[16] Within three months – by 20 December 1886 – the committee had reported back to the Prince accepting that the Institute should indeed be an 'emblem of the unity of empire' but stipulating also that it should have 'some practical and useful purpose'.[17] Such purpose, in its opinion, needed especially to focus on the regeneration of British and imperial industrial and commercial power in the face of economic depression and growing German and American com-petition. To this end, their report included a number of far-sighted proposals in the domain of information. These involved the 'formation of Colonial and Indian libraries and establishing in connection therewith reading, news and intelligence rooms' and 'the collection and diffusion of the fullest information in regard to the material condition of the colonies' to be focused on an 'emigra-tion office'.[18]

The publication of the organizing committee's report was followed in early 1887 by a period of public discussion regarding the projected role and pur-poses of the Institute. From a twenty-first-century perspective this discussion makes remarkable reading, especially because of its relatively sophisticated rhetoric concerning the role of information in commercial and economic life. At a meeting called to receive the committee's report in January 1887, T. H. Huxley, doyen of the Victorian science lobby, made his support clear for the informational functions of the Institute. He 'imagined it as a place where the fullest stores of industrial information would be made accessible to the public, in which the highest questions of commerce and industry would be systematically studied and elucidated'. Huxley saw such knowledge as a vital weapon in 'an industrial war of far more serious import than the military wars of the [nineteenth] century's opening years'.[19] Abel himself was clearly influenced by these ideas. In April 1887, he began to flesh out in more detail his plans for the Institute. In a long paper delivered at the Royal Institution he elaborated a multifaceted vision of what *The Times* subsequently labelled 'a sort of brain centre of the empire' which would 'receive intelligence from all quarters and diffuse it no less widely'.[20] The elements of this scheme were to comprise a 'commercial museum' of samples of empire raw materials and manufactures; involvement in technical education through the 'distribution of information relating to technical schools throughout the empire'; a system of correspondence linking a network of commercial and industrial agents utilizing the communications potential of electric cable; and the emigration advice bureau envisaged in the committee report. Last but not least, Abel proposed a 'commercial intelligence' department, which he argued would underpin the economic integration of empire. Through such a bureau, Abel suggested, 'the capitalist may be assisted in discovering new channels for enterprise in distant portions of the empire, the resources of which are awaiting application by the judicious application of capital'.[21]

Contemporary critics of the plans for the Institute[22] did, with some justification, perceive danger in these multifarious and potentially over-ambitious schemes. Even *The Times*, generally supportive, commented that it was 'almost tempted to ask whether there was anything the Institute is not to do'.[23] Nevertheless, preparations proceeded apace: the site in South Kensington was finalized; an architectural competition for the building was mounted and judged; and the foundation stone was duly laid by Queen Victoria in the Jubilee year on 4 July 1887.[24] The Institute's royal charter was granted almost a year later on 12 May 1888. Framed in predictably vaguer terms than Abel's detailed proposals, the charter nevertheless formalized the proposed links between information and empire. The Institute was to establish 'commercial museums, sample rooms and intelligence offices in London and other parts of the empire'. It was to 'collect and disseminate such information relating to trades and industries, to emigration and other purposes ... as may be of use to subjects of our Empire'.[25] *The Times*, commenting on the Charter, mused hopefully that the Institute might mark a turning point in a country that 'has never been prone to overestimate the value of knowledge as such'. It continued:

> If we can succeed in making the Institute a great intelligence centre for the whole Empire – a centre for the collection and diffusion of all available knowledge, theoretical and practical, mechanical and commercial, social and industrial – we shall find in the end that we have done far more towards realising the practical unity of Empire than we could possibly accomplish by any amount of premature and therefore ill-considered effort in the purely practical sphere.[26]

Meanwhile, detailed arrangements for the launch of what would become the Institute's Department of Commercial Intelligence (DCI) were well under way. The scheme was evidently first suggested to Abel in February 1887 by E. F. Law, a commercial attaché in the Foreign Office and a former major in the War Office Intelligence Department. Law suggested that the latter might serve as a model for an 'intelligence' unit applied to commerce and industry, which he envisaged as a 'central feature' of the Institute, facilitating 'the continuous and systematic supply of varied and detailed information on commercial matters as was manifestly beyond the reach of individual merchants and manufacturers'.[27] In a memorandum submitted to the Commercial Sub-committee of the Institute on 11 October 1888, Abel, heavily influenced by Law, outlined his plans for the department. It would be divided into four sections (Industries; Commerce; Technical and Commercial Education; and Emigration); it would develop a network of satellite 'enquiry and reference offices' throughout the United Kingdom and the Empire; and it would utilize sympathetic organizations such as chambers of commerce and technical colleges as both sources and outlets of information.[28] Also present at the meeting where these proposals were presented were representatives of UK chambers of commerce (from Manchester, Glasgow, Bradford and Birmingham); of the iron and steel and chemical industries; and of the Society of Arts, Manufactures and Commerce. They are said to have warmly approved the plans; in addition, an earlier meeting of agents general and crown agents for the colonies had reportedly shown similar enthusiasm.[29] A 'sum of money' was made available to begin preparatory work, and shortly afterwards Sir Somers Vine, who had been appointed assistant secretary to Abel, was dispatched on a world tour of the colonies and dominions to organize the appointment of a network of colonial 'correspondents'.[30] This he proceeded to do, with mixed success, during 1889 and 1890.

By 1892, when the new Institute buildings were complete, the DCI was able to begin its operations in earnest. Vine was designated officer in charge, and by January 1895 seven assistants had been appointed, largely recruited from other civil service departments; one of them, J. R. Fitzgerald, acting additionally as Institute librarian.[31] Financial restrictions resulted, however, in a strategy of 'gradual development' being the order of the day, and the DCI was initially organized along functional lines with branches responsible for reports and publications; correspondence and enquiries; maps and charts; education and transactions. However, the library linked to the department appears to have initially grown very rapidly, containing 9,000 volumes one year after its opening, attracting numerous donations and proving very popular amongst Institute fellows. A commercial reading room was also quickly established, 'equipped with a large and extensive collection of British and Colonial trade journals and market reports etc'. According to F. Henn, a librarian who entered service there in 1898, this was 'frequently consulted by businessmen and others requiring information respecting the Colonies and India', and it proved 'equal to most of the demands on its capabilities'.[32]

Advised by a 'Special Committee for Publications and the Library',[33] the DCI initially focused its energies on the production and dissemination of high-quality flagship publications. If it were to be judged by its quality alone, the first of these, *The Imperial Institute Yearbook*, published three times between 1892 and 1894, would be considered a great success. Compiled initially by J. R. Fitzgerald, the first Institute Librarian, and subsequently updated by his successor, H. H. Hebb, the *Yearbook* aimed to be an authoritative 'statistical record of the resources and trade of the Colonial and Indian possessions of the British Empire'. With clarity of format and indexing, comprehensiveness of coverage and high standards of publication, it was undoubtedly a model reference work of its time. However, its sales failed to cover its costs and after three editions it had to be discontinued. From January 1895 it was replaced by a more widely circulated *Imperial Institute Journal* which had a clear remit to disseminate current commercial and industrial information empire-wide. In hindsight this has little appearance of a cost-cutting exercise: the *Journal* was in fact an innovative and again impressive monthly broadsheet publication which contained a mix of regularly updated data (for example cable and packet rates and timetables; customs tariffs; forthcoming events), together with a cluster of special articles and reports in each issue. Continuing until the closure of the DCI in 1902, it survives as an early model example of what in the twentieth century would come to be called a current awareness service, or bulletin.[34]

More problematical for the DCI was the operation of its enquiry and correspondence service. The operation of this section was delayed until 1895 due to funding difficulties and from then until 1899 its volumes of activity were relatively small – some 250–300 written enquiries per annum and 'at least an equal number of verbal applications'.[35] However, there was undoubtedly some truth in Abel's assertion that the department was receiving 'a great variety of enquiries ... from most large towns in the United Kingdom' and from 'Canada, Australia, India, Ceylon, South Africa and the West Indies'. These enquiries included requests regarding 'existing and new products and services of supply; customs tariffs; local laws; transport facilities; agricultural prospects; import and export firms and agencies', and so on. Some enquiries, it is clear, were simple requests for data and information; however, others required what seems to have been detailed research by staff, and sometimes the advice of experts or corresponding agents in colonial locations.[36] In the end, some enquiries seem to have been beyond the resources of the DCI, which by the late 1890s was having to curtail the scope of its proposed system of corresponding agents and limit publicity about its services in an attempt to reconcile demands and costs.[37]

Partly because of these factors, in the late 1890s the public perception grew that the DCI was underutilized by companies and other commercial organizations. This impression was aggravated by revived criticism of the Institute's South Kensington location, away from the commercial heart of London, and an alleged preoccupation with the social and leisure activities of an imperial elite.[38] In June 1899, the Institute's board responded by opening a 'City Branch' in Cannon Street; two years later this moved to more spacious premises in Eastcheap, EC1. These comprised an open-access newsroom; a small commercial museum displaying samples of new products; and access to the main resources in South Kensington via telephone and special messenger. Institute staff were on hand on a rota basis. A system of charges and subscriptions was also introduced in order to raise money to expand the service: the reading room and library were free to fellows, but others now had to pay a £1 per annum subscription; enquiries attracted a sliding scale of additional changes depending on complexity, with a maximum of 10 shillings for colonial or foreign correspondence.[39]

In the event, these moves were too little and too late to save the DCI, whose demise was sealed by a conflation of wider trends. The United Kingdom Board of Trade (BOT), recognizing that only 22 per cent of British imports and 34 per cent of exports emanated from the empire,[40] had itself begun to explore the potential of commercial intelligence. In 1897 it set up a committee to enquire into the 'dissemination of commercial information': in particular the best means of conveying intelligence gathered by government departments, overseas commercial attaches, consular staff and the like to British companies. Taking evidence from a wide range of interested parties (including Abel, who was co-opted as a committee member in late 1897) the committee recommended the establishment of 'an office whose function it shall be to meet the constantly increasing demand for prompt and accurate information on commercial matters, as far as it can be met by government.'[41] Its findings were enthusiastically accepted by the Unionist coalition government of the day (most notably by social imperialist Joseph Chamberlain, who was colonial secretary at the time),[42] keen to counter the commercial and industrial advance of Germany and the United States. What became the Commercial Intelligence Branch of the Board of Trade opened its doors in the City of London in October 1899. Its remit, unlike the Institute's DCI, was worldwide.

Meanwhile, the voluntary financial model underpinning the Imperial Institute had become, as the 1890s progressed, more difficult to sustain. By

1899, discussions were under way to transfer its governance and financing to the United Kingdom government, supplemented by contributions from the dominions and colonies.[43] Despite the protests of the Institute's governors – who perceived a threat to both the DCI and the Institute in general[44] – under the Imperial Institute Act (1902) the Institute was in effect nationalized and placed under the jurisdiction of the Board of Trade. The DCI was swiftly absorbed by the larger and more comprehensive Board of Trade Commercial Intelligence Branch. The *Imperial Institute Journal* was similarly swallowed by the monthly *Board of Trade Journal*, an ironically altogether less impressive publication which made no real attempt to provide a comprehensive current awareness service along the lines of the *Institute Journal*. However, the resulting rationalization of commercial intelligence and its location in the City of London clearly made practical sense, and the new BOT office soon became a permanent part of London's commercial and informational landscape. By 1908 it was receiving 11,267 enquiries annually, up from 1614 in 1901 and 3599 in 1903, the first year after amalgamation with the old Institute service. This increase, its management claimed, provided 'conclusive evidence that the commercial and trading classes in the country recognize the importance of the [branch's] services'.[45] Many of these services, ironically perhaps, were modelled on the provision developed at the Imperial Institute, suitably modified and expanded to encompass Britain's worldwide trade. In this way, in effect, the Imperial Institute DCI had served as a prototype project in the development of commercial information services in Britain. 'Brain centre of empire' it was never, realistically, able to become; but information history confirms it to be, somewhat counter-intuitively perhaps, a pioneer ahead of its time.

'A CLEARING-HOUSE OF INTELLIGENCE AND INFORMATION': SCIENTIFIC AND TECHNICAL INFORMATION AT THE IMPERIAL INSTITUTE, 1895–1949

Although the Commercial Intelligence Department of the Institute had been launched relatively quickly, one further aspiration of the founders – that of developing a scientific centre of empire – took a little longer to establish in a tangible form. In a late-Victorian age of a newly nationalistic 'public science', the aspiration had widespread support: the period of the Institute's foundation was replete with the rhetoric of national efficiency; military preparedness; and 'constructive' state intervention in exploiting the resources of empire.[46] Supporters of the Institute in the British 'science lobby', such as T. H. Huxley, saw the Institute (together with its neighbour, the newly-established Imperial

College) as potentially a rival to the much-envied German Imperial Institute, founded at Charlottenburg in 1879. In more immediate terms however, the first director, Frederick Abel (himself, as we have seen, a military scientist), hoped to enhance the 'commercial museum' remit of the Institute by creating laboratories furnished to analyse and assess samples of the botanical and mineral resources of the empire and the potential products that might result.[47] In 1895, after obtaining a grant from the Goldsmith's Company and the Royal Commissioners of the 1851 exhibition, a 'Scientific and Technical Department' (henceforth S&T) of the Institute was inaugurated. Chemical and physical laboratories were equipped, and Wyndham R. Dunstan, an academic chemist and previously director of the research laboratory of the Pharmaceutical Society, was appointed as head.

Perhaps remarkably, given the Institute's financial and strategic difficulties, the S&T quickly met with considerable success. Its primary activities – the scientific testing and commercial assessment of the raw materials and new products of empire – satisfied a largely unmet need, especially in the colonial empire, were there were few available facilities to undertake this work. By 1898, the S&T was beginning to take on both commercially sponsored commissions and those requested by colonial governments. By 1902, 24 scientific reports of a high professional quality were being produced annually.[48] These achievements reflected well on Dunstan, who on the death of Abel in 1903 succeeded him as Institute director. Despite the transfer of Institute governance in that year to a Board of Trade largely uninterested in government-sponsored science, Dunstan energetically began to expand the S&T section, assisted in part by the patronage of a Colonial Office (CO) committed to Joseph Chamberlain's policies of 'constructive development'. Through its seat on the advisory committee of the Institute and its encouragement of sponsorship of investigative work by colonial administrators, the CO between 1903 and 1914 came to regard the S&T section as a 'department for the material development of the colonies'.[49] Dunstan ably led this project, expanding the staff to a complement of 25 permanents posts by 1910, the majority of them highly qualified scientists.[50] In addition, the department acquired external funding to manage two large-scale projects between 1902 and 1914: one, funded by the British Cotton Association on the quality of empire-grown cotton; another, funded by the CO, comprising a mineral and geological field survey of northern Nigeria. By 1912, the department was producing 475 scientific reports annually on these and other investigations; by 1908, 2792 analyses of minerals were being undertaken. External requests for information had also risen from approximately 200 per annum in 1905 to 521 in 1909.[51]

The effect of this expansion on the Institute's information services was, however, not entirely unproblematic. Most of the specialist information staff of the Commercial Information Department appear to have left the Institute in 1903. As a result, the quasi-professional organization of services and informational innovation apparent in the DCI in the late 1890s seems to have dissipated: effectively now scientists, rather than experienced clerks, had to re-invent information provision. However, relatively quickly, Dunstan established the *Bulletin of the Imperial Institute* as a regular quarterly publication reporting the Institute's scientific output. The growth in external enquiries also gradually led to the involvement of many scientific staff in information provision, researching secondary sources for clients rather than exclusively engaging in experimental investigation. A number of independent organizations providing various kinds of information about the empire also took up residence in the Institute in this period: the British Women's Emigration Association; the Colonial Nursing Association; the Imperial Co-operation League; the Association of Tropical Agriculture and Colonial Development; a Tropical Disease Bureau; and the University Bureau of the British Empire. In this way, by 1914, the Institute had become, as Dunstan noted in a report to the CO, 'a central clearing-house for [Empire] information'.[52] When war broke out that year, the Institute responded by setting up a Technical Information Bureau designed to help solve the (now) well-documented crises of industrial supply emanating from the cessation of Anglo-German trade. Initially this bureau seems to have met with some success, generating a marked increase in enquiries from industry and identifying new sources of manufacture and supply in both the United Kingdom and the Empire.[53] However, as the war progressed the impact of the Bureau, and that of the S&T section as a whole, appears to have diminished – in part because many of its staff became unavailable since, perhaps significantly, they were not exempted from military service.[54]

In hindsight, it is clear that the Great War marked the high-water mark of Dunstan's plans for transforming the Institute into a centre of imperial science. For the dominions and India, despite their military support of Britain, the war loosened the economic bonds of empire and left them with a renewed sense of their national independence in terms of economy, industry and science.[55] In Britain, it prompted a nationalistic focus on the modernization of the domestic industrial base, resulting in the creation of the Department of Scientific and Industrial Research (DSIR), with its research associations, stations and their information bureaux.[56] 'Imperial' science and technology began to seem an unlikely concept to many, and in 1918 a parliamentary committee under the chairmanship of the Unionist (and imperialist) MP W. A. S. Hewins, recommended that the Institute's scientific work be run down. For five years or so Dunstan, leaning on the imperialist sympathies of the CO and post-war Conservative ministers such as Milner and Churchill, effectively resisted the Hewins proposals and secured financial survival. However, in 1923 another enquiry, this time under Colonial Office under-secretary W. Ormsby-Gore, had a more lasting impact on the Institute's scientific work. It suggested that the laboratories 'carry on only the work of preliminary analysis and investigation of raw materials'. The Institute should, it proposed, be merged with the Imperial Mineral Resources Bureau (whose work it partly duplicated), and become a 'clearing house of intelligence and information' on the raw materials of the empire.[57] This change of focus was largely accepted in government and embodied in the Imperial Institute Act (1925), which transferred the administration once again to the (now renamed) Department of Overseas Trade. Concurrently, Ormsby-Gore had also recommended the run-down of the exhibition and publicity sections of the Institute; however this was not reflected in the Act, which called for the retention of a 'public information and instruction' remit in support of empire.[58]

'Information' hence became from 1925 the prime objective of the Institute, both in the shape of new intelligence bureaux focusing on empire resources, and in the guise of a re-invigorated public relations operation which promoted the imperial idea. The latter function, as John Mackenzie illustrates in detail, thrived between 1925 and 1939 in response to a resurgence in imperial sentiment, the activities of the Empire Marketing Board (founded in 1926) and the support of politicians such as colonial secretary Leopold Amery.[59] Less visibly, the scientific and technical information bureaux were rationalized on professional lines, mirroring the contemporary growth of these new kinds of services elsewhere in British industry and commerce (ASLIB, the Association of Special Libraries and Information Bureaux had been founded in 1924).[60] Two scientific departments, plant and animal products and mineral resources, were established, employing by the late 1930s 'some forty scientists'.[61] Each had an 'intelligence' section, which dealt with enquiries, and an 'indexing' section, which organized and catalogued material – by 1926 these sections employed nine specialist staff. A separate 'statistics' section, with 6 staff, and the Institute library, with four staff, supported both departments.[62] At the hub of each Intelligence section was a card index, organized under subject headings by commodity, which had originally catalogued information from the Institute's own investigations. Increasingly, however, references to a wide range of periodicals, monographs and 'grey literature' (materials that cannot be easily found through conventional channels) were included in the index. By 1939, the indexing sections were scanning and indexing some 4170 new books, official reports and pamphlets and about 900 periodicals comprising 26,000 separate issues.[63] The indexes were used to satisfy a wide range of requests in relation to the raw materials of empire: 'cassava from St Lucia ... cashew nuts from Ceylon ... Radium minerals from Canada ... bituminous material from Palestine'.[64] Enquiries came in, according to successive annual reports, from the length and breadth of the empire: by 1937 the plants intelligence section was handling 1192 per annum, the minerals section 1101.[65]

All in all there is little evidence to suggest, from a study of these information services, that after 1925 scientific and technical information work became less important in the Institute. It may well be, as Mackenzie suggests, that it became less 'prominent ... compared with the propagandist and educational objectives',[66] but even if its public profile became lower, the substance of S&T was clearly maintained, if not increased. A comprehensive and authoritative publications profile was developed. The quarterly *Bulletin* was expanded to incorporate informational tools such as subject bibliographies and current-awareness updates. The *Annual Statistical Summary of the Mineral Industry of the British Empire and Foreign Countries* developed into a key resource with an international reputation in the field.[67] Both directors during this period, Sir William Furse (1925–34) and Sir Harry Lindsay (1934–49), were non-scientists but appear to have promoted the specialist information services with vigour. The Institute was quick to join the aforementioned ASLIB, appearing on its first membership list published in 1927.[68] Institute staff participated regularly in its events and conferences in the 1930s, and Lindsay was elected ASLIB President for 1937–8 and served again throughout the early war years between 1939 and 1942.[69] During this period he addressed ASLIB conferences twice regarding the work of the Institute's specialist information services, most latterly in 1944 when he contributed to a symposium on 'The Empire Contribution to the Flow of World Information'.[70] As this appearance suggests, the Institute's work continued, although on a reduced scale, during the Second World War – as well as absence for military service, 14 specialist staff were transferred to the Ministry of Economic Warfare, where they formed an 'intelligence' section, and 11 more were seconded to undertake information work elsewhere.[71]

The swift end of scientific information provision at the Institute, when it came, cannot justifiably therefore be ascribed to any lack of managerial or other internal commitment. Rather, it was basically the result of larger historical forces beyond the Institute's control: most obviously the realization by the British state, by about 1946–47, of the redundancy of Empire and its replacement, over the next 15 years or so, by a British 'Commonwealth' of independent states. As part of this process the notion of 'imperial' science (which had in fact emerged to play one last encore at the Royal Society Empire Scientific Conference in 1946) dissolved quite quickly and was replaced by a more devolved system of scientific communication linked to the development of national institutions in the dominions and former colonies.[72] In this context there was little intellectual, political or financial support for centralized, metropolitan information services such as those of the Institute. As early as January 1946 the new Labour government signalled its intention to discontinue the scientific work of the Institute; in 1949 its remit for information and intelligence provision was revoked by an Order in Council, and its libraries and other information resources were transferred to the Colonial Geological Bureau and the Plant and Animals Advisory Bureau respectively.[73] After one final enquiry into its future – the results of which appeared in the Tweedsmuir Report (1952) – the Institute was rebranded as the Commonwealth Institute, with primary objectives concerning education and culture.[74] Its buildings – except for the Campanile Tower, which still stands on the site of Imperial College – were demolished and it moved to Holland Park. The divorce of information provision from 'imperial' Britain, after a marriage of almost 70 years, was largely complete.

CONCLUSION: THE INSTITUTE, EMPIRES AND INFORMATION HISTORY

The verdict of colonial, and especially postcolonial, history has generally been hard on the Imperial Institute. By and large, it has been dismissed as a late-Victorian imperialist folly, swimming constantly against the tide of history and, in its serious scientific and commercial work, engaged in the morally dubious business of exploiting the 'natural resources' of empire. The British government, even in its imperialist phases, never wholeheartedly supported the venture and, as we have seen, this led to chronic financial instability and curtailment of plans and aspirations. Only sporadically (perhaps under Dunstan, between 1903 and 1914, and later, between 1926 and 1939) did the Institute display any clarity of purpose. This left the field open for early criticism of its management which castigated its elitism, complacency and amateurism.[75] Dominion and colonial scepticism, too, was present almost from the beginning: as early as 1892 the *Melbourne Age* had described the Institute as a 'British asset' staffed by 'hangers-on of the aristocracy... [where] not so much as a balance sheet is supplied for colonial criticism'.[76] Even by the 1930s, when the Institute had established its administration on a much more professional footing, the issues of multifunctional muddle remained. The centre for 'imperial display' and propaganda that the Institute had gradually become seemed at odds with its still extensive scientific and economic functions. Amid this, the potentially unifying information role was understated and undervalued as routine and mundane. Indeed, in the 1943 edition of the Institute *Bulletin* commemorating the fiftieth anniversary of its opening, little official tribute was paid to the commercial and scientific information services or their staff.[77]

Such issues should not, however, be allowed to obscure the organizational and professional achievements of the Institute's information and intelligence bureaux. The re-appraisal of these here, through the lens of information history, results in a substantially less negative assessment of their achievements and legacy. The scientific and technical information work, considered in the second main section of this chapter, had its origins in an era of national and 'imperial efficiency' when information first began to be recognized as an industrial, economic and military resource. This provision evolved uncertainly between 1903 and 1924, but it was later re-organized along (for the time) highly efficient lines. By the 1930s the Institute's various S&T services were recognizably part of a network of state and quasi-state bureaux which formed an embryonic 'national infrastructure' for scientific and technical information. Their skilled labour force, comprising in the main well-qualified scientists turning their hand to new techniques of documentation, typified the professionalization of information work in early twentieth-century Britain, based as it became on the application of 'scientific' methods to information problems.[78] Perhaps surprisingly, as we have seen, it was not really until after the Second World War that the 'imperial' dimension of the S&T services came to be questioned; nevertheless, in the postcolonial age they were quickly disbanded. Their offspring, however, flourished in mid-century Britain and the Commonwealth, when a myriad of specialized bureaux emerged to form the basis of pluralist scientific and industrial information networks partly funded by the state.[79] The Institute's S&T information service – in tandem with fellow members of ASLIB in the 1920s and 1930s – can justifiably be viewed as a precursor and forerunner of these.

Less enduring than the scientific and technical operations, but in the context of information history perhaps of more unique importance, was the Commercial Intelligence Department, examined in the first main section of the chapter. Beginning its operations in 1888, the department was arguably the first true commercial information service in Britain, and one of the first in the world.[80] It was founded in an era that substantially predates the establishment of private-sector company libraries in Britain – they generally emerged after 1914 although, famously, Levinstein Dyestuffs had opened a library in the 1870s and the Board of Trade itself had had a commercial library since 1834.[81] However, the emphasis on commercial 'intelligence', current information and dissemination, embodied in the DCI's objectives, was undoubtedly new. Although some of these ideas were adapted from military and overseas intelligence as it had evolved in the Victorian civil service, the application of intelligence techniques to commercial ends was nevertheless a true innovation. Like many pioneer ventures, of course, the DCI was probably ahead of its time, and it met with mixed success. The expected demand for commercial information about the empire, fuelled by visions of trade wars and tariff reform, largely failed to materialize. Nevertheless, the quality of the DCI's publications and enquiry services was impressive: sufficiently so that the Board of Trade itself set up an enquiry into the wider potential of commercial intelligence services in 1897. As we have seen this was followed by the launch of the Board's own Commercial Intelligence Office in 1899, a service which eventually absorbed the Institute's DCI in 1903. In this way the DCI in effect served as a prototype for the twentieth-century expansion of commercial information services in Britain, and arguably worldwide. That it was established within an empire, as opposed to a free-market, context is perhaps testimony to the power of imperial sentiment in late-Victorian Britain.

Indeed, the ways in which the late-Victorian rhetoric of empire became entangled with the new idea of information is, in the end, one of the most arresting features of this account of the Imperial Institute. The founding of the Institute clearly coincided with a point in time (about 1890) where Victorian Britain was beginning to become aware of the value and significance of information in its own right: in T. H. Huxley's words 'that our people were becoming alive to the necessity of organization and discipline of knowledge'.[82] Such awareness was powerfully apparent in the early debates about the Institute's role and purpose: its supporters, as we have seen, envisioning it as a 'centre for the collection and diffusion of all available knowledge'. This discourse, as Duncan Bell observes, was closely linked to the late-Victorian preoccupation with renewal of empire, and the creation of a 'Greater Britain' made possible by the globalization of electric telegraph cable and its supposed 'annihilation of distance'.[83] To this was added a specific informational dimension in which the chaos and diversity of empire would be overcome by the collection and dissemination of intelligence and knowledge. Anticipating H. G. Wells and later prophets of global information utopias such as Manfred Kochen and Ted Nelson,[84] the Institute's imperialist supporters deployed the ancient metaphor of the body in their descriptions of the new networks and systems. At its centre, the empire of information was to be regulated by a 'brain centre' (the Institute), linked to 'local ganglions [provincial institutes] each with its own supply of efferent and afferent nerves'. This 'magnificent conception', according to *The Times*, promised the Empire 'a unity ... which it does not at present enjoy as fully as it might'. 'For scientific and commercial purposes', it went on, 'the Empire will become one body, in which each separate point will find its proper office and will discharge it with most benefit to the whole and to itself'.[85]

The Imperial Institute, of course, was never able to realize such an empire of information. Despite their professional successes, its information services were eventually subsumed by a combination of the logic of the free market – hence the takeover of its Commercial Intelligence Department by the relatively internationalist Board of Trade in 1903 – and by the growing independence of dominions and colonies suspicious of metropolitan control. 'Provincial institutes' of science and technology linked to the Institute were never established. All of this suggests that the demise of the Institute, in the 1950s, might be said to mark the passing of 'imperial' schemes and systems of knowledge. A longer view, however, would observe that the mid-twentieth century marked not the end of an age of empire and information, but more precisely the obsolescence of a particular, European, colonialist phase. As the twentieth century progressed, imperialism endured and mutated: adopting global and economic, rather than national and cultural, characteristics, and becoming what the Marxist theorist Rosa Luxemburg in 1913 saw as the 'political expression of capital accumulation in its race to take possession of the remains of the non-capitalist world'.[86] In our twenty-first-century information society the institutions of this latter-day imperialism are consequently of a different scope and order from those envisaged by the late Victorians: global, commercial, multicultural and, from the 1970s onwards, powered by the technologies of the information revolution. Informational imperialism now is, nonetheless, all the more powerful and all the more omnipresent: in surveillance states; in multinational media; in global financial systems; in the 'underdeveloped' world. New imperia of information expand and prosper despite the demise of the Imperial Institute and its colonial counterparts some 50 years ago. These imperia affirm, in a now postmodern world, the continuing correspondence between information and empire: a theme that, on the evidence at least of this limited study, will continue to animate both information and imperial historians for foreseeable decades to come.

NOTES

1. The classification of types of information system here is derived from D. Headrick (2000), *When Information Came of Age: Technologies of Knowledge in the Age of Reason and Revolution 1700–1850* (Oxford: Oxford University Press), pp. v–vii.
2. See A. Mattelart (1996), *The Invention of Communication* (Minneapolis: University of Minnesota Press) for an imaginative commentary; D. Headrick (1988), *The Tentacles of Progress: Technology Transfer in an Age of Imperialism 1850–1940* (Oxford: Oxford University Press), pp. 97–144, provides an empirical account of these technologies.

3. The notion of 'information order' is taken from C. Bayly (1996), *Empire and Information: Intelligence Gathering and Social Communication in India 1780–1870* (Cambridge: Cambridge University Press), pp. 1–9, where it is applied to British rule in North India.

4. On the wider impact of empire on European knowledge and vice-versa see E. Said (1978), *Orientalism* (London: Routledge and Kegan Paul); E. Said (1993), *Culture and Imperialism* (London: Chatto and Windus). Also, J. Mackenzie (1999), 'Empire and Metropolitan Cultures', in A. Porter (ed.) *The Oxford History of the British Empire: The Nineteenth Century* (Oxford: Oxford University Press), pp. 270–93 provides an introduction to the impact of empire on British culture.

5. That is, an information revolution not simplistically linked to the twentieth-century development of the computer. See K. Robins and F. Webster (1999), *Times of the Technoculture: From the Information Society to the Virtual Life* (London: Routledge), pp. 87–108; Headrick, *When Information Came of Age*; A. Black, D. Muddiman and H. Plant (2007), *The Early Information Society: Information Management Before the Computer* (Aldershot: Ashgate).

6. See, for example, A. Olden (1995), *Libraries in Africa: Pioneers, Policies, Problems* (Lanham, MD: Scarecrow); P. Sturges (2001), 'The Poverty of Librarianship: An Historical Critique of Public Librarianship in Anglophone Africa', *Libri*, 51, pp. 38–48.

7. It has been argued that 'even the new library history has been surprisingly deficient in its failure to assimilate [the theme of] national identity'. See G. Peatling (2004), 'Public Libraries and National Identity in Britain, 1850–1919', *Library History*, 20 (1), p. 33.

8. See, for example, D. Coombs (1988), *Spreading the Word: The Library Work of the British Council* (London: Mansell); A. Arberry (1967), *India Office Library: A Historical Sketch* (London: Commonwealth Office).

9. J. Mackenzie (1984), *Propaganda and Empire* (Manchester: Manchester University Press), pp. 122–46, provides the standard general introduction to the Institute's history, although this is arguably overly dismissive of its achievements. W. Golant (1984), *Image of Empire: The Early History of the Imperial Institute 1887–1925* (Exeter: Exeter University Press) is rather more sympathetic, but focuses mainly on science. G. Bremner (2003), 'Some Imperial Institute. Architecture, Symbolism and the Ideal of Empire in Late Victorian Britain', *Journal of the Society of Architectural Historians*, 62 (1), pp. 50–74, comprises an interesting analysis of the Institute's architecture and displays in the context of changing ideas about empire.

10. See Bremner, 'Some Imperial Institute', pp. 61–6, for a discussion of the Institute's contemporary architectural context. By 1955 Lord Hudson, chairman of the Institute Council, would describe its architecture as 'perfectly abominable', quoted in Mackenzie, *Propaganda and Empire*, p. 142.

11. Mackenzie, *Propaganda and Empire*, p. 122.

12. H. Lindsay (1939), 'The Imperial Institute as an Information Centre', in ASLIB, *Report of Proceedings of the Sixteenth Conference* (London: ASLIB), p. 12.

13. The records of the Imperial Institute can be found in the National Archives, Kew, London. They are mainly contained in the files PRO 30/76/1–319. Other relevant National Archives records include Board of Trade Papers (BT 13/28–29) and Cabinet Papers (CAB 37/49).

14. Bremner, 'Some Imperial Institute', p. 51.
15. Imperial Institute (1894), *The Year Book of the Imperial Institute* (London: John Murray), pp. 803–4.
16. Abel is popularly remembered as the inventor of cordite. For a summary of his life see H. Matthew and B. Harrison (eds) (2004), *Oxford Dictionary of National Biography* (Oxford: Oxford University Press/British Academy), pp. 62–3.
17. Imperial Institute (1886), 'Report of the Committee', *Journal of the Society of Arts*, (35) 1179, pp. 87–90.
18. Imperial Institute, 'Report of the Committee', p. 87.
19. *The Times*, 13 January 1887, p. 9.
20. *The Times*, 23 April 1887, p. 12.
21. 'Sir F. Abel on the Imperial Institute', *The Times*, 23 April 1887, pp. 4–5.
22. There were many critics of the plans for the Institute, ranging from anti-imperialists to others, such as Huxley, who were supportive but critical of the South Kensington site and agitated for a location in the City of London, the empire's commercial heartland as they saw it. See Bremner, 'Some Imperial Institute', p. 79.
23. *The Times*, 23 April 1887, p. 12.
24. The competition was won by London-based architect T. E. Colcutt.
25. The Imperial Institute (1888) *Charter of Incorporation*, pp. 6–7. PRO 30/76/308.
26. *The Times*, 6 February 1888, p. 9.
27. F. Abel (1897), *Memorandum on the Nature and Progress of Work Carried out at the Imperial Institute*, p. 3. PRO 30/76/308.
28. F. Abel (1888), *Outline of the Proposed Intelligence Department for Industries, Commerce, Technical and Commercial Education and Emigration as part of the Working Details of the Imperial Institute*. PRO 30/76/310.
29. Abel, *Memorandum*, p. 4.
30. This was not Vine's only task – rather more importantly he was charged with raising funds in the dominions and colonies, an effort which also met with mixed success. See Imperial Institute (1894) *Year Book,* 807.
31. *Imperial Institute Journal*, 1895, 1 (1), p. 8. PRO 30/76/18.
32. F. Henn (1943), 'The Library', *Bulletin of the Imperial Institute*, 41 (1), 74–5.
33. This included some leading librarians of the day – H. R. Tedder, of the Athenaeum Club; E. Maude Thompson (British Museum); R. Rost (India Office) and C. Atchley (Colonial Office). See Imperial Institute (1892) *Year Book* (London: John Murray), p. 793.
34. The full run of the *Imperial Institute Journal* can be found at the National Archives PRO 30/76/18–PRO 30/76/25.
35. Board of Trade Commercial Intelligence Committee (1897), *Minutes of Evidence Taken before the Department Committee of the Board of Trade on Commercial Intelligence*, pp. 68–9. BT 13/29/6.
36. Board of Trade Commercial Intelligence Committee, *Minutes*, pp. 94–101. The enquiries received by the DCI are recorded in detail in these pages.
37. Abel, *Memorandum*, p. 4.
38. See C. Davis (1898), *The Facts of the Imperial Institute Ascertained Upon the Enquiry of a Fellow*. PRO 30/76/311.
39. Imperial Institute (1902), *City Branch Leaflet*. BT 13/29/6.

40. A. Thompson (2000), *Imperial Britain: The Empire in British Politics 1880–1932* (London: Longman), p. 105.

41. Commercial Intelligence Committee (1898), *Report of the Departmental Committee Appointed by the Board of Trade to Inquire and Report upon the Dissemination of Commercial Information.* Cmd. 8962 (London: HMSO), p. 8.

42. *Letter to the Secretary of the Board of Trade from Colonial Office*, 20 August 1898. BT 13/28/9.

43. F. Abel (1902), 'The Future of the Imperial Institute', *Imperial Institute Journal*, 8 (92), p. 205.

44. These complaints reached cabinet level in the government of the time, Lord James of Hereford, the Institute's president, describing the proposed BOT takeover as a 'crushing blow' to the DCI. See *Memorandum before Cabinet from James of Hereford*, 20 January 1899. CAB 37/49/4.

45. Advisory Committee to the Board of Trade on Commercial Intelligence (1909), *Report of the Proceedings, August 1905–August 1909*, 4. BT 11/3.

46. See F. Turner (1980), 'Public Science in Britain, 1880–1919', *Isis*, 71 (259), pp. 589–608. D. Muddiman (2008), 'Public Science in Britain and the Origins of Documentation and Information Science' in W. Rayward (ed.), *European Modernism and the Information Society* (Ashgate: Aldershot), pp. 201–22 discusses the informational consequences of the new public science.

47. Golant, *Image of Empire*, p. 8.

48. M. Worboys (1990), 'The Imperial Institute: The State and the Development of the Natural Resources of the Colonial Empire 1887–1923', in J. Mackenzie (ed.), *Imperialism and the Natural World* (Manchester: Manchester University Press), pp. 170–1.

49. Worboys, 'The Imperial Institute', pp. 169–173.

50. Imperial Institute (1910), *The Imperial Institute of the United Kingdom, the Colonies and India* [Guide] (London: Imperial Institute), 14. PRO 30/76/314.

51. Golant, *Image of Empire*, pp. 16–20.

52. Golant, *Image of Empire*, p. 14.

53. Imperial Institute (1914), *Report on the Work of the Imperial Institute in 1914*, pp. 4–5. PRO 30/76/327.

54. Golant, *Image of Empire*, p. 24.

55. Thompson, *Imperial Britain*, pp. 157–85.

56. For the consequences of these developments for information provision see Muddiman, 'Public Science in Britain', pp. 205–9.

57. Imperial Institute Committee of Enquiry (1923), *Report* [Cmnd. 1997] (London: HMSO), p. 28.

58. Lindsay, 'The Imperial Institute', p. 12.

59. Mackenzie, *Propaganda and Empire*, pp. 132–40.

60. For a survey of the early history of ASLIB see D. Muddiman (2005), 'A New History of ASLIB, 1924–50', *Journal of Documentation*, 61 (4), pp. 402–28.

61. Lindsay, 'The Imperial Institute', p. 12.

62. Imperial Institute (1926), *Annual Report* (London: Imperial Institute). PRO 30/76/327.

63. Lindsay, 'The Imperial Institute', p. 16.

64. Lindsay, 'The Imperial Institute', p. 14.

65. Imperial Institute (1937), *Annual Report* (London: Imperial Institute), 30–44. PRO 30/76/327.
66. Mackenzie, *Propaganda and Empire*, p. 132.
67. Lindsay, 'The Imperial Institute', p. 16.
68. ASLIB (1927), *List of Members and Associate Members to 17 May 1927*. Box 51, ASLIB Archives, London.
69. ASLIB (1939), *Report of Proceedings of the Sixteenth Conference* (London: ASLIB), p. 7.
70. ASLIB (1945), *Report of Proceedings of the Nineteenth Conference* (London: ASLIB), pp. 21–50.
71. H. Lindsay (1941), 'The Imperial Institute and its Work for the Empire', *The Analyst*, 66 (783), p. 223.
72. See Royal Society (1948), *The Royal Society Empire Scientific Conference June–July 1946, Report* (London: Royal Society). The Empire Scientific Conference itself recommended 'the establishment of a network of information services throughout the Dominions' (p. 668). Little came of these proposals in practice: after World War Two, India and the dominions, like Britain, concentrated on the development of national scientific and technical information services; the other former UK colonies more gradually developed services along the models espoused by UNESCO.
73. *Machinery of Government, Imperial Institute: Notes of a Meeting Held at the Treasury*, 11 January, 1946. PRO 30/76/306; *The Future Constitution and Purpose of the Imperial Institute* [Press release], 31 March 1949. PRO 30/76/306.
74. Ministry of Education (1952), *Report of the Committee of Enquiry into the Imperial Institute* (London: HMSO), p. 2.
75. For example, see Davis, *The Facts of the Imperial Institute*.
76. *Imperial Institute Newspaper Cuttings No.1, 1892–3*, 11, PRO 30/76/9.
77. *Bulletin of the Imperial Institute*, 1943, 41 (1). One and a half pages are devoted to the history of the library in this volume.
78. See Muddiman, 'Public Science in Britain', pp. 205–209.
79. For an overview of the evolution of these services in mid-twentieth-century Britain see J. Burkett (1979), *Library and Information Networks in Britain* (London: ASLIB). For an example of Commonwealth development (in Australia) see A. Johns (1968), *Special Libraries: Development of the Concept, Their Organization, Their Services* (New Jersey: Scarecrow Press).
80. Other early services were surveyed in the evidence considered by the Board of Trade Commercial Intelligence Committee in 1897. They included business enquiry services established in 'commercial museums' in Vienna (1873), Brussels (1882) and Philadelphia (1893). See Board of Trade Commercial Intelligence Committee, *Minutes*, pp. 104–76.
81. For an introduction to early company library development in Britain see A. Black (2007), 'Enterprise and Intelligence: The Early Company Library in Context', in A. Black, D. Muddiman and H. Plant (eds), *The Early Information Society*, pp 149–85.
82. *The Times*, 13 January 1887, p. 9. For further discussion regarding the chronology of the concept of information in nineteenth-century Britain see T. Weller and D. Bawden (2006), 'Individual Perceptions: A New Chapter on Victorian Information History', *Library History*, 22 (2), pp. 137–56; and A. Black and D. Muddiman (2007), 'Reconsidering the Chronology of the Information Age', in Black et al. (eds), *The Early Information Society*, pp. 237–43.

83. D. Bell (2007), *The Idea of Greater Britain: Empire and the Future of World Order, 1860–1900* (Princeton: Princeton University Press), pp. 81–91.
84. See the discussion in D. Muddiman (1998), 'The Universal Library as Modern Utopia: The Information Society of H. G. Wells', *Library History*, 14 (2), pp. 96–8.
85. *The Times*, 23 April 1887, p. 12.
86. R. Luxemburg (1963), *The Accumulation of Capital* (London: Routledge and Kegan Paul). Cited in Mattelart, *The Invention of Communication*, p. 177.

7

'A VALUABLE HANDBOOK OF INFORMATION': THE STAFF MAGAZINE IN THE FIRST HALF OF THE TWENTIETH CENTURY AS A MEANS OF INFORMATION MANAGEMENT

Alistair Black

The glitz and glamour of the so-called 'information society' blinds us to the multitude of precursors of digital information and communication technology and culture. Partly in response to the historical blind spots created by information millenarianism, in recent years historians have highlighted a large number of the information society's pre-computer roots and antecedents.[1] Adding to this body of historical literature, this chapter examines the history of the humble in-house staff magazine in Britain in the first half of the twentieth century, especially in terms of its role as an 'information glue' in organizations that across all sectors of society and the economy during this period were becoming larger and more fragmented, thereby requiring new ways – 'informational' ways – of managing them. In this respect, the views of the editor of *The Black Diamond*, the staff magazine of the coal shipping company William Cory & Son, are worthy of note. In the first issue of the magazine, in 1925, he explained that the publication would not only carry articles that were light, humorous and of current interest but also act as a means whereby all members of the company 'may acquaint themselves with the Company's operations and trading'; it would be a magazine which, in due course, would 'form *a valuable handbook of information* [author emphasis] relative to the Countries, Cities and Ports, in and around which the Company's business is conducted'.[2]

Since the end of the nineteenth century, the staff magazine has been a very visible methods of communicating information in organizations, and often externally also. By the middle of the twentieth century, in large and even medium-sized companies, such publications were commonplace. A survey conducted by the Office Management Association in 1952 found that out of 323 firms questioned, 136 (or 42 per cent) produced a house magazine for staff.[3] Some publications could be classed as major journalistic endeavours. For example, by the early 1920s the in-house magazine of the soap manufacturer Lever Brothers, titled *Progress*, had secured a massive circulation of a quarter of a million worldwide, and was said 'to appeal to the great Lever Brotherhood in every land'.[4] By August 1956, British Petroleum's staff magazine, which ran to a healthy 56 pages, had a monthly circulation of over 20,000.[5] Such was the importance of the staff magazine that conferences of invited editors were held to discuss issues relating to the medium, such as those organized by the Industrial Welfare Society in 1921 and 1939.[6]

Work to date on the early history of the staff magazine – and it is a mystery why this fairly common component of work in the early-twentieth century has received relatively little attention – has focused on the issue of management control in the workplace in the context of business and management history. Griffiths has shown that staff magazines were effective vehicles for transmitting to the workforce, including managers, a company's culture: that is to say, its system of shared values and its strategic direction. Companies have historically viewed staff magazines, Griffiths argues, as a means of moulding employees to fulfil three roles: that of ambassador (to be courteous in communication with 'outside' parties); salesman (to vigorously promote the interests of the company) and activist (to become activists in relation to wider political, legal and economic issues facing the company).[7]

Yet, as is revealed on the cover of the first issue, in 1920, of *The Thalos Review*, the staff magazine of a London and Thames estuary oil storage company,[8] content could be eclectic, topics in this case ranging from company news, recollections of working lives and short stories, to photography, reports on holidays and competitions (Figure 7.1). This high degree of 'internal specialization', and the wide variety of reader audiences, thus makes the staff magazine potentially the subject of multiple historical investigations. This chapter's primary lens of analysis is that of information management, though because this is an aspect of broader organizational management the chapter also necessarily attends to issues of control and management history located outside the information management domain. Information management is, of course, simply one of

The Thalos Review.

THE OFFICIAL ORGAN OF
THE LONDON AND THAMES HAVEN OIL WHARVES
AND LONDON OIL STORAGE COMPANY, LIMITED.
HEAD OFFICE : 3, ST. HELEN'S PLACE, E.C. 3.

Copyright. | No. 1. JUNE, 1920. | *Price Sixpence.*

THAMES HAVEN WHARF THIRTY YEARS AGO.

CONTENTS.

Figure 7.1 Front cover of *The Thalos Review*, 1 June 1920. Reproduced with the kind permission of Shell International.

a number of lenses through which one can try to uncover the meaning of the early staff magazine. Other research might prioritize the history of: the workplace; social class; leisure; gender; authorship; publishing; literacy; the economy; or business.

The sample of magazines analysed for the purpose of this chapter (25 publications from 16 firms are cited here) is small relative to the thousands of publications that went into circulation. Also, the sample contains represents private enterprises, whereas staff magazines were certainly present in government departments,[9] and in non-governmental, non-profit organizations like libraries and hospitals, for example.[10] However, the magazines discussed here represent a wide range of industries and services, reflecting the varied workplaces in which they appeared.

A PRE-HISTORY OF THE 'DIGITAL AGE' MANAGEMENT DISCOURSE

In the digital age the discourse of management has been re-invented through the creation of a variety of new terms and concepts, including information management, the e-organization, the learning organization and knowledge management. However, although the vocabulary is new, many of the principles underpinning them are not. Indeed, these principles can be traced back to the period in which the staff magazine originated and began to flourish.

In its pure, theoretical form, today's e-organization offers employees the capability of speedy, if not instant, access to information that is relevant to their jobs and needs speedily, if not instantly, from any location and at any time.[11] It is said that we have entered an era of 'just-in-time knowledge'.[12] The desktop and mobile information technologies that facilitate this are heralded as revolutionary and transformative. However, this millennial zeal is deflated by the argument that the information-rich organization is not a product of the digital age, but of the age of corporate capitalism commencing in the late nineteenth century. At this time, firms and government bureaucracies began to increase in size and grew more complex, a trend that continued apace during the heated merger activity of the First World War and the inter-war period (a number of the magazines cited here refer at certain points to enlargement, stock-market floatations, amalgamations and takeovers affecting the business of their parent companies).[13] Hierarchies deepened and chains of command lengthened. As a result, internal communication and information systems of various kinds – aimed at reducing distance and strengthening interfaces between branches, departments or subsidiaries – became much more important in the quest for efficiency and, in the case of the private enterprise, for profit. Means were developed of monitoring and recording activity in organizations (information drawn up the hierarchy). On the basis of the information received, it was anticipated, more effective decisions could be made, and instructions and protocols formulated and disseminated (information sent down the hierarchy).[14]

The development of 'informational capabilities'[15] by organizations was part and parcel of the move away from owner-control towards control by experts and managers, including general executives, financial planners, research and development technicians, protocol administrators, technical librarians, registry supervisors and public relations specialists. The shift to a 'scientific' method of managing organizations – the visible hand of management supplementing the less predictable, invisible workings of the market mechanism – was multifaceted and drove forward the first information management revolution (information management being a process that is contextualized in the organization). Pioneers of the revolution hoped it would yield dividends in terms of the management not only of the large corporations of the immediate pre-1914 decades (and the even larger giant corporations that emerged in the heated merger activity and rationalization of the First World War and inter-war years)[16] but also in the bureaucratic world of the government department.[17] The first information management revolution entailed the introduction of new technologies *and* techniques of information recording, compilation, copying, storage, organization, retrieval, analysis and transmission. Important innovations here were the standardized printed form; the formal office memo; the fountain pen; the typewriter; the addressing machine; photography of various kinds, including the photostat and microfilm; the stencil duplicator; carbon paper; the telephone and teleprinter; calculating machines; punched-card machines; the vertical file and the filing cabinet; the central registry or filing room; new graphic means of presenting data, such as the Gantt charts; the printed protocol; and the in-house information bureau.[18] Another innovation was the in-house staff magazine.

A further context in which staff magazines developed was the process which now attracts the labels 'organizational learning' and 'knowledge management'. Organizations are collections of individuals, and if an individual learns then the organization can be said to be learning too (the 'learning organization').[19] In retrospectively applying this formula to the early twentieth century, however, one is immediately confronted with the conflicting Taylorist aim of a 'deliberate gathering, on the part of those on the management side, of all of the great mass of traditional knowledge which in the past has been in the heads of the workman'.[20] If knowledge in organizations is transferred from the minds of workers to the system, then the term 'learning organization' is undermined because it does not include intellectual capital possessed by the worker. There are two points to be made here. Firstly, the penetration of Taylorism, Fordism and scientific management in the early-twentieth-century British economy may not have been as deep as in the United States, in which case awareness of the importance of 'individual learning' remained significant. Secondly, in those sectors and companies where scientific management (or simply aggressive streamlining or rationalization) occurred, then individual learning may have been promoted as a reaction to the alienation it wrought. Either way, the information resource that was the staff magazine can be seen to have contributed to a 'learning organization' paradigm that applied to employees as well as to the system.

The formal theorizing of organizations as intelligent, information-dependent entities that can 'learn' is a relatively recent development. In post-industrial economies labour has come to be seen less as a cost and more as an investment. Human capital formation is now more likely to be seen as a process whereby units of labour are not simply imbued with the skills required to carry out specific tasks, but are capable of creativity conducive to increases in productivity. Like any resource, it is argued, employee and organizational knowledge acquisition can be managed, a perception which has given rise to the term 'knowledge management' (a corruption, it has to be said, of the more cumbersome but correct term 'knowledge-creation management', publicized by Nonaka and Takeuchi in their 1995 book *The Knowledge-Creating Company*).[21] However, although the terms might be new, the phenomenon of the learning organization and the practice of knowledge management are over a century old.

Criticism of 'knowledge management', as a management fad and as a concept manufactured by management consultants,[22] has lent weight to the argument that 'information management' remains a perfectly adequate term to describe what intelligent learning organizations have been doing since they first appeared in the late nineteenth century: that is to say, aiming to improve efficiency by planning, collecting, organizing, using, controlling, storing, disseminating and disposing of its information; and by getting the right information to the right person, in the right format and medium, at the right time.[23] If information flows in organizations are well managed, then the more likely it is that the individuals they contain will become more knowledgeable. The distinction should be made, however, between the sharing of information in an organization (knowledge absorbed through open-forum, flat structures of operation) and the top-down dissemination of information (knowledge instilled in the interests of control). A further distinction that needs to be identified is the supply of information to increase the store of existing knowledge, on the one hand, and the provision of infrastructures that enhance the capacity of individuals to produce knowledge, on the other (what McElroy calls 'supply-side' and 'demand-side' knowledge management, respectively).[24] Throughout its history, as the evidence presented below shows, the staff magazine has fulfilled these different approaches – knowledge shared/demanded/pulled, and instilled/supplied/pushed – to the management of information and organizational learning

CHANGES IN THE WORKPLACE

The control and supply dimensions of information management prompt the question of control in the workplace more generally, and, in addition, the extent to which the changing nature of work in the late twentieth and early nineteenth centuries throws light on the emergence of the staff magazine. Although there was variance between industries, occupations and regions, it is widely accepted that, against a backdrop of unrelentingly hostile international markets, the period from around 1880 to the Second World War saw an increase in the tempo of work as well as its increased regularization, mechanization, bureaucratization, fragmentation, depersonalization and deskilling (including a loss of discretion and knowledge).[25] Workers were also subjected to tighter discipline and supervision, initially through the appearance of the foreman acting on behalf of the owner-manager, and then through the imposed mechanism of scientific management systems (although, as argued above, the extent to which pure scientific management regimes were introduced in Britain should not be exaggerated).

The alienation which this engendered resulted, at different times and in various ways, in disaffection in the workplace. For Hobsbawm, this disaffection forced the crystallization of a virulent working-class consciousness. For others, notably E. P. Thompson, new working-class antipathy was a fresh manifestation of a working-class consciousness forged much earlier in the history of industrialization; whilst Joyce plays down the class aspects of workers' dissatisfaction, pointing to the importance of other forms of self-identity that might be gendered, regional, national, religious or political.

However, irrespective of the class dynamic, the period in which the staff magazine was born and achieved popularity was characterized by disquieting changes in workplace culture. Workers accepted these changes because certain benefits began to come their way and, generally speaking, employers became more conciliatory and imaginative in their management of labour, moving away from the crude tactics of the lock-out, victimization and eviction. As union membership mushroomed (by 1920, 50 per cent of the workforce was unionized compared to just 10 per cent in 1880),[26] employers became reconciled to the realities of collective bargaining, and workers' disaffection and claims. Workers, for their part, over the decades being considered here, were to a significant degree assuaged by such advances as a reduction in working hours, a shorter working life, more regular work, rising real wages, less dangerous working conditions, paid holidays and various welfare and social benefits.[27] It is in the context of the more consensual approach to management adopted by employers – though it is important not to underestimate the operation of direct and coercive controls – that the staff magazine should be seen. The staff magazine represented a subtle, indirect addition to the arsenal of management controls operated by employers.

WHOSE MAGAZINE?

Staff magazines produced in private enterprises have often been referred to as 'company magazines'. The degree of autonomy or editorial independence they did (or did not) enjoy is thus an important question to address. The magazine of the amalgamated Motor Union Insurance Company, United British Insurance Company and Federated British Insurance Company was called, simply and tellingly, *Our Magazine*.[28] The *Aquarius*, organ of the employees of the London Metropolitan Water Board, first published in 1905, was produced by the organization's Staff Association and was very much about the Association's various social activities. An example of an 'authentic', autonomous publication is *Costing Comments*, an ephemeral magazine produced for a brief period (1930–32) by staff in one of the numerous departments of the Prudential Assurance Company (the company's main journal was *The Prudential Bulletin*). Each issue contained a mock, comic monthly diary of events. Some issues contained news cuttings and photographs, accompanied by humorous commentary. The magazine was neither overtly political nor conflictual, in the industrial relations sense, but it did try to subvert establishment culture by poking fun at office life and its bureaucratic procedures, not least timekeeping.

The first issue, in 1935, of the magazine published in the London construction company Wates, titled *Wates House News*, announced that it was 'a journal produced by and in the interests of the staff of the House of Wates'. Under the headline 'Ourselves', the magazine's opening editorial explained that 'this is a staff magazine in the real sense – written and produced by members of the staff of Wates. Whether it is good or otherwise depends entirely on ourselves'.[29] However, it was the company's directors who provided the means and the facilities to produce it. Similarly, *The Home and Colonial Stores Magazine* was said to be self-supporting so far as its contents were concerned, but the company's directors would 'gladly shoulder the financial responsibility'.[30]

Financial independence was difficult to achieve. To attract popularity, magazines had to be moderately priced. The *Aquarius* began life in 1905 on a half-yearly subscription of one shilling payable in advance, but the price was soon changed to 2d per monthly issue (the *Daily Mail* at the time cost one half-penny); this was effectively the same yearly rate but with the convenience of pay-as-you-go. It looked to a circulation of 500 to break even. Priced sixpence at its launch in 1920, by 1927 *The Thalos Review* was being sold for just tup-pence. Annuals might be priced a little higher. For example, the glossy *Marlbeck Annual* was priced at sixpence. Revenues from sales were sometimes supple-mented by charges for advertisements, but this source of funds was limited and so company managers often agreed to defray all expenses that magazine projects could not themselves meet.[31]

Even though much of the material to fill the pages of publications came from the staff, most company magazines were exactly that, magazines *of* the company, funded and monitored by the company. The first magazine pro-duced by Lever Brothers, the *Port Sunlight Monthly Journal*, established in 1895, styled itself as 'an amateur magazine written by and for the employees'.[32] But the magazine was ultimately a company project – 'We want our readers to write it and *we shall edit it* [author emphasis]', declared the company.[33] All copy that was to appear in *The Black Diamond* had to pass through the hands of a 'Censor Committee' appointed by the Board of Directors.[34]

In terms of time consumed and energy expended, staff magazines could truly be classed as staff products (although there were at times complaints from editors about shortage of copy, especially a lack of contributions from women).[35] Editors – speaking for themselves but also on behalf of sub-editors), helpers and contributors as well as 'local correspondents' in remote parts of the organization – were keen to point out that staff journals were produced in their spare time.[36] But despite efforts made by editors and staff to construct and shape their publications, few magazines could avoid evolving a corporate feel. A good deal of deference was shown to company managers.[37] Some mag-azines carried biographies and photographs of the organization's hierarchy: its chairman, directors and senior officers.[38] Readers of *Our Magazine* were in each issue treated to an article depicting a day in the life of a manager.[39] The *Aquarius* carried a series titled 'Our Chiefs'. It was generally accepted that their publications could be read by people outside of the organization. Often, in fact, specific reference was made, or thanks given, to customers, associ-ated companies or members of the supply-chain.[40] This marketing dimension to magazines thus underscores the fact that mostly they were primarily the organ of the company, and *staff* magazines in name only.

INFORMATION FOR MOTIVATION

The magazine of the margarine maker and oil refiner Jurgens Ltd was described by its editor as a 'Welfare organ' which held no brief for any sectional interest – beyond 'the gospel of *cheer up*'.[41] However, despite such claims of neutrality, the underlying purpose of these magazines was the pursuit of efficiency and profit, and the calming and cohesion of the workforce. Magazines sought to incorporate the worker, making him or her feel less like a 'wage slave'.[42] In 1907 senior directors of the firm that made the famous Colman's Mustard hoped their magazine would strengthen the 'esprit de corps' which had always characterized their enterprise.[43]

A study of late-twentieth-century company magazines has revealed that managers used them as a means, amongst other aims, of motivating the workforce.[44] This was also the case with regard to earlier in-house journalism. The company Cook, Son and Co. started its staff magazine, the *Ravensbourne Gazette*, in 1917 in direct response to the Great War.[45] Articles attempted to rally the journal's readership behind the war effort and the troops. News of the company's men fighting at the front was complemented by articles on patriotic and motivational topics: 'Shakespeare and England'; 'Character'; 'The Conquering British Race'; and 'Liberty, Equality, Fraternity'. 'Courage, Cheerfulness and Resolution' were urged by one magazine after the outbreak of war in 1939.[46]

Naturally, motivational messages were also in evidence in peacetime. The *Prudential Bulletin* was also used by management to rally the 'troops' with articles carrying titles like 'Enthusiasm', 'Optimism' and 'Survival of the Fittest'.[47] *Naft-i-Iran* (*Oil in Iran*), organ of the Anglo-Persian Oil Company, later British Petroleum, declared that its publication 'will increase the pleasure we take in our work and heighten our devotion to the great Company to which we are all proud to belong'.[48] Motivational commentary was rarely directly political, although during national crises, such as the national coal strike in 1921 that affected industry widely, some editors and managers were unable to resist commenting. 'Unity is Strength' announced one magazine at the time, whereas national disunity was believed to be a recipe for disaster.[49] Another magazine, through the mouthpiece of its editor, viewed one of its roles as promoting 'economic sanity and industrial harmony'.[50] At the other end of the political spectrum, in the winter of 1905, the relatively independent magazine of the London Metropolitan Water Board helped organize a fund for the unemployed.[51]

Motivation often took the form of half-baked discourses on workplace psychology. Mantras, statements and arguments connected with the psychological requirements and effects of work abounded. The first issue of *The Home and Colonial Stores Magazine* in 1920 carried a pithy quotation by Victor Hugo: 'A day will come when the only battlefield will be the market open to commerce and the mind opening to new ideas.'[52] In addressing questions of common sense and personal success the managing director of Thomas Marshall (Marlbeck) Ltd, Leeds, wrote that

> The town of failure has inhabitants but no visitors, because you do not pass through it on your way to anywhere else. It is not a Junction but a Terminus. There are, however, three wide roads inviting one to the City centre – Panic Avenue, Guessing Lane and Worry Road.[53]

On other occasions, the same journal published an article on work and well-being, in which it was proclaimed that 'Of all the abilities, the capacity for work is the most useful and necessary, and its possession is a glorious power'; and also exclaimed that 'The father of Success is Work. The mother of Success is Ambition. The eldest son is Common Sense.'[54] 'There's no such word as can't', preached one editor in addressing the staff on the subject of the success and happiness of the company.[55]

INFORMATION FOR ORGANIZATIONAL LEARNING

The staff magazine clearly served, on an emotional level, as a rallying call for employees to devote themselves to the company, but it also worked on the rational level of aiming to secure corporate progress through an increased flow of pertinent information resulting in a more skilled and knowledgeable workforce. As one managing director put it in acknowledging this twin ambition: 'Each year sees us stronger in loyalty, knowledge and enthusiasm'.[56] The staff magazine was seen to have the potential to 'educate each member of the Staff, and especially the junior members, to a more comprehensive knowledge of the progress of the company', and in doing so create a 'happy family'.[57]

In addition to the aim of making workers more 'company minded' by explaining company policy, strengthening morale, building unity and breaking down cliques, magazines were started and supported because of their effectiveness as a medium for instruction; as a means of informing workers what was expected of them, and to promote 'obedience to rules and regulations by pointing out the reasons why conformity is essential'.[58] Customary methods of informing, or instructing, the workforce have ranged from the informal to the formal. In the former category one could include the staff magazine as well as the process of serial transmission, where instructions are allowed to trickle down the hierarchy and are reinforced by word of mouth (or may fail to be so, indeed, if distorted or if exploited for the purpose of resistance). The formal category might include direct supervision and knowledge transfer, training programmes, meetings, protocols, manuals, rule books and notices.

Notices and circular letters from managers and directors were a common means of conveying instructions, as at the Saltaire textile mill near Bradford where this format was used to disseminate information on processes and operational matters ranging from retirement and new management arrangements to holiday closures and stocktaking.[59] Another format was the booklet of instructions and general rules.[60] However, there is evidence that notices distributed were not always seen,[61] while lengthy bureaucratic instruction and rule books were, as now, not easily digestible. As rule-of-thumb working declined, the protocol came into its own. The protocol was crucial to the business life of the confectionery giant Rowntree and Co. of York. Until 1922 responsibility for factory and office rules, procedures and discipline rested with the factory manager. After this date, responsibility was transferred to an organizational office, whose function was to issue protocols in the form of 'standing orders' and 'instructions'. These were essentially handbooks (issued to managers and directors, and sometimes overlookers) which were returned to the organizational office at regular intervals for amendment. The office also issued a weekly bulletin containing information on such matters as: appointments and promotions of directors, managers, section heads and higher grade overlookers; new posts created; departments created, abolished or re-organized; the transfer of responsibilities between departments; and changes in procedures, rules and policies relating to wages, overtime, unemployment, pensions, holidays, health, safety, disciplinary matters and hygiene. The bulletin also served as a 'works diary', providing dates and details of general holidays, absences of managers, stocktaking, cleaning and painting, and information about lectures, classes and special events.[62]

The weekly bulletin at Rowntree meant that its staff organ, the *Cocoa Works Magazine*, could devote much of its copy to social matters and motivational messages from managers. However, in other magazines, instructional material had greater visibility. The subtitle of *The Prudential Bulletin* revealed its controlling information management purpose: 'A medium for the circulation of official instructions and other matters of interest to staff.' The *Carrow Works Magazine* published a regular feature titled 'Social Life', which provided workers with information and instructions regarding the company's welfare provision: pension and savings funds, the benefit society, sick visiting by the company nurse, the reporting of accidents and canteen provision. In 1937 the *Marlbeck Annual* carried instructions on how to save waste in the production process, and how to economize on office stationery.[63]

As a substitute, or adjunct, to face-to-face training, identified in the magazine of one department store as the 'Cinderella of retailing',[64] articles appeared on how to improve skills for the job, such as in the area of salesmanship,[65] or on new developments in office work. Reflecting the tremendous changes that were taking place in office management, in-house journals often carried articles that educated staff on various advances in information and communication technology, from typewriters and filing systems[66] to mechanical accounting machines[67] and the telephone.[68] Regarding the latter, in much the same way as people today debate the advantages and disadvantages of e-mail, staff were encouraged to consider the pros and cons of the telephone – a time-saver on the one hand, encouraging of verbosity and too-speedy answers to enquiries on the other – and reflect upon this in their use of the telephone at work.[69] Staff were taught how to converse correctly on the telephone, and also how to protect the equipment: 'dust your telephone regularly, replace the receiver with the earpiece down after use, keep the cords free from knots and leave the telephone ready for the next person who is to use it'.[70]

A major role of the staff magazine was to keep workers informed of activities and personnel elsewhere in organizations that were rapidly increasing in size, potentially inducing alienation and breakdowns in internal communication. Awareness of the difficulties of communication brought about by enlargement was illustrated in a humorous cartoon published in 1921 in an issue of *The Pheasant*, magazine of Jurgens Ltd, which depicts staff using megaphones to talk to each other and making their way around the workplace on conveyor belts.[71]

It was not only that production or service units were expanding naturally, as trade increased. Expansion also resulted from merger activity. The amalgamation shortly after the First World War of the London and Thames Haven Oil Wharves Company and the London Oil Storage Company (two rival but geographically distant oil storage firms on the Thames and its estuary) prompted the formation of an in-house magazine, *The Thalos Review*. The first issue of the magazine explained that its purpose was 'communal', to enable people to 'get into touch' with fellow workers 40 miles away, to 'make the real connection between us more apparent'.[72] The subtitles of *The Home and Colonial Stores Magazine* ('A Link Between the Staffs of the Home and Colonial Stores Ltd. and its Associate Companies') and *The Black Diamond* ('For Circulation Among the Staff of William Cory & Son, Ltd., and Associated Companies') are self-indicative of the honeycombed structure of large early-twentieth-century companies.

Acknowledging that each member of the Home and Colonial Stores was a small cog-wheel in a vast machine, a global company machine in fact, the editor of the company's staff magazine explained that the organization and its associated Companies

> have assumed such wide proportions and cover so immense a field, that it is thought highly desirable to try and link up more closely in bonds of mutual interest the thousands connected with the organisation. It is a matter of regret – yet unavoidable – that the members of the staff in Aberdeen are not able to be on close terms of intimacy and friendship with the staff at Penzance; that the Directors cannot be personally acquainted with each of the members; but it is hoped this Magazine will forge a common bond which will tend to bring all those concerned in the fortunes of the Home and Colonial Stores into closer touch with one another.[73]

The staff magazine was seen by management as a means of 'getting together': 'It is difficult for the departments, offices, factory and workrooms, owing to their remoteness, to become fully acquainted with each other … Therefore, we hope that this [magazine] will form another link in the chain.[74]

Of *The Prudential Bulletin*, first published in May 1920, it was believed that it would supply 'timely information on knotty points and general matters as they crop up, [and] will avoid a great deal of correspondence'. The first number of the magazine was said to assume

> the character of a composite circular containing useful hints from various Departments upon points that are continually arising in the course of correspondence received from the outdoor staff [insurance salesmen in the field] … and to give and receive through its columns a steady stream of mutual assistance.[75]

This purpose was recognized by one of its readers when in its second issue he described the magazine as 'A Mart and Exchange of Prudential ideas'.[76]

The avoidance of a cellular outlook was also the mission of the Anglo-Persian Oil Company's *APOC Magazine*. The magazine's aim was 'to assist the liaison between the various associated and subsidiary companies from whose [sic] articles and interesting items of news are received from time to time'. The aim was to produce a reading public 'covering a wide field, covering in fact the complete orbit of the company'.[77] The purpose of inaugurating a staff magazine in the company was spelt out by the chairman, Sir Charles Greenway:

> This is a company of which we can all be proud. Its very immensity, however, and the rapidity with which it has developed, make it that much more difficult for the individual worker to keep in touch with all its activities. The salesman is apt to forget the chemist, the refiner may overlook the work of the engineer, both are perhaps not so much aware as they should be of the officers and crews who conduct our tankers over the oceans, and all know little of the geologist who seeks oil for us in every corner of the earth. It is important, therefore, that the members of all these different branches of the Company's operations should be brought into touch with one another and that everyone should become familiar not only with its own special field of work but with what is being done by others to assist in building up and consolidating the structure of this huge undertaking. This is the purpose and ideal which have led to the publication of a Company magazine ... that it will increase our knowledge of our own Company and of the oil industry in general, that it will make everyone better acquainted with the various branches of the organization.[78]

In 1895 the soap manufacturer Lever Brothers launched its first magazine, the *Port Sunlight Monthly Journal*. It promoted itself, on its title page, as 'by far the best means of combining the component parts of our varied [company] life into a whole'.[79] Cohesion through the communication of information and the building of knowledge in the workforce was the stated aim of its successor publication *Progress*, the front cover of which informed its readers that it was 'a means of inter-communication between the Head Office and Works at Port Sunlight [the company's model factory], the Branch Offices in the United Kingdom, and the Offices, Agencies, Oil Mills and Affiliated Companies Abroad'.[80] Intrinsic to the *Progress* project was the desire to see the organization learn more effectively. The magazine was seen as a substitute for the decline in personal communication between management and worker which was a natural consequence of the enlargement of the firm. It was also seen as a way of bringing members of the workforce into contact with each other, a 'vehicle of inter–communication between all the members of our staff in all parts of the world'.[81]

In Wates Limited the company's chairman was in no doubt as to the value of the staff magazine, *Wates House News*. In a personal message printed in the inaugural issue, he noted

> a real need for a journal which will help to knit us together and to keep each in touch with the activities of the other ... the magazine, which, whilst retaining its light and humorous side, can also do a great deal of good in disseminating some of the vast store of expert knowledge which is available in the firm ... I hope that the serious and educational side will receive its due share of attention.[82]

One of the features of *Wates House News* was a regular 'around the departments of the organization' column. Such columns were very common in early staff magazines and matched their objective of organizational learning.[83] *Our Magazine* ran a monthly column titled 'In the Provinces', with reports from various motor insurance offices around the country. The *Brown Muff Bulletin* started a light-hearted 'Page of Personalities' series in 1930, depicting caricatures of the various heads of departments and a light-hearted description of their jobs and domains.

An important aspect of the staff magazine in regard to organizational learning was the correspondence column, which facilitated not just social exchange but also reflective commentary on operational matters. It was a place where, it was said, staff could 'get in touch with each other, give expression to our views, vent our thoughts and glean instructive information'.[84] Occasionally correspondence about the company came from outside it. The *Marlbeck Annual* carried in each issue an essay by a 'visitor' to the company, from which employees could learn supposedly objective lessons about their working environment.

A final organizational learning facility offered by the staff magazine was in the area of what we now term social networking. A good proportion of the staff magazine of the oil company Shell in the 1930s, aptly named *The Pipe Line*, was devoted to individual members of staff and might include: news from the company's workers in the Dutch East Indies; reports of births of children to company employees; news about personnel changes gathered from installations and divisions of the company around the country; obituaries; and news of social activities and clubs.[85] Also published in the 1930s, the *Marlbeck Annual* carried detailed accounts of the year's social networking, including the annual dinner-dance, photography and cartoon competitions and swimming, cricket and rambling clubs. Essays by staff who had been on holiday or who had travelled on behalf of the company were often published. In both wars, news of staff in the forces occupied a large amount of space.[86] One magazine, quoting a counterpart in the United States, wanted to hear from anyone who had 'taken a vacation, married ... bought a horse ... made a speech ... received a rise, won anything, done anything, been in a fight ... because that's news'.[87]

INFORMATION FOR EDUCATION AND CULTURE

Aside from being 'interesting and entertaining', staff magazines aimed to 'elevate and instruct'.[88] Magazines had to have a light-hearted side to maintain popularity. On the back of this, they were able to serve up more educational and cultural fare. Editors were quite serious about the literary and professional merit of their enterprises: 'We herewith enter the charmed circle of journalistic enterprise', wrote the editor of one magazine.[89] Another described his publication as 'a young shoot on the tree of literature'.[90] Articles on how to tidy the garden, or on the history of board games,[91] jostled for position alongside more heavyweight offerings. The *Tanzaro Magazine* is a good example of a sober, cultural publication that aimed to scale the literary heights (appropriate for a company, Jewsbury and Brown Ltd, that produced non-alcoholic wines, squashes and cordials). The first four issues in 1930 contained a lengthy serialized story. The *Marlbeck Annual* ran an annual literary competition.[92] The *Carrow Work Magazine* carried a good deal of educational and cultural content: for example, articles on 'The Sun, The Moon and the Stars', and on 'Life at a German Technical College'.[93] Front covers were often artistic, conveying a sense of cultural worth (Figure 7.1).

By aiming to elevate educationally and culturally, staff magazines hoped to enhance the capacity of employees to 'make' knowledge, to exploit the store of tacit knowledge – to borrow from the 'knowledge management' lexicon – owned by each individual in the organization. As if anticipating knowledge management's teaching, in the late twentieth century, of the importance of 'tacit knowledge', magazines recognized 'a desire amongst some of the staff, for an opportunity of expressing themselves upon subjects and topics with which they are conversant, and ... to discover the hidden talent, or maybe to secure a resurrection of those talents which have lain dormant'.[94] One magazine hoped its launch would provide 'an outlet for those talents which at present remain dormant, waiting perchance for a little encouragement to blossom forth'.[95] The *Aquarius* was direct in its stated aim of building up a body of contributors with literary talent, and a series of short stories duly flowed from the pens of staff. The *Carrow Works Magazine* anticipated that its publication would add 'a fresh store to the literary interests' of the people connected with the company and encourage 'talents which might otherwise remain undiscovered'.[96] One objective appeared to be the fostering of latent talent, and the showcasing of it in competition with the output of other staff magazines and, by definition, the quality of the staff of rival companies.[97]

Many magazines attempted to educate their readers to look beyond their immediate jobs and learn about wider matters affecting the company's business – what one might call 'collateral information'.[98] Articles frequently appeared inviting employees to keep up with the wider developments, technical and otherwise, in the sectors in which their companies operated. *The Thalos Review* was assiduous in providing collateral information for its readers, with each issue having a section titled 'Technical Matters'.[99] The title 'Rayon – its virtues and failings', which appeared in the *Marlbeck Annual*,[100] tells its own story in this regard. Readers of *Our Magazine* were able to keep up with developments in the insurance and motor industries via extracts and articles reprinted from newspapers and journals. Readers of *The Aquarius* were kept up to date with articles on water policy and the water industry. The typical content of *Wates News* in the late 1940s comprised motivational messages from managements as well as news about people in the company, but it also contained news about contracts, building technology and the building industry generally, as well as wider issues such as the economy and the labour market.

Unlike in the early phases of industrialization in Britain,[101] companies were very keen that their workforces became more broadly educated, whether through the staff magazine or externally. The magazine of the retailer Brown, Muff and Co. advised that

> Knowledge is all around you waiting to be picked up. You can borrow books from the local libraries and from us [from the company's library]. Excellent night-school and technical lectures can be attended ... aim at acquiring the widest knowledge possible about the class of merchandise that you handle and extend the study of the merchandise to the firms making it.[102]

Technical education achievements and qualifications obtained externally were publicized and celebrated in a 'gallery of fame' way.[103]

INFORMATION, HERITAGE AND THE CORPORATE MEMORY

A main component of the pre-computer information management revolution was the planned construction of the corporate memory. This was achieved through procedures for keeping and organizing records.[104] Corporate memory was also strengthened by the appearance of detailed internal administrative reports. As companies grew larger and more complex, there was a need to distil administrative procedures into internal assessments which could prove useful to future planners. For example, the exigencies of the First World War encouraged officers in MI5, Britain's counter-intelligence agency, to write a series of summaries, and reports on the organization's administrative arrangements were commissioned and written shortly after the war.[105] As they grew in stature and longevity, companies began to feel the need to write their histories – to reflect status, celebrate ancestry and benefit posterity. The production of company histories escalated markedly in the early twentieth century.[106] There was also a commensurate increased interest in preserving archival sources, including scrapbooks and files of newspaper cuttings concerning company affairs, to support this emergent form of historical discourse.

The sense of urgency to establish heritage and protect the corporate memory found a helpmate in the staff magazine. An article in Brown, Muff and Co.'s *The Beam* in 1934 reviewed the company's 'wonderful progress during the past twenty-five years'.[107] The *Thalos Review* reprinted reports on the recent business history of the company that had first appeared in the *Financial Times*. In the frequent periodic reviews of changes in, and performance of, companies over the previous year or longer time span,[108] writers were clearly aware that they were contributing to a historical record for the future: 'We like to feel that our "Annual" [magazine] will live as our History Recorder', wrote one editor.[109] A number of magazines printed reminiscences of work in the company by employees of long standing.[110] In the case of the debut issue of *The Thalos Review*, the importance of an article in which a member of staff offers recollections of one of the branches of the company is signalled by an illustration of his company's site 30 years earlier (Figure 7.1). Adding to the heritage and status of companies, histories of the towns, cities or local areas in which businesses were situated were common components of magazines.

The staff magazine offered historical content in order to secure, or influence, a company's history in the future. There was also an awareness that *current* content would come to have an historical value. 'The hope is that it will form an attractive record of our activities and interests', announced the editor of the Anglo-Persian Oil Company's magazine.[111]

CONCLUSION

In examining the role of the information professional in our digital age, a commentary in 2001 had this to say about the value of digital technologies in moulding the 'networked organization':

> the interaction of people outside controlled hierarchical structures is proving to be a real strength. Team and project-based working, multi-disciplinary

groups, formal and informal conversations, are all emerging as the platform for developing corporate flexibility.[112]

The power of digital technologies in facilitating such organizational cohesion and communication enhances, in the words of the commentators, 'corporate capability'.[113]

The enhancement of corporate capability was also the aim of the staff magazine in its formative decades in the first half of the twentieth century; and like digital technologies, this particular product of the pre-computer information management revolution, although in many ways reinforcing hierarchical flows of information, created interactions between people based on 'informal conversations'. In-house staff magazines are still in existence and have their place, but in our net-centric world the major medium of informal corporate conversation is now the organizational home page, and the links it provides to further pages of news and information, for both staff and external readers. It functions in much the same way as early staff magazines functioned. Electronic communication has added to the range of tools used to foster organizational learning, develop corporate identity and build brand; but these were also the aims of the staff magazine a century earlier. History, as they say, repeats itself. The journey from paper to the electronic, from 'front page' to 'home page', has not been as adventurous or extraordinary as one might imagine.[114]

In this context, it is important to register the immense popularity of newspaper and magazine reading in the early twentieth century, sparked by the introduction of the first halfpenny daily, the *Daily Mail*, in 1896, and the first mass-circulation newspaper to use the tabloid format (half the size of the traditional news sheet), the *Daily Mirror*, in 1903. Both of these publications, and others, went on to achieve million-plus circulation figures in the coming decades. In the 1930s the circulation of the *Daily Herald* and *Daily Mirror* exceeded two million copies each. By the early 1930s the aggregate circulation of national daily, provincial and Sunday newspapers had reached 29 million.[115] As real incomes rose and literacy improved, sales of popular magazines also soared, the appearance of *Tit-bits* in 1881 having expanded the penny weekly market considerably.[116] In many respects, the early-twentieth-century newspaper and popular magazine were the 'internet broadband' of their day and it was within this broad culture of popular, ephemeral reading that the staff magazine flourished.

Beyond any broad cultural drivers of the development of the early staff magazine, the major context in which the medium grew was the revolution in pre-computer information management beginning in the late nineteenth century. The new techniques and technologies of this revolution were a response to the growing size and complexity of organizations and their operations. In-house journalism was seen as a new and useful instrument of business leadership in the struggle – against a backdrop of increasingly hostile international markets – to bridge the gaps in internal communications; combat the effects of increasing intensity of work, and reduce workforce alienation; and ameliorate the specialization that corporate enlargement and the changing structure of industries and services were bringing about. At a time when production and the workplace were being subjected to streamlining, rationalization and new scientific methods of management, the staff magazine offered explanations of these changes and strategies for coping with them, including the dissemination of messages from management that attempted to motivate staff and humanize the organization, and the issuing of instructions and information (both top-down and shared) that in today's lexicon would be termed 'organizational learning'.

A series of fairly basic questions on the subject of embryonic in-house journalism remain unanswered. What was its scale? How many organizations produced staff journals? What were the rates of circulation? What was the scope of in-house journalism, in terms of publications being located in the single workplace, or in divisional, regional, national or international arenas? What degree of editorial independence existed? What formats were adopted – for example, newsletter, newspaper, magazine? Was the type of company and the sector in which it operated a variable in determining the form and content of magazines? Who were the editors and other staff associated with the editing, and indeed production, of in-house journals? What were their backgrounds, and what degree and type of professionalism did they bring to the job? Finding answers to these questions will be helpful in any further investigation of the early staff magazine as a means of information management which – though only one of many perspectives through which the subject can be examined – commands attention by virtue of the intensity of interest that currently exists in the information society and its historical foundations.

NOTES

1. Please note that abbreviations used in the notes have been expanded in the list of abbreviations on pp. xi–xii of this volume. For examples of the literature on the early information society see, E. Black (2001), *IBM and the Holocaust: The Strategic Alliance between Nazi Germany and America's Most Powerful Corporation* (London: Little, Brown); A. Black, D. Muddiman and H. Plant (2007), *The Early Information Society: Information Management in Britain before the Computer* (Aldershot: Ashgate); W. Rayward (ed.) (2008), *European Modernism and the Information Society* (Aldershot: Ashgate); E. Higgs (2004), *The Information State in England* (Basingstoke: Palgrave Macmillan); T. Weller (2009), *The Victorians and Information: A Social and Cultural History* (Saarbrücken: VDM Verlag).

2. *TBD* (1925) 3 (3), p. 1.
3. Office Management Association (1952) *Office Administrative Practices* (London), p. 29.
4. As reported in its successor, *PSN* (1922) November, p. 1.
5. *BPM* (1956) XXXII (4), August, p. 2.
6. As reported in *TP* (1921), March, p. 31; 'Report on Works Magazines' (1940), 8 March, Mass Observation Archive, University of Sussex.
7. J. Griffiths, (1999), 'Exploring Corporate Culture: The Potential of Company Magazines for the Business Historian', *Business Archives: Sources and History*, 78, November, pp. 27–37.
8. The London and Thames Haven Oil Wharves and the London Oil Storage Company.
9. In order to facilitate flows of information through the organization it was advised that, amongst other means, a staff magazine, or 'office gazette', be produced monthly: suggested memo on subject index (by Capt. Holroyd), National Archives, KV1/53, Annexure 11, and KV1/63, Sections 15 and 16.
10. For example, *The Wicket*, the magazine of the Sheffield Public Libraries Staff Association in the 1930s; and *The Guyoscope*, magazine of the staff of Guy's Hospital, London, first published in 1905.
11. G. Hamel (1998), 'The E-Corporation', *Fortune*, http://www.strategos.com/articles/ecorp.htm. [Date accessed 21 May 2009.]
12. S. Hudson (2000–01), 'Just-in-Time Knowledge', *Knowledge Management*, 4 (4), December–January, pp. 11–15.
13. For example, 'Our Company, 1896–1922', *TBD* (1922) November, pp. 5–6.
14. J. Yates (1989), *Control through Communication: The Rise of System in American Management* (Maryland and London: Johns Hopkins University Press).
15. A. Chandler (1992), 'Organisational Capabilities and the Economic History of the Industrial Enterprise', *Journal of Economic Perspectives*, 6 (3), Summer, pp. 79–100.
16. L. Hannah (1976), *The Rise of the Corporate Economy* (London: Methuen).
17. J. Agar (2003), *The Government Machine: A Revolutionary History of the Computer* (London: MIT Press).
18. J. Beniger (1986), *The Control Revolution: Technological and Economic Origins of the Information Society* (Massachusetts: Harvard University Press); J. Orbell (1991), 'The Development of Office Technology', in A. Turton (ed.), *Managing Business Archives* (Oxford: British Archives Council), pp. 60–83.
19. C. Argyris and D. Schön (1978), *Organisational Learning: A Theory of Action Perspective* (Reading, Massachusetts: Addison-Wesley Publishing).
20. Frederick Taylor's words in 1912 to a House Committee of the United States Congress investigating practices of 'scientific management', quoted in M. McElroy (2003), *The New Knowledge Management: Complexity, Learning, and Sustainable Innovation* (London: Butterworth Heinemann), xxiii.
21. I. Nonaka and H. Takeuchi (1995), *The Knowledge-Creating Company: How Japanese Companies Create the Dynamics of Innovation* (Oxford: Oxford University Press), p. 3, state that 'organisational knowledge creation' is the 'capability of a company as a whole to create new knowledge, disseminate it throughout the organisation, and embody it in products, services and systems'.

22. See especially T. Wilson (2002), 'The Nonsense of Knowledge Management', *Information Research*, 8 (1), October, http://informationr.net/ir/8–1/paper144.html. [Date accessed 12 April 2009.]

23. Adapted from the definition of 'information management' given in *The Competitive Intelligence Glossary*, http://www.quantum3.co.za/CI%20Glossary.htm. [Date accessed 21 May 2009].

24. McElroy, *The New Knowledge Management*, pp. 13–15.

25. A. McIvor (2001), *A History of Work in Britain, 1880–1950* (Basingstoke and New York: Palgrave Macmillan).

26. McIvor, *A History of Work in Britain*, p. 243.

27. An example of such social-welfare benefits is that provided by the West Midlands iron manufacturer John Lysaght (see entry in *Oxford Dictionary of National Biography*) who operated a humanitarian system which, in the 1880s, included the provision of a factory canteen, a large meeting hall and recreation centre, a well-stocked library and a sick and medical club for the workforce.

28. First published in January 1923.

29. *WHS* (1935), 1, p. 1.

30. *THCSM* (1920), November, p. 1.

31. As in the case of *TTR* (1920), June, p. 2

32. Stated on title page of *PSMJ* (1896), 2 (1).

33. *PR* (1899), October, p. 2.

34. *TBD* (1922), November, p. 3.

35. For example *TB* (1934), January, p. 1.

36. For example *MA* (1936), Christmas, 1; *TBD* (1924), April–June, p. 30. Such involvement has also been noted as early as the 1840s in terms of public contributions to popular periodicals such as the Illustrated London News. See T. Weller (2008), 'Preserving Knowledge through Popular Victorian Periodicals: An Examination of the Penny Magazine and the *Illustrated London News*, 1842–1843', *Library History*, 24 (3), pp. 200–8; and T. Weller (2009), *The Victorians and Information: A Social and Cultural History* (Saarbrücken: VDM Verlag).

37. As illustrated in 'Managers, past and present', *TCWM* (1908), April, pp. 83–5.

38. For example, see early issues of *OM*, commencing in January 1923.

39. 'A Day in the Life of a Branch Manager', *OM* (1927), December, pp. 259–60.

40. For example, *MA* (1938), Christmas, p. 5.

41. *TP* (1920), June, p. 2.

42. *TP* (1921), March, p. 31.

43. *TCWM* (1907), October, p. 3.

44. I. Spurr (1990), 'An Analysis of the Content of Employee Periodicals Produced by Britain's Largest Companies' (unpublished MPhil thesis, City University, London).

45. Another magazine, *The Call to Arms*, a monthly journal begun in 1916 in Lever Brothers, was inaugurated, as the first issue stated, 'for the information and entertainment of the brave lads who are serving King and country in the Great War'.

46. *MA* (1939), Christmas, p. 4.

47. These titles appeared in issues of September 1922, March 1923 and May 1923, respectively.

48. Quoted in 'BP house journals', *BPM* (1956), XXXII (4), August, p. 2.

49. *THCSM* (1921), January, p. 1.
50. *TP* (1921), March, p. 31.
51. *TA* (1905), December, p. 1.
52. *THCSM* (1920), November, front cover.
53. *MA* (1937), Christmas, p. 10.
54. *MA* (1936), Christmas, p. 12; (1935) Christmas, p. 14.
55. *TB* (1935), July, p. 134.
56. *MA* (1935), Christmas, p. 5.
57. *TBD* (1922), November, p.1
58. G. Bentley (1953), *Editing the Company Publication* (New York: Harper and Brothers), p. 4.
59. Notices to staff and managers (1918–35), Salts Ltd, Saltaire, West Yorkshire Archives Service, 9D94/1/4/12.
60. For example, Brown, Muff and Co., *Employees' Instructions and Book of General Rules* (c. 1918), West Yorkshire Archives Service, 35D78/18. The booklet ran to over 40 pages.
61. *SMBMC* (1933), December, p. 2.
62. Documents mentioned here can be found in R/DH/00, Rowntree and Co. Archives, Borthwick Institute, University of York.
63. *MA* (1937), Christmas, p. 9.
64. *MA* (1936), Christmas, p. 28.
65. *TB* (1934), April, p. 20.
66. 'On Office Systems', *TTR* (1927), March, pp. 16–18.
67. *MA* (1936), Christmas, p. 17.
68. 'Automatic telephony', *TBD* (1923), January–March, pp. 43–5.
69. 'The Telephone – Blessing or Bane?', *TTR* (1926), June, p. 521; *TTR* (1927) March, p. 17.
70. 'Lecture on Telephones', *TB* (1934), March, p. 10.
71. *TP* (1921), June, p. 18.
72. *TTR* (1920), June, pp. 1–2.
73. *THCM* (1920), November, p. 1.
74. *SMBMC* (1933), December, p. 1.
75. *TPB* (1920), May, Editorial.
76. *TPB* (1920), June.
77. Quoted in *BPM* (1956), XXXII (4), August, p. 3.
78. Quoted in *BPM* (1956), XXXII (4), August, p. 2.
79. *PSMJ* (1896) 2 (1).
80. *PR* (1900), October, p. 1.
81. *PR* (1899), October, p. 2.
82. *WHN* (1935), 1 June, p. 2.
83. For example, 'We have to be Fast: Typing in the Sales Department is a Real Hustle', *WHN* (1935), 1 June, p. 7. News from departments was also a feature of the *MA* and the *RG*.
84. OM (1923), March, p. 45.
85. *TPL* (1931), 21 January.
86. As in the *MA* (1939).
87. *TP* (1921), June, p. 2.

88. *TCWM* (1907), October, p. 4.
89. *TCWM* (1907), October, p. 4.
90. *TTR* (1920), June, p. 1.
91. *TR* (1922), December, pp. 227, 233–4.
92. *MA* (1935–9).
93. *TCWM* (1907), December, pp. 54–6, 57–9.
94. *TBD* (1922), November, p. 1.
95. *OM* (1923), January, p. 1.
96. *TCWM* (1907), October, p. 3.
97. *TBD* (1922), November, p. 4.
98. Bentley, *Editing the Company Publication*, p. 81.
99. Containing articles, for example, on castor oil, oil storage tanks and whale oil.
100. *MA* (1936), Christmas, p. 68.
101. It is argued that in the era of proto-industrialization, literacy did not necessarily translate into higher wages and productivity; as time passed, however, its increasing importance is undeniable: see H. J. Graff (1981) 'Literacy, Jobs and Industrialisation: The Nineteenth Century', in H. J. Graff (ed.), *Literacy and Social Development in the West: A Reader* (Cambridge: Cambridge University Press), pp. 232–60.
102. *TB* (1937), September, p. 339.
103. For example, *MA* (1935), Christmas, p. 20.
104. E. Hudders (1916), *Indexing and Filing: A Manual of Standard Practice* (New York: The Ronald Press Company); J. Kaiser (1908), *The Card System at the Office* (London: McCorquodale and Company).
105. National Archives, KV1/63, Section 13.
106. E. Green (1991), 'Business Archives in the United Kingdom: History, Conspectus, Prospectus', in A. Turton (ed.), *Managing Business Archives* (Oxford: Business Archives Council), p. 7.
107. '1909–34', *TB* (1934), May, pp. 32–3.
108. '35 years of progress', *MA* (1935), Christmas, p. 59; 'An Historical Year', *MA* (1939), Christmas, pp. 60–1; 'Our company, 1896–1922', *TBD* (1922), November, pp. 5–6.
109. *MA* (1936), Christmas, p. 1.
110. For example, 'How I Learnt my Lesson: By a Machinist', *MA* (1936), Christmas, pp. 66–7.
111. Quoted in *BPM* (1956), XXXII (4), August, p. 2.
112. A. Abell and N. Oxbrow (2001), *Competing with Knowledge: The Information Professional in the Knowledge Management Age* (London: Library Association Publishing and TFPL), pp. 8–9.
113. Abell and Oxbrow, *Competing with Knowledge*, p. 9.
114. My thanks to Tony Bryant for suggesting the home/front page analogy.
115. A. Jones (1992), 'The British Press, 1919–1945', in D. Griffiths (ed.), *The Encyclopedia of the British Press, 1422–1992* (London: Palgrave Macmillan), pp. 47–55.
116. D. Reed (1997), *The Popular Magazine in Britain and the United States 1880–1960* (London: The British Library), pp. 93–9.

8

MODELLING RECENT INFORMATION HISTORY: THE 'BANDITRY' OF THE LORD'S RESISTANCE ARMY IN UGANDA

Paul Sturges

INTRODUCTION

The use of models is at least implicit in much modern historical scholarship. These can be economic history models capable of processing great volumes of statistics with predictive potential, or the more descriptive models that give form and shape to an essentially verbal structure of argument. This chapter will make use of, and assess, a model of the second type, designed to structure understanding of the role of information in civil conflict. An ongoing episode in the history of Uganda, the insurgency or banditry of the Lord's Resistance Army (LRA), 1986 and onwards, is the case under study. This may seem a strange choice of topic, but in fact it responds to a suggestion by Boyd Rayward that the history of the colonial wars of independence might prove interesting from an information-centred perspective.[1] The author has responded to this suggestion[2] and it is a small stretch to turn this towards post-colonial conflicts such as that in northern Uganda. An earlier version of the present chapter,[3] used by kind permission of the editor and publishers of *Information Development*, did precisely that, but without the emphasis on the significance of the model that will be offered here. Part of the fascination of studying information seeking and use in the Acholi areas of northern Uganda, around the provincial capital of Gulu, is that it offers an information landscape of a bleakness that is in striking contrast to the lush natural environment of the area. Only the

155

situation in failed states like Somalia and the Democratic Republic of the Congo is likely to be worse.

In what follows, an attempt is made to model an information history synthesis of the conflict with material taken from the literature on the conflict, looked at in the context of ideas obtained during two short visits to Uganda (in 2004 and 2007) and in particular through discussions with Ugandan journalists in Kampala and Gulu. Before looking directly at information and communication in the region, an outline of the recent history of northern Uganda is required and, since the LRA is commonly characterized as a bandit movement, the relevance of the concept of the bandit needs to be examined. Then some distinctive features of the region as an information environment will be described. After this the nature and effects of the LRA conflict and its information-related elements will be identified and discussed in the light of the model already mentioned. Finally, some tentative conclusions about this extreme environment and the role of information in its future will be drawn.

NORTHERN UGANDA – BANDITRY OR REBELLION?

Northern Uganda is different from the rest of the country in an important way: the people of the region speak the Acholi language, a dialect of Lwo. This is a non-Bantu language not mutually intelligible with the languages of southern Uganda. Until the end of British colonial rule in Uganda in 1962, there was an implicit policy of filling official posts with people from the southern kingdoms and recruiting for the army from the north. A largely artificial Acholi military identity developed on this basis, and after independence the Acholi presence in the army gave them a disproportionately significant role in the bloody and damaging fluctuations of Ugandan history. Power successively passed from Obote to Amin, to Obote again, then to Okello and, in 1986, to Yoweri Museveni. The important fact as far as recent Acholi history is concerned is that Museveni is a southern president who overthrew an Acholi-supported regime. Acholi soldiers retreated north to their homeland, or across the border into Sudan, fearing massacre at the hands of troops loyal to the government. Their subsequent efforts were directed into an unsuccessful rebellion under the name of the Uganda People's Democratic Army (UPDA). The failure of this and other contemporary insurgencies left the region impoverished, demoralized and in fear of the state and its armed forces.

The nature of the conflicts that followed is the distinctive feature of recent northern Uganda history, and the reason why circumstances in the region continue to present considerable problems for the information seeker. The failure of the UPDA and other conventional political/regional movements was immediately followed by the emergence of the Holy Spirit Movement (HSM) of Alice Auma, usually known as Alice Lakwena after her chief 'spirit adviser'.[4] Alice mobilized the Acholi in an initially successful insurgency that pitted warriors protected by anointment with shea butter oil and holy water, and using rocks that were to turn miraculously into grenades, against tanks and artillery. The bloody defeat of the HSM's invasion of the south at Jinja and Alice's escape (on a bicycle, it is said) did not, however, bring an end to what might seem to outsiders the Acholi recourse to the irrational. From the wreckage of the HSM came the movement that soon adopted the name 'Lord's Resistance Army', led by Joseph Kony, reputedly a cousin of Alice's. Since 1987 Kony has fought the Ugandan army with remarkable success, in the early years according to some accounts commanding as many as 5000 men. His success was, however, at a terrible cost to the region as the LRA consumed and savaged its own home ground. Although the LRA has always claimed the status of a rebel movement and characterized itself as seeking the spiritual renewal of the Acholi, the government calls its fighters bandits, common criminals and terrorists. What does this particular categorization of the LRA mean? 'Terrorist' is the modern word to denigrate a political movement that resorts to clandestine force, but 'bandit' suggests a fundamentally criminal motivation. However, 'bandit' is not necessarily as negative a term as it might seem.

It is now 40 years since Hobsbawn published the fullest version of his survey of banditry worldwide, elaborating the idea of the 'noble' or 'social' bandit that he had first put forward ten years earlier.[5] Hobsbawn contended that history reveals certain bandits who, like Robin Hood, were believed to rob the rich to feed the poor, and were consequently something more than common criminals. This idea met challenges from the outset. A recent revisiting of the idea concludes that Hobsbawm's reliance on folkloric and literary sources exaggerated the relationship between peasant and bandit, but that 'thanks to his provocative model, subsequent scholars have dug deeply into the lives of bandits around the globe.'[6] Bhatia points out that naming is an important factor in global ideological struggles.[7] Whether you call a movement terrorists, bandits or rebels matters in the mobilization of opinion and the nature of responses adopted by governments, law courts and society generally. Specifically, a bandit movement is, by definition, denied a claim to political legitimacy. This in turn gives those in power licence to ignore any grievances that the movement, however unacceptable its methods, might justifiably represent.

If, however, Kony and his followers can be seen as attracting a certain level of local sympathy and support they might, however unlikely this might seem on the face of it, deserve at least the status of Hobsbawm's 'social bandits'. Furthermore, their claim to be a legitimate rebel movement might seem more credible. Vinci set out one of the most detailed accounts of how the LRA actually operates, and what this means in explicitly political terms.[8] He then went on to address the question of how the categorization that is applied to a movement points towards a form of response, and worked this notion through in a functional analysis of the LRA.[9] This hard-headed approach to the LRA phenomenon moves the discussion away from natural revulsion towards the deeds of Kony and his followers, towards the kind of analysis that can throw some light on northern Uganda as an information and communication environment. The region certainly does offer a distinctive information landscape, as will be set out in the following.

THE INFORMATION CONTEXT OF
NORTHERN UGANDA

When discussing the patterns of information and communication activity in an area as troubled as northern Uganda, the first thing to remember is that little is what it seems to be. Expectations imported from Europe or North America are quite simply disappointed at every turn. Important communication takes place through channels including many that would not be considered significant in developed countries, and information is often found in the kind of packages that sophisticated communications media generally do not carry. To some extent this is a function of conflict. As p'Lajur puts it:

> There is lack of information, concealment of information, propaganda and misinformation, between the warring parties and the affected community. In order to suppress information, the government downplays any negative image and is not interested in exposing what is going on in the war zone.
> On the other hand, the LRA has never encouraged the use of media in the same way other rebel movements the world over would.[10]

This is true, but not the whole story. Many of the distinctive features of the region as an information environment are rooted in older patterns, which have reasserted their ancient strength and significance. Others are specific consequences of events or policy in the region.

The significance of religious beliefs and the traditions associated with them should never be underestimated in the societies of the developing world. This is certainly true of the Acholi people. As Doom and Vlassenroot put it, 'the Acholi world is a spiritual community, densely populated with spirits, forces and powers.'[11] The despair of the defeated Acholi people during the mid-1980s made the appropriation of their armed struggle by spiritual leaders such as

Alice Auma quite natural. Her spirits, particularly Lakwena, spoke of heal-
ing and purification in ways which caused thousands of Acholi to take part
in the HSM's disastrous military campaign against Museveni's government
forces (the National Resistance Army, or NRA). Kony also received spirit messages, some from Lakwena himself, as well as from others including Silly Sindy
and Major Bianca who dealt with battle tactics and intelligence matters. Like
Alice, Kony established 'yards' in which the purification of his followers and
the reception of his messages could take place. At the same time, the guer-
rilla tactics of the LRA have been devastatingly effective. The spirit messages
received by Kony were complemented by the experienced military leadership
of ex-UPDA commanders such as Odong Latek, Charles Tabuley and Vincent
Otti.

The structures of spiritual communication employed by Alice, Kony and
other spirit mediums are rooted in tradition, but that tradition has been
expanding and changing during the period concerned. Christian influences
are visible in the practices and beliefs they adopted. The traditional spirit
mediums and healers were known as *ajakwa*, but Alice claimed to be a *nebi* (a
prophet in the biblical sense), spending 40 days and 40 nights in the wilderness
at some point during 1985. Alice laid down a series of rules for her followers
couched in biblical style:

> The rules vary somewhat between testimonies but are consistent in their
> prohibition of wearing lucky charms, consulting other healers and medi-
> ums, sexual intercourse, alcohol, tobacco and certain foods (white ants,
> pork, sometimes mutton). Other prohibitions that appear frequently are on
> food cooked in saucepans, eating with anyone who has not been anointed,
> killing snakes, becoming angry, and theft.[12]

Later, a rule that 'Thou shalt have two testicles, neither more nor less' was
added. Allen actually speculates that this might have had humorous intent.
Kony also stressed the Ten Commandments and other Christian elements
in his messages. In the 1990s when he spent much time across the border
in Sudan, allegedly subsidized by the Sudanese government to counter the
Christian rebels of southern Sudan (the Sudan People's Liberation Army, or
SPLA), he also introduced Muslim elements. Traditional religion is seldom a
hermetic system, and in times of turmoil it is likely to be more receptive to new
influences. The important thing to note is that whatever form it takes, it can
dominate thought and behaviour and, by extension, define both the nature of
communication and the information content of communication on its native
ground.

The governance of the Acholi region of northern Uganda since the 1980s has arguably been based on a cynical assessment of how a troublesome area can best be neutralized, and possibly also used to further wider political aims. Widespread and extreme violence against the Acholi people by the NRA in its successful campaign against the UPDA in 1986 has not been forgotten, even though it has largely been replaced by a kind of calculated neglect. Despite major campaigns against the LRA (Operation North in 1991, and the Ironfist offensives of 2002 and 2004) the government's efforts to drive out the LRA by military force have been ineffective and poorly motivated. Peace talks in 2006 at Juba, southern Sudan, failed but by then the LRA had moved their bases to the Democratic Republic of the Congo, from which they raided widely throughout the region and accumulated supplies. A major Ugandan government military operation, codenamed Lightning Thunder, in late 2008 broke up their bases but failed to capture Kony and his commanders. The LRA unleashed a bloody response on nearby Congolese villages and began to add to their basic strength of 600–800 men by a new programme of abductions (Human Rights Watch, 2009). At the time of writing they remain a formidable force, available for hire in the regional conflict and still exerting their threat over Acholiland. This may well suit Ugandan government agendas more than it might seem. The NRA (now the Uganda People's Defence Force or UPDF) has shown considerable military inadequacy. In March 2002 Museveni spoke of drunkenness, indiscipline and laxity in the army.[13] Reports of inadequate equipment and resources have also frequently surfaced. A lack of real interest in pursuing the conflict is suspected.

It is commonly suggested in Uganda and the region that President Museveni has an expansionist military strategy that involves playing off the many factions and military entities of eastern Congo, so as to exert control and draw mineral revenues from a swathe of resource-rich but irretrievably anarchic territory. There are also Uganda's interests in southern Sudan to take into account. Alliances with Sudanese separatist movements such as the SPLA have given Uganda influence over a large part of a neighbouring state that otherwise might be an enemy or rival. Westbrook summarizes publicly-expressed Acholi grievances as follows:

> Support being given by Uganda's government to the SPLA; the LRA receiving support from the Sudanese government; individuals in the Army, and some civilians, benefiting economically by supplying the war effort; some foreign powers' use of Uganda, and Acholi in particular, as a base for fighting the [Sudanese] government of El Bashir; and a lack of trust between the population and the government of Uganda.[14]

Furthermore, the inability of the UPDF to exert control over an impoverished and devastated region of its own country is often attributed to a lack of interest in achieving full control. That is to say, northern Uganda is less trouble to the government, and arguably more use to it, as a military fiefdom. Those who put forward variations on this theory cite the profits that army officers are believed to draw from exploitation of supply contracts, plunder and the presence of 'ghost soldiers' on their payroll. They see northern Uganda as a comparatively subdued territory, threatened (in the eyes of the outside world) by an inhuman bandit, but contributing to the unspoken policy of a corrupt and Machiavellian government. Inhibiting and suppressing communication in such a region has the look of a natural and effective strategy.

The obvious distortion of the communication environment by the prolonged northern conflict takes some very specific and damaging forms. First there is the state of the transport infrastructure. Roads are in very poor repair nationally, but in the north the conflict has made travel on them extremely dangerous. Even in daylight the lush vegetation and long grasses provide cover for ambushes. The north has recently seen the benefit of road-work programmes, partly to facilitate troop movements, but also to create a 'gateway' for trade with the Sudan. If the current cessation of hostilities continues, the benefits of the road works will be considerable. This could include bringing life back to what p'Lajur describes as 'a vast no-man's land along the common border with Sudan, which is [un]inhabited. The rebels can hide there for as long as they want. There are neither human beings nor infrastructure to facilitate monitoring of rebel movements.'[15]

Government counter-insurgency strategy has involved moving the population into protected villages, the Internally Displaced Persons (IDP) camps. Doom and Vlassenroot describe them as follows:

> Some villages are permanently occupied, while others exist for those who go to work on the fields but take shelter overnight in the camps. Villages are often located next to military bases. Officially the villages are there for the protection of civilians, but obviously forced resettlements also serve military aims.[16]

Estimates of the number of people in IDP camps vary over time: Van Acker suggests 1,200,000 whilst others, including Apuuli, suggest up to 1,400,000 at the end of 2003.[17]

The damage to agriculture consequent on moving people away from the land has been enormous. Lack of access to basic market intelligence in the

camps makes re-establishing agriculture and distribution structures very difficult. To make things worse, the economic damage of the LRA conflict has
been compounded by other disasters. The effects of endemic lawlessness in the
Karamoja, just to the east of Acholiland, were exacerbated when the cattle
raiders of that region took advantage of opportunities to acquire large quanti-
ties of weapons in the late 1980s.[18] Once heavily armed, they drove off virtually the whole of the Acholi herd, estimated at 285,000. The Acholi saw this
loss of their wealth and self-respect (as cattle owners) as government-condoned.
'For the Acholi, it appears clear that Kampala is giving the Karamojong a
free hand to further destroy their cultural and moral heritage.'[19] Cooped up
in the camps, dispossessed of their cattle and unable to cultivate their fields,
with few opportunities for employment, victims of poor sanitation and the consequent outbreaks of disease, the people of the region have suffered a painful
moral deterioration.[20] The lives of children, and their education, have suffered
particularly. The threat of abduction by the LRA led to the phenomenon of
the 'night commuters', children who at the end of each day left their homes in
the camps or remaining villages to go into Gulu and other towns to sleep in
locations they felt would be comparatively safe. With family life, education,
economic activity and social organization all deeply damaged by the protected
villages scheme, the population has effectively been deprived of what might be
called 'normal life'. The negative consequences for Acholiland as an information and communications environment are considerable.

THE MODEL

Models that might explain the operations of the LRA, including Collier's
Greed or Grievance model of civil conflicts, have been somewhat inconclu-
sively tested by Jackson.[21] The author's own model of information in national
liberation struggles is less ambitious than most of these, but by bringing an
information and communication focus to conflict it offers a distinctly different perspective.[22] The model takes into account both an insurgent (or bandit)
movement's information and communication activities, and the information
aspects of official counter-insurgency programmes. It is built upon a three-
fold pattern of information and communication elements. The first of these
identifies three *domains* of information activity: the field, centre (or headquarters) and the media. The second divides information activities into three
types, according to whether they are concerned with input (acquisition and
processing of information), output (the dissemination of messages), or information suppression. Each of these types of activity is further divided into
overt and covert aspects. Types of information activity, of whichever aspect,

can then be placed in a rough-and-ready relationship to the domains. Thus, the domain of the field is wholly covert, with both input and suppression; in the media domain activity is overt, with both output and suppression; and at the centre there is basically overt input and covert output.

The model can be expressed graphically as a circle divided into three sectors, with these sectors further subdivided.[23] Arranged in this way, input activities have as their centre a vertical axis dividing overt and covert aspects of input, and the field and centre domains. The arrangement does not then tidily show output at the end of the extension of this axis (which comes between

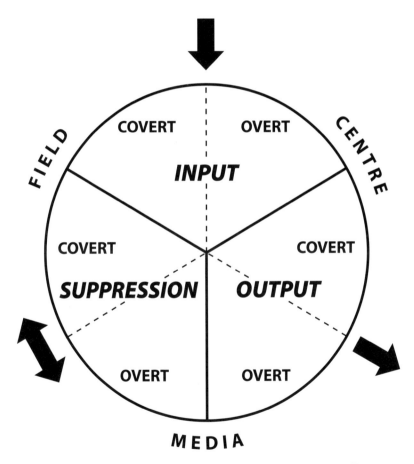

Figure 8.1   Information Model of Civil Conflict, or The Millstone Model[24]

the suppression and output activities in the media domain). Rather, it skews output outcomes to the axis dividing overt and covert output. The skewing of the input-output relationship indicates the non-linearity of the actual circumstances of civil conflict and emphasizes the significance of suppression which sits at the end of a third axis, between covert suppression of information in the field and its overt aspect in the media domain. The model then can be applied to both insurgent and government activity. In relation to the Namibian liberation war, it was claimed that by using the model the successful outcome of SWAPO's struggle could be predicted, despite the ineffectiveness of the military side of the insurgency. Here, the model will be applied chiefly to the LRA itself, as a means of assessing its position on the rebel-to-bandit spectrum, and what emerges is very different.

THE CONFLICT IN NORTHERN UGANDA AND THE MODEL

Centre: Input – Overt

At the centre, the question as to the LRA's true status is brought into sharp focus. The Ugandan government and the UPDF have all the conventional structures of governance and military command, but what does the LRA reveal? The simple answer seems to be a mad tyrant and his henchmen. What is more, the most striking aspect of overt input to the LRA's 'policy' has come, at least in the early years, in the form of spirit messages. But as Nabudere puts it, 'the fact that spiritual forces guide Kony does not mean that he does not know what he is fighting for.'[25] One could also add, 'and how to fight for it effectively'. To extend this a little further, the LRA is clearly strategically aware, as witness its alliances in the Sudan conflict and its ability to identify, take and hold territory in the chaos of contemporary Congo. The horrible but dramatically effective outflanking of the Ironfist offensives of the early 2000s, with bloody raids deep into Acholiland, is further proof of an effective headquarters function. Quite clearly the spirits are not the LRA's only source of strategic intelligence, although the actual nature of the movement's communication network is far from overt.

What can the government rely on at the strategic level? Very little, the evidence of generally ineffective response to LRA military activity suggests. This is not quite the case, however. The government is able to offer safety and rehabilitation to LRA fighters, most of whom were not willing recruits in the first place. The policy of amnesty has been a considerable success and, at the same time, a constant source of strategic and tactical information. The process was set on its way by the Amnesty Act of 2000. The conditions of the act were publicized, principally by Mega Radio, and during 2003 and 2004 there was a flow of surrendering LRA fighters amounting to over 5000. The idea of amnesty seemed to accord well with the Acholi concept of *timo kica*, which means both amnesty and forgiveness. However, the Ugandan government has sought to exclude Kony and his commanders from the provisions of the act, and has referred the case of the LRA to the International Criminal Court.[26] The criminalization of the LRA's leadership has not prevented one of Kony's main commanders, Patrick Makasi, deserting with detailed information on the LRA's Sudanese-supplied weapons stockpile.[27] Others, Okot Odhiambo and Dominic Ongwen for instance, have also reportedly discussed surrender and the consequent prospect of trial in open court.[28]

Centre: Output – Covert

If we look at messages put out by the LRA command, the most prominent flow is actually in the form of the child abductions.[29] There is a crude but effective statement in the very existence and repetition of this policy: a mixture of defiance and threat to Acholiland and to Uganda itself. The abducted children are used as soldiers, workers, porters and sexual slaves, but they are also, at the same time, recipients of and possibly channels for elaborated versions of LRA messages. Vinci describes processes of initiation through traumatization that enable the LRA to control its child soldiers without the use of drugs (as is commonly the practice with other child armies).[30] Taking the argument a little further, Doom and Vlassenroot suggest that

> These young people are thought to be the nucleus of a new Acholi identity. They are supposed to be a blank sheet of paper that may be filled in with Kony's commandments.[31]

The extent to which there is personal communication between Kony's child soldiers and family or community is obscure, but they do re-enter the community, as deserters or temporary fugitives, and carry the message with them. The issue of the LRA mutilations could also be discussed under this heading, but will be dealt with later.

On the government side, there is a considerable capacity to communicate at levels below the formal surface through the agency of the camps. Formal communication in the camps does not function effectively, and the extent to which this is a deliberate or at least accepted policy needs to be asked. It has clear negative consequences which may well be germane to government policy

objectives. The communication environment in the camps has been characterized as follows:

> It is an issue of conflict within the camps, between those responsible for
> the transfer of information, who neglected to relay the information to the
> majority, and the grassroots dependent on their leadership for timely infor-
> mation sharing. In doing so, the [local councils], camp leaders and bosses
> have control over who gets first access to food, medicine and supplies, and
> also who participates in activities, be it talking to NGOs and researchers,
> or participating in political activities.[32]

What is being described here has the nature of messages expressed through
the day-to-day exercise of power over the essential features of people's lives in
a way that parallels the LRA's message through abduction.

Media: Output – Overt

The existence, or not, of formal messages that enter the media domain is a
central feature of the arguments that the model suggests. The LRA is quite
simply not a communicating entity in a sense that fits the expected categories
of media exploitation. The core of the problem is that the LRA apparently
lacks a formal political programme. As Jackson put it, 'the LRA is one of the
most enigmatic of all movements in Sub-Saharan Africa, and it is not clear
whether it actually has any final goals.'[33] Vinci identifies the communication
element of this: 'The conscious motives of the LRA leadership may be impossible to define since they rarely communicate with the outside world.'[34] It is this
seeming lack of political aims, or a will to communicate them, that has led to a
more or less universal condemnation of the LRA as being outside the political
spectrum: simply a bandit movement.

The few statements on programme that have been made by the LRA do not
really answer these charges. A summary of the content of these, reported by
Allen, lists:

- An all-party national political conference followed by general elections
- Creation of a Religious Affairs Ministry to 'see an end to the use of
  witchcraft and sorcery by the promotion of the Ten Commandments'
- Rehabilitation of the economy and national infrastructure
- A programme for national unity based on inter-tribal marriages and
  language instruction
- Education for all
- Encouragement of foreign investment

- Independence of the judiciary
- An ethnically balanced national army
- Improved diplomatic relations with neighbouring states
- Relocation of the Ugandan capital to Kigumba.[35]

Give or take one or two of the more unusual demands, this has elements in common with hundreds of such programmes worldwide. The problem is that the LRA has done virtually nothing to promote this agenda. The occasional distribution of leaflets, a few internet postings and a short-lived radio station, Radio Free Uganda, in 1999 constitute only a minimal publicity effort.

It is necessary to look elsewhere for the true centre of the LRA's programme, and its means of presenting it to the world. With the few exceptions just mentioned, the LRA communicates its messages in ways that would have been just as available and comprehensible one thousand or ten thousand years ago. To describe the message of the LRA as a cry of pain from a defeated people would be not inaccurate. The programme of the LRA is quite simply the obtaining and retention of power through physical force, with human beings as its media and content. Although the intentions behind that quest for power are obscure and incoherent and their actions thoroughly aversive and counter-productive, if they seek power for any reason it is as an expression of a cultural and linguistic identity. People understand their messages, and although most are repelled and terrified by the LRA there are indications of a certain grudging acceptance that, in some way or other, the LRA still represents Acholi goals.

As has been suggested earlier, it would be quite easy to characterize the policy of the government as equally Machiavellian. There is all the paraphernalia of meetings, consultations, policy initiatives and statements, but what lies below this surface? The surface itself is normal. For instance, radio is used to good effect in conveying the official side of events. Mega Radio was set up as a government communication medium (with financial assistance from the UK Department for International Development), and it is credited with considerable success. A form of evidence for this is the reports that Kony and his commanders have phoned in to make points on air and dispute what they have heard. There is also a very interesting press environment. *New Vision* and its companion *Sunday Vision* are government papers in the sense that they have a sizeable government investment, with the capacity for control that this implies. However, the evidence of these papers' extremely lively and frequently quite open journalism, and the content of their independent rival newspapers, suggests that this is control at arm's length.

In Gulu in 2008 there were most of the facilities of modern communication: NGOs and local government had internet access; a range of newspapers were sold on the street by persistent vendors; and mobile phones were apparent everywhere. This, however, is untypical of the region as a whole, and has only been the case for the last year or two. Take the example of a journalist working in Gulu. Not so long ago, he would have found it exceptionally difficult to report local events for a national newspaper, even if censorship was not applied. Word of mouth would be the main means of alerting him to a possible story. Access to the location of stories, if not actually prohibited, would depend on him obtaining a lift on a military or government vehicle. Submitting the story to a newspaper would depend on his queuing to use the fax machine at the post office. All of this might reduce the currency and detail of the story to the extent that it would lose out in the contest for page space. But today, widespread mobile phone access, more frequent traffic on the roads and email contact between journalists and newspapers have changed this, even though the environment remains sensitive and even threatening for the reporter. All of this could be seen as representing subtle and effective government exploitation of media, but behind it is still the language of ruthlessly-applied power.

Media: Suppression – Covert

On LRA suppression of media communication there is little to say. On one hand there is Kony himself as a media user, balanced against the evidence of government success in inducing LRA desertions through the dissemination of their messages. On the other hand, the LRA suppression of media is implicit in the brainwashing techniques referred to above. Looking at the government, it has to be conceded that its interference with the press is comparatively light in comparison with that in many parts of the world. A well-known incident in 2002, in which it temporarily shut down *The Monitor* newspaper, shows it as intolerant of criticism, but surprisingly sensitive to opinion. Its own newspaper, *New Vision*, opposed the closure in solidarity when it discovered that public disgust was actually hitting its own sales. The government then conceded the contest. But once all this has been said, people's access to information in rural Uganda is poor. This could read 'extremely poor' in the case of Acholiland. The street newspaper vendors of Gulu do not make it out to the camps, and the newspapers themselves show little motivation to spread their words to these difficult markets. The genuinely improved access opportunities beginning to spread out from Gulu do not change the fact that for the majority of the population of the region, their information environment is so constrained that it must be seen as a substantial contributor to their abysmal quality of life. Media communication is weak, and direct suppression is hardly necessary.

Field: Suppression – Covert

If the strategy of power and the language of violence identify the communication media and the information messages of the LRA, the use of murder, mutilation, rape and abduction is their chosen means to inhibit communication. One of the most brutal of insurgent and bandit groupings on the African continent, the LRA sends out unmistakable messages written in blood to those in its field of war:

> The LRA's brutality allows it to use mutilation as a method of communication and control over the population. Ears and lips are cut off as a signal to beware of informing on the LRA. Bicycle riders have their legs cut off because bicycles, a major mode of transportation, also bring communication. Rape is often public, as a way to humiliate both the victim and his or her family members.[36]

Less publicized is the history of massacre and individual murder on the part of the government, but its use in the past and the threat of its use in the future is arguably the reason for Acholi discontent and the undoubted sympathy, however slight, that the LRA still attracts. As suggested earlier, the camps are a massive mechanism for the suppression of communication. This might seem a paradox: 'Coop the people up together and they will communicate less effectively'. Of course people talk in the camps, and that talk is unlikely to be very friendly towards the government. But in the getting and disseminating of information the inhabitants of the camps are effectively disadvantaged to a very high degree.

Field: Input – Covert

In this final segment of the model the sequence adopted above can be switched by talking of government field intelligence before talking of the LRA. The only conclusion that the constant failure to lay a hand on Kony or deal a knockout blow to his forces can suggest is that government field intelligence gathering is a near-total failure. They may have aircraft, motorized transport and sophisticated surveillance technology, but when it matters they appear to be blind and ill-informed.

The LRA, in contrast, has excellent basic military intelligence. It could not have survived, let alone so frequently embarrassed the government and carried out as many successful operations as it has, if it did not have detailed information from the field of conflict. To some extent this is achieved by old-fashioned scouting on foot. The author remembers with a shiver of horror a newspaper report anticipating one of the LRA's incursions, because local people had become aware of their scouts moving through the countryside. Good intelligence also necessarily involves the use of informants and agents. At the 1998 trial of Francis Kilama, a Uganda National Parks employee, it was alleged that he used the office radio to assist the LRA in planning attacks.[37] If he was guilty as accused, he was unlikely to have been the LRA's only agent, and rumour tells of networks of assistance and information throughout the area. Effective rebel movements are heavily dependent on local support and protection, and even bandits have their networks of helpers. To co-ordinate action based on the intelligence they acquire, the LRA have not been slow to appreciate the value of modern communications technology. They have acquired satellite phones (over 150, according to Crilly)[38] and used them for communication between the detached columns that carry out raids or form and disperse when their bases are attacked. If there is an identifying feature of the LRA as a communicating entity, it is definitely their field intelligence techniques and networks.

Summary

By setting out aspects of information and communication under the various categories demanded by the model, it can immediately be seen that the pattern found in other conflicts is not replicated in this case. Some types of activity are densely represented, frequently in striking and disturbing forms; other types of activity are basically absent. The LRA scarcely shows any interest in formal communication, yet it has excellent intelligence-gathering capacity. It talks the language of spirit messages and symbolic actions (mutilation and rape), and seeks to press its case through naked armed force. The conflict in northern Uganda is not a classic liberation struggle in which one has reason to expect the whole range of 'gun and ballot box' communication. Yet the LRA have not been simply violent criminals. They have been able to engage a certain level of grudging support on their home ground and their programme, such as it was, arose directly out of real grievances. Over the years they have been driven out of their Acholiland home ground, and their status in their present locations in the Congo is much less obvious. Yet somewhere in the consciousness of Kony and some of those close to him there may still lurk the germ of their original status: that of putative liberators.

CONCLUSIONS

The elements that combine to make northern Uganda an extreme and prob-lematic information and communication environment begin with the common

African problem of peoples and regions that are detached from the states that exercise power over them. This marginalization is, in the case of northern Uganda, made worse by broader government agendas and power strategies in which the welfare of the region has been openly neglected. As Vinci puts it, 'while the LRA's tactics may be barbaric in the extreme, they are rational and are directed at achieving ends. And, even though Joseph Kony may be insane in reality, it is clear that the LRA as an organization is acting in a strategic, instrumental manner.'[39] Some commentators call the LRA a self-sustaining militia, and this may well be the most accurate term available. The logic of this is that the LRA should not be treated simply as a bandit movement, but as in many ways a rebellion that can be addressed by measures that include information and communication elements.

Ideally, the communication aspects of a solution should begin with some kind of truth and reconciliation process:

> Fact-based and fact-finding problems are central to the intractability of this conflict. Distortion on all sides has occurred and continues to occur. Issues ranging from human rights abuses and by whom they were committed to why the war has continued need to be resolved. There is a need for an independent, probably international in character, fact-finding commission to look into these issues.[40]

But this is not enough by itself: it needs to be accompanied by measures that neutralize the threat of the LRA, and empower the hundreds of thousands in the camps to function economically, socially and politically.

Such a secure basis requires not only a more clear-cut resolution of the campaign that the LRA has fought for so many years with such terrible consequences. It also requires that the community should be made fit to move itself out of the deprivation arising from the conflict. A key contribution to such a process could take the form of information-based work in the community: in the camps in particular. Buttedahl and Nkurunziza identify a need for 'civic literacy', and arising from this the creation and fostering of institutions and media of communication.[41] They clearly regard Ugandan government decentralization programmes as offering the possibility of long-term solutions to the problems of northern Uganda. However, they point out that '[i]lliteracy and poverty are also huge barriers to communication. The inability to read and write causes severe handicap when trying to either pass messages up the chain or gain information from local government. Newsletters and posters are only good if you can read them.'[42] A population empowered by literacy and, through it, granted access to institutions can begin, with appropriate help, to put right many of the horrific circumstances of the region. The message is that ultimately ideas, debate and consensus-building are the only effective responses to violence as form of communication, and to the seizure of power as a political goal.

If one were to ask whether this approach and the model used here could be used in other circumstances (the history of information-based competition between business corporations, for instance) the answer would be yes. There are at least three areas brought into clear focus by the model that would repay attention in other environments. The first of these is the primacy of oral communication. Although, given peaceful conditions, people habitually communicate to a considerable degree through written and transmitted media, the extent to which they use oral communication for the most vital messages and discussions is neglected. The vogue for knowledge management to some extent acknowledges this. Second, the role of secrecy needs to be brought to the fore much more than is usual in information science. True, industrial secrecy and confidentially agreements are recognized as factors in business-sector information work, but concealment is generally more common and more important than is recognized. Thirdly, mis/disinformation is widely present in politics, business and other aspects of society. Even the practices of the scientific establishment, with regard to what is true and what is not, must be questioned. In fact, much that is dismissed as 'noise' in the context of conventional communication models deserves to be given real attention. Whilst the model offered here might not work equally well in all information environments, wherever there is an issue of conflict its categories are relevant and revealing.

NOTES

1. B. Rayward (1996), 'Introduction', *Information Processing and Management*, 32 (1), pp. 1–2.
2. P. Sturges (2004) 'Information in the National Liberation Struggle: Developing a Model', *Journal of Documentation*, 60 (4), pp. 428–48; P. Sturges, M. Katjihingua and K. Mchombu (2005), 'Information in the National Liberation Struggle: Modelling the Case of Namibia', *Journal of Documentation*, 61 (6), pp. 735–50.
3. P. Sturges (2008), 'Information and Communication in Bandit Country: An Exploratory Study of Civil Conflict in Northern Uganda', *Information Development*, 24 (3), pp. 204–11.
4. T. Allen (1991), 'Understanding Alice: Uganda's Holy Spirit Movement in Context', *Africa*, 61 (3), pp. 370–99; H. Behrend (2003), *Alice Lakwena and the Holy Spirits War in Northern Uganda* (London: James Currey).
5. E. Hobsbawm (1969), *Bandits* (London: Weidenfeld and Nicolson).
6. R. Slatta (2004), 'Eric J. Hobsbawm's Social Bandit: A Critique and Revision', *A Contracorriente, A Journal on Social History and Literature in Latin America*, 1 (2), p. 30.

7. M. Bhatia (2005), 'Fighting Words: Naming Terrorists, Bandits, Rebels and Other Violent Actors', *Third World Quarterly*, 26 (1), pp. 5–22.

8. A. Vinci (2005), 'The Strategic Use of Fear by the Lord's Resistance Army', *Small Wars and Insurgencies*, 16 (3), pp. 360–81.

9. A. Vinci (2006), 'The "Problems of Mobilization" and the Analysis of Armed Groups', *Parameters*, Spring, pp. 49–62.

10. J. p'Lajur (2006), 'The Challenges of Reporting the Northern Uganda Armed Conflict', in A. Mbaine (ed.), *Media in Situations of Conflict: Roles, Challenges and Responsibility* (Kampala: Fountain Publishers), pp. 72–3.

11. R. Doom and K. Vlassenroot (1999), 'Kony's Message: A New *Koine*? The Lord's Resistance Army in Northern Uganda', *African Affairs*, 98, pp. 5–36.

12. Allen, 'Understanding Alice', p. 377.

13. F. Van Acker (2004), 'Uganda and the Lord's Resistance Army: The New Order No One Ordered', *African Affairs*, 103, pp. 335–357.

14. D. Westbrook (2000), 'The Torment of Northern Uganda: A Legacy of Missed Opportunities', *Online Journal of Peace and Conflict Resolution*, 3 (2), June, p. 8. Available at: http://www.trinstitute.org/pjpcr/p3_2westbrook.htm. [Date accessed 3 June 2007].

15. p'Lajur, 'The Challenges of Reporting', p. 79.

16. Doom and Vlassenroot, 'Kony's Message', p. 31.

17. Van Acker, 'Uganda', p. 336; K. Apuuli (2004), 'The International Criminal Court and the Lord's Resistance Army Insurgency in Northern Uganda', *Criminal Law Forum*, 15, p. 401.

18. N. Byamukama (2006), 'Conflict in Karamoja: Bridging the Information Gap through Human Rights-based Communication', in A. Mbaine (ed.), *Media in Situations of Conflict* (Kampala: Fountain Publishers), pp. 87–102.

19. Doom and Vlassenroot, 'Kony's Message', p. 13.

20. T. Allen (2006), *Trial Justice: The International Criminal Court and the Lord's Resistance Army* (London: Zed Books), p. 53ff.

21. For grievance models see P. Collier and A. Hoeffler (2004), 'Greed and Grievance in Civil War', *Oxford Economic Papers*, 56 (4), pp. 563–95; P. Jackson (2002), 'The March of the Lord's Resistance Army: Greed or Grievance in Northern Uganda?', *Small Wars and Insurgencies*, 13 (3), pp. 29–52.

22. Sturges, 'Information in the National Liberation Struggle', pp. 428–448.

23. Sturges, 'Information in the National Liberation Struggle', p. 436.

24. With thanks to Gillian Veen for recreating the digital version of this model.

25. D. Nabudere (2003), *The Hidden War: The Forgotten People* (Kampala: Human Rights and Peace Centre, Makerere University), p. 41.

26. Allen, *Trial Justice*, p. 1.

27. R. Crilly (2008), 'Lord's Resistance Army Uses Truce to Rearm and Spread Fear in Uganda', *The Times*, 12 December, available at: www.timesonline.co.uk/tol/news/world/africa/article5348890, [Date accessed 19 March 2009].

28. P. Eichstaedt (2009b), 'Congo's Other Killing Corps', *Global Post*, 1 March, available at: www.globalpost.com/print/409592. [Date accessed 19 March 2009].

29. P. Eichstaedt (2009a), *First Kill Your Family: Child Soldiers of Uganda and the LRA* (Chicago: Lawrence Hill Books).

30. Vinci (2006), 'Problems of Mobilization'.

31. Doom and Vlassenroot, 'Kony's Message', p. 25.
32. P. Buttedahl and D. Nkurunziza (2005), *An Assessment of Civic Literacy in Uganda's Local Government* (Kampala: Peace and Conflict Studies, Makere University), p. 11.
33. Jackson, 'March of the Lord's Resistance Army', p. 40.
34. Vinci, 'The Strategic Use of Fear', p. 361.
35. Allen, *Trial Justice*, p. 43.
36. Vinci, 'The Strategic Use of Fear', p. 370.
37. Doom and Vlassenroot, 'Kony's Message', p. 34.
38. Crilly, 'Lord's Resistance Army'.
39. Vinci, 'The Strategic Use of Fear', p. 377.
40. D. Westbrook (2000), 'The Torment of Northern Uganda: A Legacy of Missed Opportunities', *Online Journal of Peace and Conflict Resolution*, 3 (2), p. 11, available at: http://www.trinstitute.org/pjpcr/p3_2westbrook.htm. [Date accessed 3 June 2007].
41. P. Buttedahl and D. Nkurunziza (2005), *An Assessment of Civic Literacy in Uganda's Local Government* (Kampala: Peace and Conflict Studies, Makerere University), pp. 16–18.
42. Buttedahl and Nkurunziza, *An Assessment of Civic Literacy*, pp. 11–12.

9

REWRITING HISTORY: THE INFORMATION AGE AND THE KNOWABLE PAST

Luke Tredinnick

Does history any longer have meaning in the information age? Baudrillard has described history as 'our lost referential, that is to say our myth'.[1] History seems to slip away in the precession of simulacra accompanying mass media and digital computing: ever-present if inauthentic versions of the past overwhelm any sense of historical continuity. Arguably we live in an era of timeless time, or time without chronology in which the very patterns of our daily lives are disrupted.[2] Some theorists suggest we have reached the end of history;[3] others that real historical research is no longer either possible or desirable.[4] In the ephemeral spaces of the information society, history apparently lacks purchase. As an emerging discipline, information history must take seriously the proposition that information itself possesses historical agency. It must develop ways of understanding the past that address both 'information as a central theme' and its 'impact upon existing historical theses'.[5] This chapter argues that structural transformations in the production and consumption of information accompanying the transition to the information society require us to rethink both the nature of history and our relationship with the past. They do so because of the tendency of mass media and digital computing to undermine the ontological stability that writing was assumed to possess in the modern age. A subtle complicity exists between writing and history. In unpicking that complicity we might uncover new kinds of previously marginalized historicity.

Over the past twenty years a lingering crisis has slowly played itself out in the discourse of scholarly history. Driven by epistemological scepticism,[6] postmodernist historiography has emerged to challenge many of the received assumption of historical research, drawing attention to history's highly literary nature. In many ways history can be situated as a predominantly literary activity: a process of rewriting the written records of the past. Hayden White for example described history as 'a verbal structure in the form of a narrative prose discourse'[7] with an 'ineluctably poetic nature'.[8] Ankersmit suggests 'that historical knowledge is as much "made" (by the historian's language) as it is "found" (in the archives)'.[9] Munslow that 'history is best understood as what it plainly is – a narrative about the past'.[10] But while this literary nature of historical research is widely acknowledged,[11] postmodernist scepticism goes further, questioning whether history can ever transcend its status as a literary activity to reveal the truths of past experience. It should already be clear that I have some sympathy with these perspectives. However, I do not find them adequate. The problem of history in the information age is not predominantly epistemological; it is also ontological. It concerns not only the literary nature of historical accounts, but also the ontological stability of the historical trace itself, which shares with those accounts a dependency on the medium of writing. Structural changes to the production and consumption of information have destabilized the historical trace, undermining a key tenet of scholarly history: the idea of a knowable past.

The postmodernist history theorist Keith Jenkins has noted that the *past* and *history* are different things adding that they 'float free of each other; they are ages and miles apart'.[12] The phenomenal reality of past experiences is only rarely seriously doubted,[13] but the possibility of adequately representing those experiences in historical works remains more problematic. Jenkins highlights the gulf between the truths of history and the truths of the past, questioning whether they are ever really commensurable. Most historians believe they are. Fulbrook notes that 'most historians make at least an implicit claim for some degree of truth value for what they are saying'.[14] The incomplete nature of the surviving record, the further filtering, selection and arrangement that is subsequently made, and the re-presentation of those traces in predominantly narrative forms mean that historical interpretations always retain a degree of contingency. The truths of the past belong to the past. Nevertheless through disinterested critical distance historical accounts can approach objectivity, validating their claims against the events and experiences they seek to both contain and understand. The historian aspires to understand the past in Ranke's terms 'as it really was' whilst acknowledging the ultimate impossibility of that aspiration. In this way history can become more than a purely literary or fictive activity. Alun Munslow explains:

> Modernist or 'proper' history bases its claims to legitimacy as a discipline by discovering the meaning of a past reality: a meaning that is enduring and can be described or represented faithfully by the suitably distanced historian.[15]

History is therefore generally situated as a broadly empirical pursuit grounded in the surviving traces of the past by which the past is rendered knowable. Fulbrook notes 'there is extraordinarily widespread agreement that sources are the bedrock of historical research';[16] Eaglestone argues this 'is perhaps the central convention of the genre of history, and differentiates it most clearly from fiction'.[17] The surviving traces legitimize scholarly history, both testifying to past experience and validating particular historical interpretations.

It is in this assumption that the truths of past experience are revealed by the surviving record, not merely in the in the process of transforming those records into historical narratives, that the challenge to history in the information age is located. I want to frame that idea by another passing comment by Keith Jenkins, who draws here on the cultural critic and theorist Tony Bennett. This is therefore an uncompromisingly unconventional view of the historical process, and that it precisely its value:

> What is at issue in historiography – and indeed what can only ever be at issue – is what can be derived and constructed from the *historicised* record or archive. It is the 'historicised' nature of the records/archives that historians access that must be stressed here. For such records and archives are, as Bennett explains, only too clearly highly volatile and mutable products of complex historical processes in that, apart from the considerable amount of organised labour (librarians, archivists, archaeologists, curators) which goes into their production (preservation, cataloguing, indexing, 'weeding out'), the composition and potential of such traces/records vary considerably in terms of their potential use over time.[18]

Jenkins does not explore the consequences of this further, but from arguments presented elsewhere, it is reasonable to assume he might understand the historicized record to function primarily in ideological terms, valorising certain perspectives and marginalizing others.[19] There can be no doubt that what comes to be constituted in the historical record significantly influences the kinds of histories that can be made. Furthermore information professionals in their various guises contribute to this process as Jenkins implies. Elsewhere I have noted that decisions made in collection management are explicitly ideologically situated, even though the information professions tend not to frame their work in ideological terms.[20] Changes to what come to be constituted as the record in the library and archive also change the kinds of histories that can be written. This already historicised nature of the trace problemetises scholarly history's assumption that the past is rendered knowable by what is revealed in the historical record. It implies that historical narratives are already written into the record by those very historical processes to which it also testifies. Information history perhaps has an important role to play in critiquing how information as a product of particular social and cultural contexts, mediated by particular institutions such as the archive or library, and embedded within particular historically situated social processes comes to influence the ways in which we frame our understanding of the past. By telling the story of the record, its production, consumption and retention, it might uncover new kinds of historical experience.

This idea becomes critical to the problem of history in the information age because of explicit changes to the nature and status of record-making; it is the inadequacy of the digital record that causes history to lose its purchase. Throughout the period of high modernity the making of records was generally driven by what Weber described as administrative rationality, implying deliberate and purposeful actions.[21] In information rich societies by contrast records are often produced as a by-produce of our use of digital technologies. Almost everything we do leaves a trace inscribed in the digital sphere. But although information is proliferating exponentially,[22] and in the process both inscribing a more complete picture of our lives than ever before and making possible new kinds of historical research,[23] much of it remains highly ephemeral. The average lifespan of a website for example is less than seventy-five days.[24] This intrinsic ephemerality is exacerbated by the volatile nature of digital media; Conway has noted that 'our capacity to record information has increased exponentially over time while the longevity of the media used to store the information has reduced equivalently'.[25] Digital content lacks *persistence;* the material record often survives unless it is deliberately destroyed; the digital record is usually lost unless it is deliberately preserved. Consequently, while the information age 'will undoubtedly have recorded more data than any other period in history, it will also almost certainly have lost more information'.[26]

The volatile nature of the digital record has led to ongoing concerns about the preservation of digital culture. Some theorists fear the emergence of a new dark age, in which not records survive to testify to present experience.[27] Others fear digital technologies make history itself impossible, rendering the pasts of the future unknowable. Vincent suggests that 'a study based on the written word cannot survive the marginalization of paper'.[28] He argues that that 'we may be on the verge of a new prehistory' adding that

> Electronic communication means no history. The fashion for open access means no history. The mass production of evidence, and its mass destruction on an industrial scale, means no history.[29]

Historical scholarship is faced with a looming crisis of relevancy and legitimacy, driven in part by the changing status of the record within the situated habits and traditions of the information age. But if the volatile nature of the digital record suggests from one perspective the emergence of a new dark age or the end of history, from another it suggests only that there is something wrong with way in which scholarly history has embedded the idea of a knowable past in its persistent written traces. If we want to maintain that history still has meaning, we therefore need to explore what that meaning can be in an age when the historical trace is itself subject to such comprehensive destabilization. Information history must address not only the story of the record, but also how that story might transform what history can mean in the information age.

In part this must entail a re-examination of the influence of historically situated modes of communication on the ways in which we interpret the traces of the past. Because the idea of the already historicised record presents a more challenging set of problems than those Jenkins suggests. While on the one hand the written record is always already worked-over in the ways he describes, on the other writing itself also involves historically situated traditions, values and beliefs. Mayhew has noted of the record that 'both the message it embodies and the medium through which that embodiment occurs are themselves historically contingent'.[30] And following McLuhan we now know well enough that both medium and message must make a contribution to the agency writing may have.[31] But the idea of *medium* should not be reduced to the mere carriers that McLuhan implied; it is the entire set of social practices and values that accompany the uses of writing, perhaps what Williams nebulously termed 'structures of feeling'.[32] It follows that as uses of writing change, from for example analogue to digital, or manuscript to print, the ways in which we understand the experiences it inscribes may also change. Printing helped underpin Enlightenment rationalism and the idea of a knowable past by stabilizing writing in the printed text. Digital technologies are progressively undermining those ideas by destabilizing writing once again. To understand the challenges to historical scholarship posed by the information age we therefore need to explore how the notion of a knowable past emerged under particular technological conditions in the production and reproduction of writing; we need to see ways of historicising the past as themselves products of particular historically situated traditions, values and beliefs.

The pursuit of a knowable past made accessible through interrogation of the meanings inscribed in the surviving historical traces reflects a dominant mode in current historical research, but it is not the only possible way of historicising the past. One of the earliest English uses of the word *history* with something like its modern connotations occurs in Gower's *Confessio Amantis*, written in an age on the very cusp of print. Gower's idea of *histoire* neither implied historical veracity nor any attempt to objectively document past experiences. History was a framework for hanging moral truths 'essampled of these olde wyse' for the benefit of 'oure tyme among ous hiere'.[33] It was intrinsically present-centred. Within a century Caxton used *history* to suggest the continuous methodical record of events and circumstances.[34] What Tosh terms *historical consciousness*[35] arguably germinated in late manuscript culture and began to take root in the transition to print. We might therefore imagine from what has been suggested above that print reproduction rapidly changed the ways in which we relate to the past. But the histories written in the subsequent centuries were not empirical accounts; historical works continued to be ecumenical about evidence, lacking later scholarship's rigorous classification of source materials,[36] and frequently placing scripture, literature, myth and tradition on an equal footing in ways that reflected 'the Enlightenment's pre-historical notion of historical change'.[37] Marwick has suggested that even by the Eighteenth century, 'in their contempt for basic scholarship and research...historians showed an unjustifiable carelessness'.[38] History 'continued to be marked by a combination of moral engagement and literary endeavour'[39] that exposed its characteristic present-centeredness.

It took a more radical break to separate historical writing from the highly literary contexts in which it was traditionally embedded. Between Caxton and Collingwood mass publishing emerged to unsettle the cosy hegemony of literary culture. This reflected changing socio-cultural contexts following in the wake of the industrial revolution rather than any significant shift in the technology of the press. The 1709 Statute of Anne and 1886 Berne Convention enabled the more effective economic exploitation of written works. Abolition of the 'taxes on knowledge' between 1853 and 1861, including advertisement duty, stamp duty on newspaper, and paper duty, further helped emancipate the printed word.[40] Educational reforms throughout the nineteenth century greatly increased literacy and created a new reading public.[41] The Improving transport infrastructure facilitated the distribution of books and journals.

Contemporary commentators noted the change to reading habits throughout this period, one observing that 'people are used to reading nowadays in places where twenty years since a book was hardly available' and another that 'a passion for reading becomes commoner from day to day and spreads among all classes'.[42] The emergence of mass publishing was widely regarded with mistrust; many feared it would drown literary culture under the 'smother of new books'.[43] The inevitable tension erupted in a sustained epistemological crisis of sometimes veiled and sometimes vitriolic antagonism, epitomized for example by Arnold, Leavis and Eliot.[44]

It was amid these wider social changes during the nineteenth century that history became uniquely associated with the idea of an empirically knowable past.[45] This transition reflected not merely an increased sophistication in historical methods borrowed in part from philology and the emerging social sciences,[46] but also a conscious effort to break with the long tradition of broadly historical writing. The first act of scholarly history was to differentiate the new empirically grounded pursuit of an objective past from the literary histories that came before; history was established as a discipline 'independent from philosophy or literature'.[47] It explicitly proclaimed itself a science; 'professional' history replaced 'amateur' history as the foundation of our relationship with the past.[48] In fact, history could never fully secure these claims; its status as an empirical pursuit remained in question throughout the late nineteenth and twentieth centuries. But the doubt was itself sufficient to impress that it could be more than merely a literary activity. In this context it is as well to pose a question put by Foucault:

> We should be ... asking ourselves about the aspiration to power that is inherent in the claim to being a science. The question or questions that have to be asked are 'what kinds of knowledge are you trying to disqualify when you say that you are a science?'[49]

Tosh has argued that 'near-universal literacy raises the stakes' of historical writings by enabling 'the mainstream establishment interpretations' to 'penetrate everywhere'.[50] Scholarly history retreated before the rising tide of literacy into a positivist mode that attempted perhaps not to understand the past as such, but only to secure control over historical writing against a burgeoning literary culture. If the kinds of histories that had previously regulated the past were confounded by the expansion of the presses, the impulse became to re-regulate the past in new less accessible ways. Not any kind of history would now do, only those rooted in difficult to access historical archives and records. The man of letters, a 'whose synoptic vision ... is able to survey the whole cultural and intellectual landscape of his age'[51] was superseded by the scholarly historian; that synoptic vision replaced by an increasingly compartmentalized historical knowledge. History was 'professionalized' in the same moment that literary culture was regulated in scholarly criticism[52], although the impulse to protect 'minority culture'[53] drove the two once closely associated disciplines in different directions: towards realism and idealism respectively. Munslow has suggested that the rise scholarly publishing 'braced the nineteenth-century disciplining of the past'.[54] History re-emerged in forms of new writing that in their regulation of the past sought to both conceal their literary nature and eradicate the influence of the present.

The new empirical history was able to rescue the past from its more mythapoeic field and render it empirically knowable in part by exploiting the ontological stability with which printing seemed to allow writing to be regarded. It therefore became complicit in the values of print culture: both relying on them and amid the explosion of knowledge in the nineteenth century also extending them. Burrow has argued that printing 'made less immediate difference than might be supposed';[55] the real 'printing revolution'[56] was not located in the technology of the press, but in the conventions governing the creation and consumption of writing that technology made possible. These conventions developed gradually as print culture strengthened its grip, culminating in the late eighteenth and early nineteenth centuries at the very moment that scholarly history was developing its empirical stance. Printing offered the promise of an ontologically stable form of writing that would offer up its meanings more easily[57]; the exegesis of medieval interpretation declined as standardized grammar, morphology and syntax each helped secure the correspondence of world and word.[58] The development of descriptive bibliographic frameworks reinforced the idea of textual unity in the material artefact, and directed interpretation towards authorial intention.[59] Text became less a site of the cultural production of meanings, and more a vessel for memorializing individualized original expression. The constant iteration of memorial truths that characterize what Burrow termed 'intermittent culture' was replaced by the gradual accretion of knowledge in a 'continuous culture'.[60] It has even been argued that printing underpinned the Enlightenment,[61] although it is probably more accurate to say that printing enabled Enlightenment rationalism to make certain assumptions about the ontological status of writing which in turn helped secure its progressive epistemological ideals. The printed text became a stable vessel for knowledge, separating the *known* from the *knower* in the processes of its production, transmission, and aggregation.[62] Scholarly history drew itself up on the scaffolding of essentially metaphysical notions about the ontological status of writing and its epistemological function that largely reflected the conventions of print reproduction.

The ontological stable text helped imply the putative objectivity of historical accounts. Munslow has argued that the separation of knower and known is central to modernist historiography.[63] Scholarly history depended on the notion that the truths of the past exist independently of the historical work. By isolating the text from the contingencies of tradition, memory, and oral culture printing impressed the idea that historical accounts could be more than merely the highly situated subjective narratives they so clearly were. It impressed that they could reveal the true meanings of the past, rather than merely appropriating the past and imposing their own meanings. In abstracting the individual written work from the wider textual field and imbuing it with an authenticity associated with authorial intention inscribed in an original creative act, printing also abstracted the historical account from the mythapoeic field in which past and present are fused by clearly contemporary values. The finalized printed work also implied a final objective history on which individual accounts could converge. The imposition of authorial authority over the written work was also an imposition of the historian on the real past. The historical work was not open to interpretation because it was already an *interpretation;* any negotiation about the truths that it claimed was deferred to the sources. Scholarly history therefore assumed for itself a sphere outside of the historical process from which it could project its interpretations onto a phenomenal past; a s.phere in Barthes terms 'occupying a part of the space of books'.[64]

It is in the tendency of digital technologies to undermine the apparent stability of writing, destabilizing the assumption that the past is rendered knowable through its surviving traces, that the crisis of history in the information age is situated. The whole social context in which writing is produced and consumed has changed in ways that inevitably influence how we frame the idea of a knowable past. Susan Blackmore has distinguished between two modes of cultural reproduction: copying the instructions and copying the end-product.[65] The age of print generally relied on copying a material product; an original exemplar becomes the basis of all subsequent copies. As a consequence form and meaning become united in the materiel artifact; writing became in Buckland's terms a *thing*.[66] Digital texts are conversely algorithmically produced at the point of consumption; their reproduction occurs by copying the instructions for recreating them during the cycle of transmission and use. Digital technologies have therefore effected the virtual eradication of the material basis of the written work. Digital writing is not indelibly inscribed in its medium, but is recreated with every use. From this apparently minor change in the mode of reproduction the very different qualities of digital textuality flow.

If mass media introduced a 'secondary orality' associated with radio, television and cinema,[67] we are perhaps witnessing a secondary literacy associated
with digital computing.[68] Writing is now thoroughly integrated into our social
lives: we put it to greater and more varied use than ever before. With its use
in asynchronous communications such as email, instant messaging, discussion
groups, and social networking services, digital writing has adopted some of
the characteristics of speech. New grapholects, such as txtspeak and leetspeak,
have emerged to supplement standardized written forms. The emphatic mood
has been extended with the use of acronyms and emoticons to expand writing's emotional range in imitation of speech. These *ostensibly* new uses of writing undermine conventions particularly associated with print reproduction.
Spelling, capitalization, grammar and punctuation are all perhaps used more
playfully.[69] Writing has also become the site of performance with specific kinds
of language play emerging in virtual environments, such as identity play.[70]
Digital writing has become a kind of hybrid of spoken and written forms;
it is both a medium of communication and of record, carrying meaning in
new ways.[71]

The decentralized contexts of its creation and dissemination make much
digital writing resistant to the kinds of fixed final form associated with print.
Writing itself and written works have become more mutable and more malleable. This is exemplified by the wiki, in which the textual work is constantly
evolving to meet the shifting expectations and needs of its users. Digital texts
are often subject to this kind of constant drift. In digital contexts writing is
often highly participatory and derivative; many digital texts do not emerge in
single original creative acts, but in mash-ups, collaborations, and adaptations
epitomized by slash fiction. Digital texts are consequently more explicitly situated as participants in an intertextual space. Their meanings are often generated in the relationship forged between works, both by allusion, and by the
fabric of hypertext itself. Something like this is explicit in the epistemology of
the Web; Berners-Lee has noted:

> I liked the idea that a piece of information is really defined only by what it's
> related to and how it is related. There is really little else to meaning. The
> structure is everything.[72]

As a consequence digital texts find new meanings in the dialogues they create
within their ephemeral contexts, not only through the explicit contextualization implied by hypertext itself, but also from *ad hoc* contextualization that
emerges through search engine results sets, social bookmarking services and
the like. The fabric of digital textuality is geared towards what Henry Jenkins

has termed *participatory culture*,[73] implying a pluralizing of textual authority that goes against the 'stabilizing, individualizing, internalizing effects' of printing.[74]

Changes of this kind fundamentally alter the way in which we approach the idea of an already historicized record situated within the persistent traces of digital culture. Emerging into the contested sphere of mass publishing history could hardly help reflecting in its attitude to sources assumptions about the status of writing that had underpinned Enlightenment rationalism. Those assumptions enabled source-writing to become subject of critical empirical investigation; to become in Eaglestone's terms 'reliable' and 'testable'[75] (or rather *reliable* precisely because it becomes *testable* against qualities impressed on the textual work). Elton suggested that 'criticizing the evidence means two things: establishing its genuineness, and assessing its proper significance'.[76] The ways this is achieved remain remarkably consistent across different schools of scholarly history. They include: establishing the type of source, how and why it came into being, what person or group created it, what attitudes, prejudices or vested interest it reflects, who it was written by or addressed to, whether the author, date and place of writing are what they purport to be, whether it can be traced back to the office or person who is supposed to have produced it, whether it is in the form expected, whether the age of paper, parchment and ink are what they should be, and so on.[77] These tests reveal a number of essentially metaphysical assumptions about the nature of source-writing: that it is essentially stable allowing access to 'the meaning of a past reality: a meaning that is enduring';[78] that it can be accurately described using certain conceptual categories, such as author, date of composition, against which we are invited 'to test its authenticity';[79] that this authenticity is secured against the site of its original production, or 'the person or group of persons [who] created the source';[80] that there is a real distinction between genuine source-writing and later interpolation that can be traced through the material history of the textual medium or 'elicited from the surface appearance',[81] and that there is some direct relationship between source-writing and past-reality that underpins the 'belief in the language correspondence of present word and past world'.[82] History could only secure its status as empirical science against its always-undermining status as a clearly literary pursuit by making precisely these kinds of assumptions, each of which help establish the written source as a testament to real past experiences.

Unfortunately the technological changes of the information age have had the effect of undermining precisely these assumptions on which history established its idea of a knowable past. They undermine the 'reliable' source by destabilizing the qualities against which it becomes empirically 'testable', exposing history's ideas about the nature of writing as entangled with the influence of print reproduction. This becomes clear in the information age because often the kinds of questions posed in source-criticism simply make no real sense when applied to the products of digital culture. Tosh insisted that 'written sources are usually precise as regards time, place and authorship',[83] but digital texts are rarely precise in quite these ways. Writing emerging in collaborative environments does not always have an author as such, cannot always be associated with a single place or date of writing, or to an office or person who is supposed to have produced it. Elton suggested that 'the real meaning of the surviving materials must be elicited from the surface appearance'.[84] But the highly mutable nature of digital writing, in which the same works may be re-presented very differently within different media and computing environments, means that the form of the document is often no real indicator or source or provenance. Because of their dematerialization, the authenticity of digital texts cannot be traced against any material history. They neither wither nor fade. Unless deliberately corrupted they survive unblemished or not at all. The empirical tests against which the authenticity of sources is secured break down under conditions of a mutable, malleable and volatile digital record.

This raises a more fundamental problem with the idea of the already historicized record as it relates to the products of digital culture. Scholarly history had assumed that aside from any deliberate interpolation in the historical record, the effects of which can be guarded against by rigorous empirical analysis, the historical sources would present themselves more or less as originally created, albeit reflecting only a fraction of what must once have existed and bearing the scars of their material history. But this assumption cannot be made of the products of digital culture. Its dematerialized nature means the digital record can be rewritten by silent hands at every turn without leaving any trace of that intervention; only convention dictates intervention should be recorded, and such conventions are dependent on intrinsically unstable socially and politically situated practices. This potential mutability creates an inescapable uncertainty about the genuineness of digital source-writing; empirical analysis cannot penetrate the dematerialized artefact to confirm its authenticity against its material history. As more of our lives are documented only in the digital realm, context-based source criticism techniques also begins to founder; the entire context becomes as untrustworthy as the individual record. The hybrid nature of digital writing, situated somewhere between the spoken and the textual work, undermines the reliability and provenance of the digital trace, and its correspondence with any real experiences it may purport to both contain and explain. Much like the histories that emerge in the oral tradition the knowable past must perhaps inevitably give way to an expedient past that quickly forgets inconvenient truths and forever rewrites itself with every generation to reflect changing concerns.[85] The past and the trace have become irrevocably detached.

There are two ways to respond to this apparent intransigence of digital artefacts to those presuppositions history incorporated into its interrogation of source-writing. It may be that they are so different in kind from the historical traces to which we are used that they cannot be regarded as historical sources in any traditional sense. In this case the history of digital culture becomes impossible until new ways are found to establish the provenance and authenticity of its source-writing; we are bought to the cusp of a new dark age or the end of history. On the other hand it may be that the tacit assumptions about the status of the historical record that make possible the idea of a knowable past are simply wrong. While our values are still largely those of the print tradition, digital textuality is not quite the same. Digital texts resist final signification and stability. They resist final classification and stable contextualization. They are always straining at the edges of their own meaning. But digital texts perhaps only reveal the resistance of all writing to final signification and closure. The medium of writing itself has not changed in any particularly significant way, only the *media* within which it is embedded and inscribed, and their concomitant modes of production and reproduction. If those superficial changes seem to expose new potentialities, new kinds of creativity, new kinds of ephemerality, a new mutability, and a new intransigence to final signification, then we are entitled to question whether these were in fact qualities always present in the written record but to which we had blinded ourselves. And if so we arrive at the worrying proposition that the mutability of the digital record threatens not only the possible histories of the information age, but the validity of all historical enquiry pursued through interrogation of the surviving traces of the past. Not only our future histories, but the whole idea of a knowable past is undone. This is an unsettling idea, but appears nevertheless to be an inescapable outcome of the ways digital communications technology are changing our understanding of the qualities of the written word.

Derrida has suggested that the 'death of the civilization of the book' is inaugurating a 'new mutation in the history of writing, in history as writing'.[86] Where Collingwood famously characterized all history as the history of thought,[87] Derrida implies it is merely the history of writing itself; an affect of the civilization of the book or a kind of trace irreducibly inscribed in the relationship between written artefacts of different kinds from different eras. This suggests that history and writing are inexorably bound; more than merely a literary activity, the idea of history is literally *exhausted* in the written work. The past is fabricated in writing; there is no knowable past outside of the text. One reason for suspecting this arises from the dissolution of the linguistic sign central to poststructuralist theory. Elsewhere Derrida argued that a logocentric bias in Western philosophy distorted our understanding of writing; dominant correspondence theories of language entailed a pervasive 'metaphysics of presence' in which external reality is said to be re-presented to the mind through language.[88] Saussure's critique of the sign implied that meaning was deferred through the chain of linguistic difference.[89] Writing involved what Barthes described as 'the generation of the perpetual signified'[90] and Eco as 'unlimited semiosis'.[91] Any correspondence of world and word was lost in the self-referential play of language; reality slipped away in the spaces between signs. This also implies the lack of a real phenomenal past in historical accounts. The past becomes a construct in the play of signification; a way of 'drawing a line around a vacant place in the middle of a web of words, and then claiming that there is something there rather than nothing'.[92] The dissolution of the linguistic sign is also therefore the dissolution of the phenomenal past in historical accounts.

Although controversial, this idea emphasizes a troubling complicity and duality in history's relationship with writing: it is both the subject of historical representation and the medium within which representation is embodied. This complicity is partially concealed by a distinction that generally emerges in history theory between the two uses that history makes of writing: the predominantly written traces of the past (primary sources), and their re-presentation in predominantly written historical accounts (secondary sources).[93] This distinction establishes a hierarchy of values that insulates the putative authenticity of the historical trace from those various interpretations in which it is given voice, and between which it is subsequently made arbiter. By securing history against the surviving record it apparently resolves any lingering suspicion that the past is constructed only in the historical text. But it creates another problem, opening up an epistemological gap between history and the past that it is difficult to close. Into that gap were poured the metaphysics of the text that helped secure the reliability and validity of source criticism. Theories of history can be characterized as those various attempts to stitch the absent past back into historical accounts without fully collapsing the history/past dichotomy. Nevertheless there remains something troubling in this generally unacknowledged complicity, and in the failure to explore its consequences. It is difficult to untangle the two uses of writing to reveal the phenomenal past. Historical scholarship looks suspiciously like a hall of mirrors in which its own image is projected onto the past into infinite regress.

An illustration of this effect emerges in Carr's argument concerning the constitution of historical fact. Carr suggested that 'the belief in a hard core of historical facts existing objectively and independently of the interpretation of the historian is a preposterous fallacy, but one which it is very hard to eradicate'.[94] Claims about the past are transformed into historical facts only when the accounts in which they appear are subsequently cited in other works.[95] The facts of history are generated in the discourse of history; primary sources are both subordinate to and largely a product of the secondary historical text. Although controversial, most criticism of this argument concerns Carr's careless conception of *fact*, rather than the process by which particular claims are authenticated within historical writing.[96] But the social process that Carr described itself suggests that scholarly history is only engaged in rewriting and reworking previous accounts. History becomes an elaborate language game played-out between historians according to tacitly agreed rules that legitimize individual interpretations, rules that do not formally address the past but only particular uses of writing. History occupies the spaces between the record and the past and does not seem to belong to either.

This socially situated process of rewriting history dissolves the distinction between primary and secondary sources and with it the idea of the knowable past. The primacy of a source is constituted in the historical account itself; it is inscribed within and mediated by the historical text. But the distinction remains important precisely because its helps secure history's 'reality effect'.[97] Barthes argued that historical scholarship exploits a sleight of hand in which the referent constructed in the historical account is projected onto a past to which it does not belong and subsequently used to validate the very accounts in which it originated.[98] This places history in Barthes' category of *mythology*, a 'second order semiological system'[99] in which sign (in this case the historical account) and signified (the historical source) together form a new sign without concrete referent (the past). The rigorous distinction between primary and secondary sources, the classification of evidence, and the props of scientific discourse all help disguise the process through which the historical past is fabricated in the text. History therefore secures its apparent objectivity by assuming a particular discursive form with agreed conventions, and by projecting its own image onto the records of the past. Each helps validate historical claims, but only against the rules of its language game. History can never transcend that language game to root itself in the knowable past. It is in this sense that history becomes 'our lost referential, that is to say our myth.'[100] History has assumed that the meanings of past realities are contained within source writing, revealed by critical analysis. Post-structuralism suggests conversely that meaning is not intrinsic to texts, but imposed by the various interpretive categories we bring to them.

The new mutation of writing accompanying the technologies of the information age does not dislocate the knowable past from the surviving written traces, but exposes the knowable past as a vanishing referent. The value of writing as a record of previous experience is secured against the idea that sources emerges at specific points in time and space as a result of the deliberate acts of identifiable persons, and inscribe meanings that reflect the experiences of those persons accurately, duplicitously or otherwise. In the more participatory spaces of digital culture these associations apparently break down; the mutability and malleability of digital writing transform it into simulacra: signs sign without referent.[101] Real historical experiences are therefore difficult to anchor against particular written artefacts. But the original creative act against which the authenticity of the text was always only a 'useful fiction' implying an unmediated access to intentional meanings that does not withstand scrutiny. Printing helped impress the idea of an ontologically stable text by petrifying writing at stages in its ongoing production, but all writing in whatever medium is already rewritten in a number of complex ways. They involve the working-over and assimilation of other written artefacts, often betraying what Bloom described as the *anxiety of influence*.[102] They are therefore subject to 'the intertextual in which every text is held',[103] being composed from allusions that are 'anonymous, untraceable, and yet *already read*' being 'quotations without inverted commas'.[104] They are complicit in the conventions of particular textual practices, from administrative processes through to the literary work. The text can never escape its enmeshment within the wider fabric of literary culture. It is hemmed in on every side by the patterns of linguistic practice, moulding the writings on which it consciously and unconsciously draws, and being itself moulded by subsequent works. If the meaning of source-writing cannot be secured against the real historical contexts in which it was produced, then the experiences is inscribes cannot be directly reveal specific historical realities.

By changing the contexts within which writing is produced, transmitted and consumed, digital technologies merely make explicit what post-structuralism implied: both that writing is simply not the kind of medium that scholarly history assumed, and that it is unable to carry meaning in the stable and enduring ways history demands. History had assumed that any meaning its source-writings convey corresponded to some real historically situated intention, whether or not reflecting things 'as it really was', as it appeared to be, or only as the writer would have liked us to believe them to have been. In this finality of meaning the creators of the traces of the past are re-presented to us in their own unchanging words, forever condemned to testify to their own apparently intentional meanings. The idea that meaning is never more than interpretation, and that interpretation is always already historically embedded, so that rather than the sources revealing their meaning to us we instead impose on them our own meanings is incompatible with this. By highlighting the mutability and lack of finality of all texts, that intentionality is not involved in meaning, that the traces of the past are lost in the play of history, and in particular that both medium and message are historically situated and temporally contingent, digital technologies exposes scholarly history's claims to uncover the true meanings of a objectively knowable past as a fiction. The vanishing referent in digital culture reveals Collingwood's assertion that all history is the history of men's minds as a fallacy, reflecting only the capacity of print reproduction to construct a metaphysics of presence out of the written word in which the figurative voice of the past comes back haunt us. History is no more the history of men's minds that it is of a true past; it is only the history of historical writing itself, and more than that the history of writing as record: the persistent trace of our attempts to assimilate previous experience into our own lives. We have not been plunged into historical darkness in the digital age, only made to recognize the little gloaming light we saw previously as darkness made visible by desire.

What then is left of the idea of history? Does history really lack all possible meaning in the information age? If the information society has in some ways undermined history, in others the past is an ever more immediate part of our social lives. Digital technologies perhaps allow a more democratic participation in historical discourse. Services like the British Library's *Turning Pages,* the digitization of the national Newspaper Library, Google Books, and the Census online open up access to the historical record, and in a very real sense do change our relationship with the past. Through them the long tail of historical record is put on public view. This has enabled new increasingly personal kinds of histories to emerge, exemplified by the popularity of genealogy, local history and life histories. Technology has allowed new kinds of specifically non-textual sources to contribute to our idea of the past, such as the oral history collection of the Imperial War Museum. It has also allowed marginal histories to find voice in digitally mediated social networks, as people come together across the world in new ways. And technology is creating new ways to experience history in film, television, video games and simulation. The immersive multimedia environments of *Jorvik*[105] and *The Canterbury Tales Visitor Attraction,*[106] or the anachronistic mash-ups of films like *A Knight's Tale*[107] and games like *World of Warcraft*[108] are in many ways no less authentic *representations* of the past than the equally fabricated reconstructions of scholarly history. In the process of making plain the influence of their medium, they reveal how scholarly history had always concealed the fictive and peculiarly literary bias of its own. The fascination with the information apparent in all spheres, from science to the humanities and social sciences, offers a real opportunity for information history to synthesize divergent aspect of contemporary experience.

The truths of history in the information age are not inscribed in the historical text, but remain contingent and plural, emerging in the whole social process, through the entire *structure of feeling* in which we are inevitably already historically entangled. This may seem to imply that history becomes subject to an unrestrained relativism where all accounts are as good as any other, robbing history of any meaning. But the anxiety that attends to the possibility of historical research in the digital age reflects only the loss of certain kinds of claims about the true nature of the historical past, not the loss of all possible rational discourse in relation to history. Are there criteria other than the true meaning of the past against which to secure history? Ankersmit argues that 'it is an empiricist superstition to believe that no such criteria can be conceived of and that prejudice, irrationality, and arbitrariness are the only options'.[109] By any reasonable assessment scholarly history was able to ground its claims more securely than other kinds of history, albeit in a way always undermined by the refusal of the past to fully divulge its secrets. But that security was bought at the cost of the diversity of experiences classified as *history*. On one level this can be framed as a means to tacitly privilege particular dominant discourses through the apparatus of power in the ways that many post-modernist history theorists imply.[110] But more importantly it involves real choices about what we understand history to be. Ankersmit argues:

> The (im)plausibility of historical accounts only manifests itself in the presence of many such accounts...Hence, the more accounts of the past we have, and the more complex the web of their agreements and differences, the closer we may come to historical truth.[111]

The plurality of history matters not merely as a means of warding off society's tendency to marginalize the experiences, traditions and beliefs of the disempowered, but also as a means of furthering our historical understanding. It allows us to choose not only between histories, but also between ways of writing history, and ways of engaging with the past. Ankersmit notes that 'we will sometimes find ourselves...not being able to distinguish between truths *de dicto* and truths *de re*' adding that that truth is 'not the arbiter of the game but its stake'.[112] Scholarly history measured itself against an extrinsic truth: the correspondence of the historical account with 'the meaning of a past reality'.[113] This inevitably tended to atomise the whole notion of historical truth in the verifiably factual statement, which never sat comfortably with the literary nature of the historical account. By contrast, the unanchored spaces of digital culture necessitate the foregrounding of intrinsic truth-judgements. The truths *de re* remain beyond our grasp, but the truths *de dicto* can be tested, not through correspondence or world and word, but correspondence of word and word. The internal consistency of historical accounts, not the external conditions under which they can be regarded as true of false, becomes critical to the ways in which we choose between versions of history. Thus we can continue to dismiss those kinds of accounts that claim the status of scholarship without embodying that claim. We can continue to reject those accounts that contradict the body of evidence, neither because they fail to reflect any true nature of past experiences, nor because they are superficially falsified by surviving evidence, but only because their claims to truth are contradicted by the manner in which those claims have been constructed and presented. Self-consistency in the historical work will come to matter more than its consistency with a true past.

So history has meaning, the past has a future, but not of a kind imagined in the period of high-modernity. The death of scholarly history is only a rebirth of the lived social history in which the past is open to reincorporation into present experience rather than rigorously regulated by the academy. In many ways this represents only a relinquishment of the shackles of empirical enquiry. This does not mean of course that there will be no more scholarly empirical history. It implies only that scholarly history represents one of the many new and emerging ways of forging a relationship with the past; neither necessarily better than all the others nor necessarily worse but only a different kinds of situated discourse with its own traditions and assumptions. The potential of digital culture is in its essentially limitless cultural bandwidth. We are not obliged to squeeze all possibly, acceptable or permissible meanings into the limited medium of the printed book, the network television channel, or the national newspaper. Endlessly proliferating, essentially unlimited and often inaccurate information is all we have. Regulation of this new historical expanse is neither particular possible nor particular desirable; better to simply explore the very different kinds of stories it may disclose. Information history is in a unique position to develop a better understanding of how the shifting qualities of information itself, and our changing attitudes toward information artefacts might transform both our historical consciousness, and how we understand the already historical past.

NOTES

1. J. Baudrillard (1994), *Simulacra and Simulation*, Translated by Sheila Faria Glaser (Michigan: University of Michigan Press), p. 43.

2. M. Castells (2000), *The Information Age: Economy, Society and Culture. Volume I: The Rise of the Network Society* (Massachusetts, Oxford & Victoria: Blackwell Publishing).

3. F. Fukuyama (1989), 'The End of History?', *The National Interest*, 16 (Summer), pp. 3–18; F. Fukuyama (1992), *The End of History and the Last Man Standing* (London: Penguin Books).

4. K. Jenkins (1999), *Why History? Ethics and Postmodernity* (London and New York: Routledge).

5. T. Weller (2005), 'A New Approach: The Arrival of Information History', *Proceedings of the XVI International Conference of the Association for History and Computing, 14–17 September*, pp. 273–8. Also see T. Weller (2007), 'Information History: Its Importance, Relevance, and Future', *Aslib Proceedings*, 59 (4/5), pp. 437–48; T. Weller (2008), *Information History – An Introduction: Exploring an Emerging Field* (Oxford: Chandos).

6. A. Munslow (2003), *The New History* (London and New York: Pearson Education).

7. H. White (1973), *Metahistory: The Historical Imagination in Nineteenth-Century Europe* (Baltimore, Maryland: Johns Hopkins University Press), p. ix.

8. White, *Metahistory*, p. xi.

9. F. Ankersmit (2001), *Historical Representation* (Stanford, California: Stanford University Press), p. 3.

10. Munslow, *The New History*, p. 1.

11. Tosh, for example, argues that 'the study of history has nearly always been based squarely on what the historian can read in documents or hear from informants. And ever since historical research was placed on a professional footing during Ranke's lifetime, the emphasis has fallen almost exclusively on the written rather than the spoken word. ... For the vast majority of historians, research is confined to libraries and archives'; J. Tosh (1991), *The Pursuit of History: Aims, Methods and New Directions in the Study of Modern History* (London and New York: Longman), p. 31.

12. K. Jenkins (1991), *Re-thinking History* (London and New York: Routledge), p. 7.

13. Munslow, *The New History*, pp. 94–7.

14. M. Fulbrook (2002), *Historical Theory* (London and New York: Routledge), p. 7.

15. A. Munslow (2006), *The Routledge Companion to Historical Studies* (London and New York: Routledge), p. 3.

16. Fulbrook, *Historical Theory*, p. 100.

17. R. Eaglestone (2001), *Postmodernism and Holocaust Denial* (Cambridge: Icon Books), p. 45.

18. K. Jenkins (1995), *On 'What is History?' From Carr and Elton to Rorty and White* (London and New York: Routledge), p. 17.

19. See Jenkins, *Re-thinking History*, p. 21.

20. L. Tredinnick (2006), *Digital Information Contexts: Theoretical Approaches to Understanding Digital Information* (Oxford: Chandos Publishing); L. Tredinnick (2007), 'Post-Structuralism, Hypertext and the World Wide Web', *Aslib Proceedings*, 59 (2), pp. 169–86.

21. M. Weber (1946), 'Bureaucracy', in H. Gerth and C. Mills Wright (eds), *Max Weber* (Oxford and New York: Oxford University Press).

22. P. Conway (1996), 'Preservation in the Digital World', *Council of Library and Information Resources*, http://www.clir.org/pubs/reports/conway2/, [Date accessed 3 May 2006]; H. Baeyer (2003), *Information: The New Language of Science* (London: Weidenfield and Nicolson).

23. For example, Brand writes: 'If raw data can be kept accessible as well as stored, history will become a different discipline, closer to a science, because it can use marketers' data-mining techniques to detect patterns hidden in the data. You could fast-forward history, tease out correlated trends, zoom in on particular moments', S. Brand (1999), 'Escaping the Digital Dark Age', *Library Journal*, 124 (2), pp. 46–8. Although naive, unreflective and uncritical, Brand does highlight how digital technologies might enable us to rethink the relationship between the past and the present, and pursue a different kind of history

24. J. Barksdale and F. Berman (2007), 'Saving our Digital Heritage', *Washington Post*, 16 May, A15.

25. Conway, 'Preservation in the Digital World'.

26. A. Stille (2002), *The Future of the Past: How the Information Age Threatens to Destroy our Cultural Heritage* (London, Basingstoke and Oxford: Picador), p. 300.

27. T. Kuny (1998), 'The Digital Dark Ages? Challenges in the Preservation of Electronic Information', *International Preservation News*, 17 (May), pp. 8–13; M. Deegan and S. Tanner (2002), 'The Digital Dark Ages', *Library and Information Update*, 1 (2), pp. 41–2.

28. J. Vincent (2005), *History* (London and New York: Continuum), p. 19.

29. Vincent, *History*, p. 19.

30. R. Mayhew (2007), 'Denaturalising Print, Historicising Text: Historical Geography and the History of the Book', in E. Gagen, H. Lorimer and A. Vasudevan (eds) (2007), *Practicing the Archive: Reflections on Method and Practice in Historical Geography*, *Historical Geography Research Series 40* (London: Royal Geographic Society), pp. 23–36.

31. M. McLuhan (1964), *Understanding Media: The Extensions of Man* (London: Routledge and Kegan Paul).

32. R. Williams (1961), *The Long Revolution* (London: Chatto and Windus).

33. J. Gower (1900), 'Confessio Amantis', in G. MacAuley (ed.) (1900), *The English Works of John Gower* (Oxford: The Early English Text Society), p. 1.

34. *The Oxford English Dictionary* (Oxford: Clarendon Press).

35. Tosh, *The Pursuit of History*, p. 9.

36. Marwick, for example, lists nine different classes of historical record: Document of Record; Surveys and Reports; Chronicles and Histories; Polemical Documents and Media of Communication; Archaeology, Industrial Archaeology, History on the Ground and Physical Artefacts; Literary and Artistic Sources; Sources which are Techniques as much as Sources, and 'Oral History' in A. Marwick (1981), *The Nature of History* (Basingstoke: Macmillan Education), pp. 139–41.These appear to be in order of their validity as evidence.

37. Ankersmit, *Historical Representation*, p. 23.

38. Marwick, *The Nature of History*, p. 35.

39. Fulbrook, *Historical Theory*, p. 13.

40. D. Read (1992), *The Power of News: The History of Reuters* (Oxford and New York: Oxford University Press).

41. E. Midwinter (1968), *Victorian Social Reform* (Harlow: Longman).

42. Cited by S. Steinberg (1974), *Five Hundred Years of Printing* (Middlesex: Penguin Books), p. 260.

43. F. Leavis (1930), 'Mass Civilisation and Minority Culture', in J. Storey (ed.) (2006), *Cultural Theory and Popular Culture: A Reader* (Harlow: Pearson Education), p. 17.

44. See M. Arnold (1869), *Culture and Anarchy: An Essay in Political and Social Criticism* (London: Smith, Elder & Co); Leavis, 'Mass Civilisation, pp. 12–19; T. S. Elliot (1948), *Notes towards the Definition of Culture* (London: Faber & Faber).
45. G. Elton (2002), *The Practice of History* (Oxford: Blackwell Publishing), pp. 2–3; R. Evans (1997), *In Defence of History* (London: Granta Books), pp. 15–44; Marwick, *The Nature of History*, pp. 36–57.
46. Evans, *In Defence of History*, pp. 15–44; Marwick, *The Nature of History*, pp. 36–57.
47. Evans, *In Defence of History*, p. 17.
48. See Elton, *The Practice of History*.
49. M. Foucault (2003), *Society Must be Defended* (London: Allen Lane), p. 10.
50. Tosh, *The Pursuit of History*, p. 9.
51. T. Eagleton (2005), *The Function of Criticism: From the Spectator to Poststructuralism* (New York and London: Verso Books), p. 45.
52. See Eagleton, *The Function of Criticism*.
53. Leavis, 'Mass Civilisation', pp. 12–19.
54. Munslow, *The New History*, p. 49.
55. J. Burrow (1982), *Medieval Writers and Their Work: Middle English Literature and Its Background 1100–1500* (Oxford: Oxford University Press), p. 123.
56. E. Eisenstein (2005), *The Printing Revolution in Early Modern Europe* (Cambridge: Cambridge University Press).
57. See L. Mumford (1947), 'The Invention of Printing', in D. Crowley and P. Heyer (eds) (2007), *Communications in History: Technology, Culture, Society* (Boston: Pearson Education), pp. 91–5; Steinberg, *Five Hundred Years of Printing*; Eisenstein, *The Printing Revolution*; M. McLuhan (1962), *The Guttenberg Galaxy: The Making of Typographic Man* (London: Routledge & Keegan Paul).
58. See A. Baugh and T. Cable (1993), *A History of the English Language* (London: Routledge); D. Robertson (1962), *Preface to Chaucer: Studies in Medieval Perspectives* (London: Oxford University Press).
59. See G. Gennette (1997), *Paratexts: Threasholds of Interpretation* (Cambridge: Cambridge University Press); J. Kristeve (1980), *Desire in Language: A Semiotic Approach to Literature and Art* (Columbia: Columbia University Press); J. Wolfreys (1998), *Deconstruction: Derrida* (London: Macmillan Press).
60. J. Burrow (1982), *Medieval Writers and Their Work: Middle English Literature and its Background 1100–1500* (Oxford: Oxford University Press).
61. McLuhan, *The Guttenberg Galaxy*; Also see Eisenstein, *The Printing Revolution*.
62. L. Treninnick (2008), *Digital Information Culture: The Individual and Society in the Digital Age* (Oxford: Chandos).
63. Munslow, *The New History*, p. 15.
64. R. Barthes (1977), *Image Music Text* (London: Fontana Press), p. 157.
65. S. Blackmore (1999), *The Meme Machine* (Oxford: Oxford University Press).
66. M. Buckland (1991), 'Information as Thing', *Journal of the American Society for Information Science*, 42 (5), pp. 351–60; See also M. Buckland (1997), 'What is a Document?', *Journal of the American Society for Information Science*, 48 (9), pp. 804–9; M. Buckland (1998), 'What is a Digital Document?', *Document Numérique*, 2 (2), pp. 221–30.
67. E. Havelock (1986), *The Muse Learns to Write: Reflections on Orality and Literacy from Antiquity to the Present* (New Haven and London: Yale University Press); W. Ong (1982), *Orality and Literature: The Technologizing of the Word* (London: Methuen & Co).

68. Tredinnick, *Digital Information Culture*.
69. D. Crystal (2001), *Language and the Internet* (Cambridge: Cambridge University Press); D. Crystal (2008), *txtng: the gr8n db8* (Oxford: Oxford University Press).
70. S. Turkle (1996), *Life on the Screen: Identity in the Age of the Internet* (London: Weidenfeld & Nicolson).
71. Tredinnick, *Digital Information Culture*.
72. T. Berners-Lee (1999), *Weaving the Web: The Past, Present and Future of the World Wide Web by Its Creator* (London: Orion Business Press), p. 14.
73. H. Jenkins (2003), 'Quentin Tarantino's Star Wars?: Digital Cinema, Media Convergence and Participatory Culture', in M. Durham and D. Kellner (eds) (2006), *Media and Cultural Studies KeyWorks* (Oxford: Blackwell Publishing), pp. 549–76.
74. D. Brewer (1982), 'The Social Context of Medieval English Literature', in B. Ford, *The New Pelican Guide to English Literature: Medieval Literature* (London: Penguin Books), pp. 15–42.
75. Eaglestone, *Postmodernism*, p. 46.
76. Elton, *The Practice of History*, 67–8.
77. Elton, *The Practice of History*, p. 70; Marwick, *The Nature of History*, p. 145; Tosh, *The Pursuit of History*, pp. 57–8.
78. Munslow, *The Routledge Companion to Historical Studies*, p. 3.
79. Tosh, *The Pursuit of History*, p. 57.
80. Marwick, *The Nature of History*, p. 145.
81. Elton, *The Practice of History*, p. 66.
82. A. Munslow (2003), *The New History* (London & New York: Pearson Education), p. 82.
83. Tosh, *The Pursuit of History*, p. 31.
84. Elton, *The Practice of History*, p. 66.
85. See Havelock, *The Muse Learns to Write*; Ong, *Orality and Literature*.
86. J. Derrida (1997), *Of Grammatology*, translated by Gayatri Chakravorty Spivak (London: Johns Hopkins University Press), p. 8.
87. R. Collingwood (1999), *The Principles of History: And Other Writings in the Philosophy of History* (Oxford: Oxford University Press), p. 77.
88. J. Derrida (1978), *Writing and Difference* (London and New York: Routledge Kegan & Paul); Derrida, *Of Grammatology*; J. Derrida (2002) *Positions* (London: Continuum).
89. F. de Saussure (1966), *Course in General Linguistics* (New York, Toronto and London: McGraw-Hill).
90. Barthes, *Image Music Text*, p. 158.
91. U. Eco (1994), *The Limits of Interpretation* (Bloomington: Indiana University Press).
92. R. Rorty (1982), *Consequences of Pragmatism: Essays 1972–1980* (Minneapolis: University of Minnesota Press), p. xxxiv.
93. Marwick, *The Nature of History*; Tosh, *The Pursuit of History*. See Elton, *The Practice of History*.
94. E. Carr (2001), *What is History* (Basingstoke: Palgrave Macmillan), p. 6.
95. Carr, *What is History*, pp. 1–24.
96. For example, Elton, *The Practice of History*, pp. 50–2; Evans, *In Defence of History*, pp. 75–102. See also Jenkins, *On 'What is History?'*, pp. 43–63.
97. R. Barthes (1967), 'The Discourse of History', in R. Barthes (1989), *The Rustle of Language* (Berkeley and Los Angeles: University of California Press), pp. 127–40.

98. Barthes, 'The Discourse of History', pp. 127–40.

99. R. Barthes (1972), *Mythologies* (London: Jonathan Cape), p. 112.

100. Baudrillard, *Simulacra and Simulation*, p. 43.

101. See Baudrillard, *Simulacra and Simulation*, pp. 1–42.

102. H. Bloom (1973), *The Anxiety of Influence: A Theory of Poetry* (Oxford: Oxford University Press).

103. Barthes, *Image Music Text*, p. 160.

104. Barthes, *Image Music Text*, p. 160.

105. See http://www.jorvik-viking-centre.co.uk/ [Date accessed July 2009].

106. See http://www.canterburytales.org.uk/ [Date accessed July2009].

107. *A Knight's Tale* (2001), Film, directed by Brian Helgeland (USA: Black and Blue Entertainment).

108. *World of Warcraft* (1994), Massively Multiplayer Role Playing Game, created by Blizzard Entertainment (US: Vivendi Games).

109. Ankersmit, *Historical Representation*, p. 35.

110. See M. Foucault (1980), *Power/Knowledge: Selected Interviews and Other Writings 1972–1977* (London: Longman); Jenkins, *Re-thinking History,* pp. 85–6n1.

111. Ankersmit, *Historical Representation*, p. 15

112. Ankersmit, *Historical Representation*, p. 35.

113. Munslow, *The Routledge Companion to Historical Studies*, p. 3.

10

CONCLUSION: INFORMATION HISTORY IN THE MODERN WORLD

Toni Weller

Information has a rich but currently under-explored history. The chapters of this book offer some new insights as to how information has been thought of, conceptualized and used in past societies. There is no single definition or single history of information; like any other historical subject it has a complex relationship with the past. This is made all the more intricate because of our own contemporary relationship with information. It has a paradoxical existence in our own society: on one hand the subject of constant political and cultural discussion in relation to personal privacy rights, data protection, the surveillance state and so on, whilst on the other hand often appearing to be an ordinary, everyday phenomenon. This latter experience is a result of our over-exposure to information: we take it for granted. Consequently, until the information turn of the late 1990s and early 2000s

> Historians have been guilty of not seeing the wood for the trees. We use different types of 'information' all the time in our research in the form of documents, letters, diaries, archives, or newspapers, so we do not easily distance ourselves from these materials as information sources in order to think about information more conceptually.[1]

Information history allows us to revisit established historical discourses and to challenge them. It offers new perspectives on contemporary information debates and concerns. It can challenge the chronology of the information age. At the end of the previous chapter, Luke Tredinnick concluded that

> Information history is in a unique position to develop a better understanding of how the shifting qualities of information itself, and our changing attitudes toward information artefacts might transform both our historical consciousness, and how we understand the already historical past.[2]

Collectively, the chapters of this book argue that information is a vital and intriguing subject of historical enquiry. History is not static: it is a dynamic process which feeds into the present as much as the present influences the questions that we chose to ask of the past. Information history is indeed in a unique position. Not only does it offer a new way of exploring the past, but it can also have a very direct impact on how we understand our own contemporary society. As Tosh has argued more generally, 'long forgotten traditions of thought may acquire fresh salience in the light of changes which are occurring now'.[3] Although each of the chapters in this book can be read individually, some common themes emerge when they are viewed more holistically: identity, the management and control of information, surveillance, conflict, the information state, information design and information culture. Such ideas feed into a bigger discourse about changing conceptualizations of information over time. These themes are immensely topical, and as part of its larger remit information history can have a role to play in ensuring that contemporary political rhetoric about the information age is balanced and accurate, situating debates within their wider historical context and creating new links between the past and present.[4]

The culture of information is a concept that has emerged in several of the previous chapters. Information culture can be understood as cultural mediums of information dissemination and exchange, but also as influencing culture through a broader sense of information as an increasingly important and recognized part of society. For Rayward, the Bureau d'Adresse and the Republic of Letters in mid-seventeenth-century France and England 'represented a fascinating forum for the merger of, or at least an oscillation between, oral and printed cultures', acting as an early form of informal information network.[5] This same combination of oral and print information culture can be seen in nineteenth-century Denmark, through the mediums of the *Illustrated News*, the almanacs and the broadside ballads, as Laura Skouvig has shown. For the educated classes, new forms of information exchange and dissemination became manifest in the modern period. The in-house company magazine, Black suggests, attempted to 'elevate and instruct' as well as being entertaining.[6] There was a recognizable shift from pre-modern to modern understandings of information, to where it was explicitly recognized within society and culture for the first time, as opposed to forming an implicit part of rhetorical discourse.[7] This explicit recognition is a defining feature of information in the modern world.

Information culture can be very ephemeral in many ways, and perhaps this is a characteristic of information itself, seen in the official government census and tax form, the in-house company magazine, or even the earlier promotional registers of the Bureau d'Adresse. Tredinnick argues that 'we might therefore imagine ... that print reproduction rapidly changed the ways in which we relate to the past', but this did not happen because information culture was retained in the written source – until the advent of the digital document at the end of the twentieth century.[8] The digital document itself has offered a change in the relationship between past and present, indicating the essential mutability of history, but as several of the chapters demonstrate, ephemeral and transitory documents can offer new ways of exploring information culture. This is perhaps most powerfully demonstrated by Stiff et al. through their exploration of the nature of the official form during the nineteenth century.

The idea of information design, of the way in which people viewed, read, understood and interacted with information underwent a shift during the modern period. As Stiff et al. have shown, the official form became 'a medium for the conduct of dialogues and interrogations between regulators and citizens'.[9] Arguably then, the ways in which information was presented and communicated plays an important role in information culture in the modern world. This can be attributed partly to new types of information available, as Postman has noted,[10] and partly to new ways of displaying information graphically. Headrick argued that, from 1700, the way in which information was displayed, classified, organized, stored and communicated took on new formal characteristics. Globes, display cabinets, dictionaries, encyclopedias, maps, graphs, even statistics, all presented information in ways different from those which had gone before.[11] If we broaden this to include visual information more generally then the illustrated publications of the in-house company magazine, the Danish *Illustrated News* and even the visual emblems of identification discussed by Edward Higgs in Chapter 2 are also representative of this shift.

The idea of the information state as a vehicle for collecting personal information on citizens tends to be located in the bureaucratic processes and the growth of government of the late nineteenth century. Alternate perspectives to this have been suggested in the preceding chapters. The collection and control of information through nineteenth-century forms, discussed in Chapter 4, is one such alternative. While these were official documents, in the case of census and tax returns, they offer a glimpse into not just what kinds of information were being collected, but how it was composed, and the reactions of those required to provide information on the forms, but who did not always comply. Renaudot's seventeenth-century manual for patients 'to identify on diagrams of their bodies the location of their condition, to describe its major characteristics in detail, to state the length of time during which the problem had been experienced and so on', offers another perspective on the gathering and central collections of information.[12] For Muddiman, the information and intelligence bureaux of the Imperial Institute were examples of organized imperial commercial intelligence and enquiry. Even the English and Danish cultural material explored by Black and by Skouvig was used to collect, control and disseminate information that was deemed 'appropriate' for readers. Crime, conflict and security were key justifications of information collection, as both Edward Higgs and Paul Sturges have shown through the entirely different contexts of early modern and industrial England, and twentieth-century liberation struggles, with the threat of terrorism, in Africa.

In the period discussed by this book, information took on a new precedence and importance alongside other social, cultural and political developments including the growth of the central state, popular and print culture, the communications revolution, literacy, conflict and globalization. The modern world emerged though a complex and interrelated series of events and ideologies, including the changing perceptions, manifestations and uses of information. By the twenty-first century information has become 'a distinguishing feature of the modern world'.[13] Responding to the historical turn towards information during the late 1990s and early 2000s, this collection of essays shares a common information discourse. Despite temporal and geographical differences, the chapters demonstrate how information as a historical category can offer some intriguing new perspectives on the past. Ultimately then, this book offers a series of discrete information histories, but also contributes to a much bigger and ongoing historiography of information in the modern world.

NOTES

1. T. Weller (2010a), 'An Information History Decade: A Review of the Literature and Concepts, 2000–2009', *Library and Information History*, 26 (1), pp. 83–97.
2. Chapter 9, this volume.
3. J. Tosh (2008), *Why History Matters* (Basingstoke: Palgrave Macmillan), p. 7.
4. One way of doing this can be through applied history. See Tosh, *Why History Matters*, pp. 61–77, and also *History and Policy*, a UK-based collaboration between the University of Cambridge, The Institute of Historical Research and The London School of Hygiene and Tropical Medicine, which encourages historians to apply

historical thinking to contemporary global situations and policy: http://www.
historyandpolicy.org/index.html. [Date accessed 27 November 2009].

5. Chapter 3, this volume.
6. Chapter 7, this volume. *TCWM* (1907), October, p. 4.
7. See N. Postman (1999), 'Information', in *Building a Bridge to the Eighteenth Century*
    (New York: Vintage), pp. 82–98, for the divorcing of information from content
    during the nineteenth century, and T. Weller (2009), *The Victorians and Information:
    A Social and Cultural History* (Saarbrücken: VDM Verlag) for the shift from pre-
    modern to modern perceptions of information.
8. Chapter 9, this volume.
9. Chapter 4, this volume.
10. Postman, 'Information', pp. 82–98.
11. D. Headrick (2000), *When Information Came of Age: Technologies of Knowledge in the Age
    of Reason and Revolution 1700–1850* (Oxford: Oxford University Press).
12. Chapter 3, this volume.
13. F. Webster (2002), *Theories of the Information Society* (London: Routledge), p. 1.

SELECTED BIBLIOGRAPHY

J. M Arnoult (1988), 'Peiresc et ses Livres', in C. Jolly (ed), *Histoire des Bibliothèques Françaises*, vol 1, (Paris: Promodis), p. 128.

J. Beniger (1986), *The Control Revolution: Technological and Economic Origins of the Information Society* (Cambridge, MA: Harvard University Press).

A. Black (1995), 'New Methodologies in Library History: A Manifesto for the "New" Library History', *Library History*, 1, pp. 76–85.

A. Black (1997), 'Lost Worlds of Culture: Victorian Libraries, Library History and Prospects for a History of Information', *Journal of Victorian Culture*, 2 (1), pp. 124–141.

A. Black (1998), 'Information and Modernity: The History of Information and the Eclipse of Library History', *Library History*, 14 (1), pp. 39–45.

A. Black (2006), 'Information History', in B. Cronin (ed), *Annual Review of Information Science and Technology Volume 40* (Medford, NJ: Information Today Inc.), pp. 441–74.

A. Black, D. Muddiman and H. Plant (2007), *The Early Information Society: Information Management in Britain before the Computer* (Aldershot: Ashgate).

P. Burke (2000), *A Social History of Knowledge: From Gutenburg to Diderot* (Cambridge: Polity Press).

M. Castells (1996–98), *The Information Age* (Oxford: Blackwell).

R. Day (2001), *The Modern Invention of Information* (Edwardsville: The Southern Illinois Press).

P. Dobraszczyk (2008), 'Useful Reading? Designing Information for London's Victorian Cab Passengers', *Journal of Design History*, 21 (2), pp. 121–141.

P. Dobraszczyk (2009), 'Give in your Account': Using and Abusing Victorian Census Forms, *Journal of Victorian Culture*, 14, pp. 1–25.

M. Esbester (2009), 'Designing Time: The Design and Use of Nineteenth-Century Transport Timetables', *Journal of Design History*, 22 (2), pp. 91–113.

M. Esbester (2009), 'Nineteenth-Century Timetables and the History of Reading', *Book History*, 12, pp. 156–185.

A. Giddens (1990), *The Consequences of Modernity* (Cambridge: Polity).

J. Habermas (1962), *The Structural Transformation of the Public Sphere* (Cambridge: Polity).

D. Headrick (2000), *When Information Came of Age: Technologies of Knowledge in the Age of Reason and Revolution 1700–1850* (Oxford: Oxford University Press).

E. Higgs (2004), *The Information State in England: the Central Collection of Information on Citizens since 1500* (Basingstoke: Palgrave),

D. Muddiman (2008), 'Public Science in Britain and the Origins of Documentation and Information Science', in W. Rayward (ed), *European Modernism and the Information Society* (Ashgate: Aldershot).

N. Postman (1999), 'Information', in *Building a Bridge to the Eighteenth Century* (New York: Vintage), pp. 82–98.

W. Rayward (1994), 'Some Schemes for Restructuring and Mobilising Information in Documents: A Historical Perspective', *Information Processing and Management*, 30, pp. 163–175.

W. Rayward (ed) (2008), *European Modernism and the Information Society* (Ashgate: Aldershot).

P. Stiff (2005), 'Some Documents for a History of Information Design', *Information Design Journal*, 13 (3), pp. 216–28.

P. Sturges (2004), 'Information in the National Liberation Struggle: Developing a Model', *Journal of Documentation*, 60 (4), pp. 428–48.

P. Sturges, M. Katjihingua and K. Mchombu (2005), 'Information in the National Liberation Struggle: Modelling the Case of Namibia', *Journal of Documentation*, 61 (6), pp. 735–50.

P. Sturges (2008), 'Information and Communication in Bandit Country: An Exploratory Study of Civil Conflict in Northern Uganda', *Information Development*, 24 (3), pp. 204–11.

L. Tredinnick (2006), *Digital Information Contexts: Theoretical Approaches to Understanding Digital Information* (Oxford: Chandos Publishing).

L. Tredinnick (2007), 'Post-Structuralism, Hypertext and the World Wide Web', *Aslib Proceedings*, 59 (2), pp. 169–86.

L. Tredinnick (2008), *Digital Information Culture: The Individual and Society in the Digital Age* (Oxford: Chandos).

F. Webster (2002), *Theories of the Information Society* (London: Routledge).

T. Weller and D. Bawden (2005), 'The Social and Technological Origins of the Information Society: An Analysis of the Crisis of Control in England, 1830–1900, *Journal of Documentation*, 61 (6), pp. 777–802.

T. Weller and D. Bawden (2006), 'Individual Perceptions: A New Chapter on Victorian Information History', *Library History*, 22 (2), pp. 137–56.

T. Weller (2007), 'Information History: Its Importance, Relevance, and Future', *Aslib Proceedings*, 59 (4/5), pp. 437–48.

T. Weller (2008), *Information History – An Introduction: Exploring an Emergent Field* (Oxford: Chandos).

T. Weller (2008), 'Preserving Knowledge Through Popular Victorian Periodicals: An Examination of The Penny Magazine and the Illustrated London News, 1842–1843', *Library History*, 24 (3), pp. 200–8.

T. Weller (2009), *The Victorians and Information: A Social and Cultural History* (Saarbrücken: VDM Verlag).

T. Weller (2010a), 'An Information History Decade: A Review of the Literature and Concepts, 2000–2009', *Library & Information History*, 26 (1), pp. 83–97.

T. Weller (2010b), 'The Victorian Information Age: Nineteenth Century Answers to Today's Information Policy Questions?', *History & Policy*, June, available at http://www.historyandpolicy.org/papers/policy-paper-104.html.

INDEX